SCENIC **DRIVING** SERIES

SECOND EDITION

SCENIC DRIVING

ATLANTIC CANADA

Exploring the Most Spectacular Back Roads of
Nova Scotia, New Brunswick, Prince Edward
Island, and Newfoundland & Labrador

CHLOË ERNST

Globe
Pequot

Guilford, Connecticut

All the information in this guidebook is subject to change. We recommend that you call ahead to obtain current information before traveling.

Globe
Pequot

An imprint of The Rowman & Littlefield Publishing Group, Inc.
4501 Forbes Blvd., Ste. 200
Lanham, MD 20706
www.rowman.com

Distributed by NATIONAL BOOK NETWORK

British Library Cataloguing in Publication Information available

Library of Congress Cataloging-in-Publication Data available

ISBN 978-1-4930-3607-3 (paperback)
ISBN 978-1-4930-3608-0 (e-book)

∞™ The paper used in this publication meets the minimum requirements of American National Standard for Information Sciences—Permanence of Paper for Printed Library Materials, ANSI/ NISO Z39.48-1992

Printed in the United States of America

Contents

Prince Edward Island

Newfoundland & Labrador

About the Author

Be it riding the Tancook ferry, timing the Fundy tides, or learning an island fiddle tune, Chloë Ernst has always enjoyed exploring the Atlantic Canadian coast. She grew up sailing among Mahone Bay's treasured islands, where her family roots go back to the 1750s.

Chloë earned an honors degree in journalism and Spanish from the University of King's College in Halifax, Nova Scotia. After writing for east coast publications such as the *Bridgewater Bulletin* and interning at *Saltscapes* magazine, she moved to Vancouver, British Columbia.

The travel writer has also written *Best Hikes near Vancouver* (2014) and *Day Trips from Seattle* (2010), published by Globe Pequot. In all, she has authored and contributed to more than a dozen travel guides for Globe Pequot, Frommer's, Fodors, as well as articles for the *Toronto Star* and other publications.

Look for updates on her travel adventures at chloeernst.com.

Acknowledgments

Plates of lobster legs in Prince Edward Island, sailing out to Tancook Island, passing through New Brunswick by train at night, or watching the sunrise on the Argentia ferry—these are just a few of my treasured Atlantic Canada travel memories.

My family often spent vacations in Nova Scotia until we moved to the province's South Shore when I was ten. Since then I've discovered the east coast in detail, including traveling thousands of kilometers for these pages.

Thank you first and foremost to those readers who picked up the first edition of this guide. Nine years on, it has been a moving experience to revisit these regions, making a new attempt to capture the beauty, mystery, and magic of Atlantic Canada. Thank you for this opportunity.

To the editors and the staff at Globe Pequot Press, I offer my thanks for your help and your dedication to local travel. To the tourism associations and proprietors around the four Atlantic Provinces, thank you for providing quality resources and excellent service. And in every province I've relied on gracious locals to help with updates for this edition.

To my parents and family, thank you for the support and love and, most of all, for always welcoming me home.

In a variety of ways, I've lost and found some people very dear to me since writing the first edition of this guide in 2010. Retracing familiar routes brought these changes, struggles, and joys into sharp perspective—giving me pause to consider what can transpire in a decade of life.

My wide and warm thanks go to all those who share the road with me. I believe life is very much like a scenic drive: it's rarely about getting to your destination—enjoy where you are in the ride.

Introduction

The Atlantic Provinces cover only a small section of the map of Canada—that is, until you're driving their coastlines. Ocean treasures are abundant: fishing outports in Newfoundland and Labrador, docked schooners and beaming lighthouses in Nova Scotia, Fundy tides revealing the ocean floor in New Brunswick, and red sandy beaches in Prince Edward Island. But Atlantic Canada—which draws its name from its location on and vulnerability to the Atlantic Ocean—also spans farmlands, river valleys, mountains, lakes, and great swaths of forest. Its histories intertwine fascinating tales of ancient First Nations communities, Viking explorers, Basque whalers, French cartographers, Acadian farmers, English merchants, outport fishermen, and entrepreneurial businesswomen.

This rich history and achingly beautiful coastal scenery, which has the magic of seeming like home even to those "from away," are even more engaging when you take the slow road.

In this guide there are 29 scenic drives to take you the long way around, stopping in end-of-the-road communities and little-visited places in New Brunswick, Nova Scotia, Prince Edward Island, and Newfoundland and Labrador. But we don't shun the favorites either: The Cabot Trail in Cape Breton, the Irish Loop on the Avalon Peninsula, and the *Anne of Green Gables* route near Cavendish are rightful treasures.

The curse and also the beauty of travel is that there will never be enough time to go everywhere. These scenic drives don't attempt to cram every attraction into one guide. Here you have highlights, covering diverse regions of the east coast. My recommendation is to work with a rule of three in planning your time: pick three places, drives, or even stops that are *your* must-visits and then plan a trip that fits your timeline.

For example, three places to watch icebergs could take you to Labrador (Drive 24), Twillingate (Drive 26), and Conception Bay (Drive 28). Three opportunities to walk on the ocean floor could take you to Ministers Island (Drive 2), Hopewell Rocks (Drive 4), and along the Glooscap Trail (Drive 9).

Three wine regions? Wolfville (Drive 10), Petite Riviere (Drive 12), and even Prince Edward Island (Drive 21).

Sandcastles? How about Parlee Beach (Drive 8), Cavendish (Drive 20), and Rainbow Haven Beach (Drive 14).

Music legends? The Cabot Trail (Drive 16), Stompin' Tom (Drive 19), and St. John's George Street (Drive 28) all have incredible entertainment.

Love ferrys? Head along the Saint John River (Drive 5), to Campobello Island (Drive 1), and out to Brier Island (Drive 11).

My point is that no trip can take you everywhere—so make the few places you go, truly worth going.

Scenic Region: New Brunswick

If you arrive in Atlantic Canada by land, your first experience will be the forests of New Brunswick. Escape the monotone of the highway to explore the province's greatest treasures, which lie mostly in the coastal regions: the world's highest tides in the Bay of Fundy, vibrant Acadian towns on Chaleur Bay, and the Reversing Falls of the Saint John River.

New Brunswick is Canada's only officially bilingual province, and seeing French-only signs or being greeted *en français* adds a new dimension to traveling here. Saint John and Moncton, the largest cities, are close to the Bay of Fundy. Fredericton, the capital, sits inland along the Saint John River. Because your enjoyment of some of the province's best attractions (such as the Hopewell Rocks and Ministers Island) will depend on the tides, New Brunswick is a province where your list of essentials includes a tide table.

The provincial history starts with First Nations, primarily the Mi'kmaq and the Maliseet, who have fished, hunted, and lived along the rivers and coasts of what's now New Brunswick for generations. Metepenagiag First Nation west of Miramichi is known as the village of 30 centuries.

French explorers and cartographers Jacques Cartier (in the 1500s) then Samuel de Champlain (in the 1600s) visited New Brunswick's coastal areas. French settlers followed, building dikes to reclaim farmland and naming the three Maritime Provinces "Acadia." Into the 1700s, the region seesawed between British and French forces.

When Britain took final control, they issued a deportation order in 1755 for the Acadians—those French that had settled in the 1600s—unless they swore allegiance to the British crown. Many were exiled from the region, imprisoned, or taken to France and US regions such as Louisiana. Thousands of people died. Some Acadians escaped deportation and moved north to settle the Acadian Peninsula along Chaleur Bay.

During the late 1700s and 1800s, Loyalists fleeing after the American Revolution, Irish escaping the potato famine, and Scots departing the Highlands all arrived in New Brunswick. In 1784 the area north of the Bay of Fundy became the colony of New Brunswick and then part of the Dominion of Canada in 1867.

The Fundy coast from the Maine border to the Nova Scotia border is the primary scenic region. The Saint John Reversing Falls, Fundy National Park, and the

The Ecological Park on Lameque Island, New Brunswick, features marshland boardwalks.

Hopewell Rocks are all stunning attractions formed by the world's highest tides, which reach up to 16 meters (52.5 feet) in the head of the bay.

Along the northeastern coast, facing the Northumberland Strait, discover the Acadian heritage of the province. In this proud region, Acadian flags—the French flag with a five-point gold star—adorn everything from lobster pots to benches and boats. Inland, rivers and culture-rich communities break the deep green of the province's great forests.

The province has many friends: it shares its longest border with Quebec, has an international crossing to Maine, faces Nova Scotia across the Bay of Fundy, and links with Prince Edward Island via the Confederation Bridge.

Scenic Region: Nova Scotia

The 7,500 kilometers (4,660 miles) of the Nova Scotia coastline feature in every scenic drive in this region. Lighthouses, fishing wharves, and historic streets are a few of the other commonalities—but greater is the diversity: from the vast Bay of Fundy tides to fog-smothered coves to the rugged Cape Breton highlands.

Sign the guestbook at the Northern Point Lighthouse on Brier Island, Nova Scotia.

Heritage inns, live music, and easily spotted wildlife abound as you explore a province almost encircled with water. Stop at the coastal beaches, parks, and viewpoints to slow down and admire the sights.

Traditionally Mi'kmaq territory, Nova Scotia is where John Cabot is thought to have landed in 1497. The French established the first permanent European colony in what was to become Canada at Port Royal on the Bay of Fundy in 1605, and French settlers—the Acadians—built dikes and farms here as they did along the New Brunswick coast. The region changed hands many times over the following century.

A 1710 conquest and the 1713 Treaty of Utrecht put Acadia in British power, leaving Cape Breton and Prince Edward Island in French hands. As in New Brunswick, British control led to the deportation of the Acadians starting in 1755 and the deaths of thousands.

Coastal access, fisheries, farmlands, forests, and other natural resources have always made Nova Scotia a desirable territory. The province is now ringed with historic fishing villages—ties to an industry that spurred wide-reaching settlement in the region.

Becoming the provincial capital in 1749, Halifax is now known for its live music and museums, although a historic British fort still watches over the port city and there are fortifications around the harbor. Most visitors will base themselves in the capital, and it's easy to make day trips to most areas of the province—except, that is, to Cape Breton Island.

Connected to the mainland by only a causeway, the northern end of Nova Scotia differs widely in its culture. Moose roam the wilds of the Cape Breton Highlands, and a rare few locals still speak in Gaelic tongues. Fiddle music, Highland dancing, and lively ceilidhs add vibrancy that's more appealing than industrial Sydney, the second largest city in Nova Scotia.

The province shares the Bay of Fundy with New Brunswick and has ferry service to the latter as well as to Prince Edward Island and Newfoundland. The summer fast-ferry route from Yarmouth to Maine had ended in 2009, but resumed service again in 2016 (ferries.ca).

In Nova Scotia, like in all of Atlantic Canada, it's truly the rural roads that take you to the local events, small communities, accessible islands, and endless beaches that make the province so precious.

Scenic Region: Prince Edward Island

Farmlands and golf courses cover the grassy acres of Prince Edward Island, or PEI. This is an easy province to navigate, where driving clear across the island can take less than four hours. But who would want to do that? Instead, PEI is a long-time favorite for exploring at the leisurely pace of summer road trips and beach vacations. The highest point on the island sits at only 142 meters (466 feet) elevation, but the scenery rolls in every direction to a sandy coastline. The picturesque landscape transitions from potato rows, hay fields, and grazing pastures to red cliffs, golden sands, and calm saltwaters.

The Mi'kmaq were the island's first residents. Much later than elsewhere in Atlantic Canada, French settlement started in the 1720s with a colony at Port-la-Joye. Acadians were deported with the Great Upheaval, and the British changed the region's French name of Île St-Jean to St. Johns Island.

A surveyor divvied the land into 67 lots and 3 royalties in the 1760s, and lotteries allocated land to mostly absentee landlords in England. Influxes of Scottish and Irish settlers in the 1800s and rich soils allowed for rapid population expansion, despite the feudal system and lack of definitive land ownership—a problem that would not be fully resolved until after Confederation.

In 1864 the Charlottetown Conference, held at Province House in Charlottetown, seeded the idea of Canada. But the island, by then renamed Prince Edward Island, held out from joining the dominion until 1873—when it was pressured

by the high cost of building a provincial railway. Part of the Confederation carrot was maintaining a year-round link to the mainland: For centuries it was the ferries and, as of 1997, the Confederation Bridge.

Today the two largest cities, the capital Charlottetown and Summerside, both face the Northumberland shores of Nova Scotia and New Brunswick. The entire island is scattered with rural communities, connected with twisting coastal routes and straight roads that parallel the original lot divisions. There are also the delightful old-timey earthy red farm lanes to drive—an experience that can take you back in time by a century.

In Prince Edward Island it is the places between that form the province's most scenic regions.

Unlike the other three Atlantic Provinces, the far extremes of the province—North Cape, West Point, Wood Islands, and East Point—are close enough to be easily explored, be it by scenic drives or the Confederation Trail. The railway, decommissioned in 1989, forms this recreational path network that spans the full length of the island.

Beaches encircle the green island, ranging in hues from white to golden to red. Farmlands are abundant, and late summer is a wonderful time to drive past the crop fields. Time here seems measured by the farm activities: from the week potato rows are ploughed to the week the hay is raked.

Scenic Region: Newfoundland & Labrador

Newfoundland and Labrador, Atlantic Canada's most visually stunning province, requires a special effort to visit. But going the distance to this easternmost part of Canada rewards unfathomably with rugged beauty, inaccessible coast, and friendly locals who will still wave a "hello" to you on the highway.

Two ferry routes (both originating in North Sydney, Nova Scotia) and an international airport in St. John's, Newfoundland, provide links to the province locals call "the Rock." Paved main routes, small coast-hopping ferries, and dirt-road highways provide access to the communities, even to remote Labrador—a vast, empty, and almost ghostly region that borders Quebec and Nunavut.

The coastline of the province measures nearly 30,000 kilometers (18,640 miles), more than any other Canadian province (although that of the Northwest Territories and Nunavut dwarfs this number). Summer icebergs, Atlantic puffins, whale pods, and caribou herds show the pure natural wonders of the province.

From the Confederation Centre of the Arts in Charlottetown, costumed guides lead walking tours around the city.

The history spans extinct Beothuks, exploring Vikings, Basque whalers, French fishermen, and English colonizers and merchants. Archaeological digs throughout the province uncover these ruins with amazing occurrence, be it the Colony of Avalon in Ferryland, John Guy's settlement in Cupids, Beothuk villages in Boyd's Cove, or a 7,500-year-old burial mound at Point Amour, Labrador.

In the unclaimed wilderness (of which there is *a lot*), hiking trails lead to ancient fossils, and inland fjords are diminutively called ponds.

St. John's, the capital and largest city, lies on the Avalon Peninsula to the east of the province. But it is in the great bare stretches of highway in Labrador and the barrens of the Irish Loop where the truly arresting beauty can be found.

Newfoundlanders are a unique, friendly bunch and they even boast their own dictionary to decipher the local dialect, quirky sayings, and unusual customs.

The human history here stretches back thousands of years and the geological history hundred of millions more. The extinct Beothuk lived on the Newfoundland coast most recently, and Inuit still live throughout Labrador. Vikings set up a small settlement in L'Anse aux Meadows about 1,000 years ago. Basque whalers visited the Labrador coast in the 1500s to hunt bowhead and right whales and render the blubber into oil. French fishermen harvested the sea bounty off the coast in the 1600s, as did the English.

From 1907, Newfoundland was the Dominion of Newfoundland under the British Crown. This ended when Newfoundland joined Confederation in 1949, but you'll still see the colors of Newfoundland's unofficial flag flying. Known as the Pink, White, and Green, the flag is said to symbolize peace between the Irish and English. The current Newfoundland flag became official in 1980.

Once-abundant cod and other fish stocks have diminished over the past five centuries of European settlement, forcing those in small fishing-supported communities—called outports—to move to larger centers.

Some outports remain active, with their fishing stages, docked vessels, and saltbox houses. It makes a coastal out-of-the-way drive in Newfoundland almost like time travel.

Geology

Shifting tectonic plates and recent ice ages have carved, pushed, and formed a diverse landscape in Atlantic Canada, a region that once abutted Africa. But the geology of each province is distinct, from the soft red soils of PEI to the jutting rocks of Newfoundland.

The Appalachian Mountains stretch up the coast into Newfoundland, defining much of New Brunswick. The Bay of Fundy, which forms a tidal funnel, is perhaps the best-known geological wonder. Grand Manan, an island off the Fundy coast, reveals some of this contrasting scenery in its sedimentary and volcanic rocks.

In Nova Scotia a fault runs from Cobequid Bay off the Bay of Fundy to Chedabucto Bay near Cape Breton. It divides the province into two geological regions: the Avalon Zone to the north and the Meguma Zone to the south. For much of geological history, the two existed on different super continents before ending up on one. Become a Nova Scotian rockhound with visits to the Joggins Fossil Cliffs between Amherst and Parrsboro, a coal-mine tour in Glace Bay, or a shoreline walk in Arisaig Provincial Park on the Northumberland Strait.

Prince Edward Island offers scant fossils on its eroding coast, but the island was once connected to the mainland until sea levels rose. The island sits on a shallow ocean shelf, and this is the best geological feature because it creates lots of coastal habitat for the island's favorite crustacean: lobsters.

In Newfoundland, get below the surface at the Johnson Geo Centre near Signal Hill in St. John's. Sunk into the hillside, exhibits show the evolution of the province nicknamed "the Rock." The most unique rock-spotting places in the province require an extra effort to reach: the fossils at Mistaken Point at the tip of the Avalon Peninsula, and the Tablelands in Gros Morne, where exposed mantle and an ancient ocean bed provided evidence for the theories of plate tectonics.

Natural World

Unfortunately most of the creatures you'll see on Maritime roads will be road-kill—mostly raccoons, porcupines, and skunks. These species along with black bears, deer, coyotes, and moose are those most commonly spotted in the Maritimes (defined as just New Brunswick, Nova Scotia, and Prince Edward Island).

Newfoundland has fewer small mammal species than the Maritimes, with no raccoons or skunks, as well as no snakes. Moose, however, seem to make up for the lack of smaller beasts and are a factor in many fatal road collisions.

Whale-watching tours in Cape Breton and along the Bay of Fundy provide excellent access to the beautiful but often-endangered sea mammals.

Bird watching in all four provinces is the most accessible wildlife experience. Along the shorelines, migratory sandpipers and piping plovers feed and nest. Newfoundland has burgeoning colonies of gannets at Cape St. Mary's and Atlantic puffins at Witless Bay. Jays, woodpeckers, and birds of prey make for more great sightings throughout the provinces, especially in national parks.

Heed advice about endangered and threatened wildlife. Don't feed animals, as this desensitizes them to humans and cars.

Outdoors Advice

Head out prepared. On the coast, which is to say the majority of Atlantic Canada, fog rolls in without warning. In summer, the severe weather is limited, but autumn hurricanes are becoming increasingly common this far north. In winter, snow can halt all travel for days.

Even on short hikes over marked trails, take the essentials: water, food, rain gear, maps, and a compass. Advise someone of your route and expected return time. Also, be prepared for bugs: from the early-season black flies and no-see-ums to the summer-long mosquitoes. Long sleeves, pants, and a good bug repellant will save much grief (and scratching).

If you must take a souvenir while beachcombing, look for sea glass, a lobster trap rib, or a fishing buoy. You're not only finding a unique beach treasure, but also collecting garbage (albeit *pretty* garbage) from the shoreline.

Fishing requires a license in Canada, although for some activities like clam digging you need only observe the daily limit. Check with a local visitor center or a park ranger for exact regulations, as well as any health-related shellfish closures (like red tide) for that area.

Emergencies & Preparedness

Most, if not all, areas use 911 as an emergency number. While a cell phone can be useful in emergencies, there is no guarantee that cellular service will be available in all areas of Atlantic Canada. This is especially true for remote and wilderness areas, and there are areas with irregular or no cellular coverage in these drives.

For those on a road trip, an auto-plan membership can provide assistance in areas where services are limited. But it's no substitute for checking gas, fluids, tires, mechanics, and the weather before departing.

For maps, all provincial tourism organizations provide hard-copy and digital guides that include detailed highway maps. Make sure you also have an offline version for all your adventures.

How to Use This Guide

This scenic driving guide is unconcerned with checklist travel: by that I mean, making sure you visit everywhere in a given area. It's about taking things slowly, going to the end of the road and back, and traversing new landscapes. The drives are spread out evenly over the four Atlantic Provinces, and I've focused on highlighting favorite historical sites, picturesque parks, protected natural areas, and friendly communities where you'll meet people like nowhere else.

Each drive includes the text with navigation directions and descriptions, plus a map and a photo. Some drives also offer side trips, or options to explore further. You'll find contact information for attractions, parks, and visitor centers, separated by drive, in Appendix A at the end of the book. Rarely do I give hours for attractions, although the vast majority of places in the region open daily from May or June to September or October.

I only occasionally list specific restaurants or accommodations. In most areas your options will number in the dozens. The tourism offices in all four provinces produce an annual magazine-like travel guide that lists accommodations, campgrounds, festivals, and attractions. Some also include shops, art galleries, and selected restaurants. Contact details for main provincial tourism offices are listed in Appendix B.

Any listed prices are in Canadian dollars. And while they were current at the time of printing, they may have since changed.

In revising the second edition, ferry services were the greatest variable in Atlantic Canada. For example the Gagetown ferry had been cancelled by 2018, and ferries in Englishtown and Campobello Island had undergone long periods of no service. For drives that include a ferry route, be sure to call ahead and confirm the ferry is running—or you may face significant changes to your travel plans.

The maps in this guide are intended to give you a sense of the route and main communities. Either a detailed and current road map, a GPS system, or offline maps, however, is an essential supplement. Look for one that lists route numbers for tertiary highways and rural roads, not just major highways. Handy extras are maps that pinpoint the location of attractions and parks.

Generally, most roads in Atlantic Canada can be called highways or routes interchangeably. In general I've delineated the two, referring to major thoroughfares as highways and local roads as routes.

Exploring all the scenic drives outlined in this guide will take you to the most spectacular spots in Atlantic Canada. But unless you are lucky enough to be on a two-month vacation, driving all in the same go is just about impossible. Choose a few to provide the groundwork of a trip or to use as a weekend-getaway or day-trip guide.

A cliché but a deserving one nonetheless: Be sure to take a sense of discovery as you turn onto an unknown route—perhaps it leads to a quiet beach, seafood canteen, friendly artist's studio, or something unknown.

Overview

Map Legend

Trans-Canada Highway/ Featured Trans-Canada Highway	▬▬▬🍁▬▬ / ▬▬▬🍁▬▬
Interstate Highway/ Featured Interstate Highway	▬▬(95)▬▬ / ▬▬(95)▬▬
Highway/ Featured Highway	▬▬(1)▬▬ / ▬▬(1)▬▬
Paved Road/ Featured Paved Road	▬▬▬▬ / ▬▬▬▬
Trail	....

- ■ Building or Structure
- ⊛ Capital
- 🕯 Lighthouse
- ▲ Mountain Peak
- ○ Town
- (1) Route Location

River, Creek, or Drainage	～～～～
Reservoir or Lake	▭
International Border	▬ ▪ ▬ ▪ ▬ ▪ ▬
Provincial Border	▬ ▪ ▬ ▪ ▬ ▪ ▬
National Park	▬▬▬▬▬
Provincial Park	▬▬▲▬▬
Wildlife Sanctuary/Reserve	▬▬▬▬▬

New Brunswick

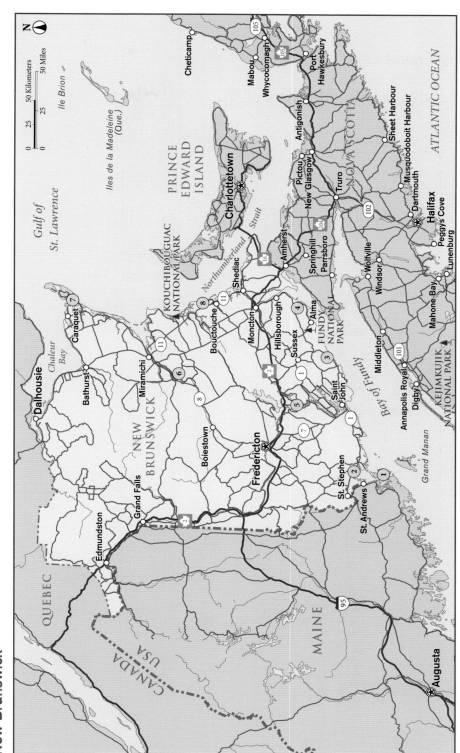

Nova Scotia

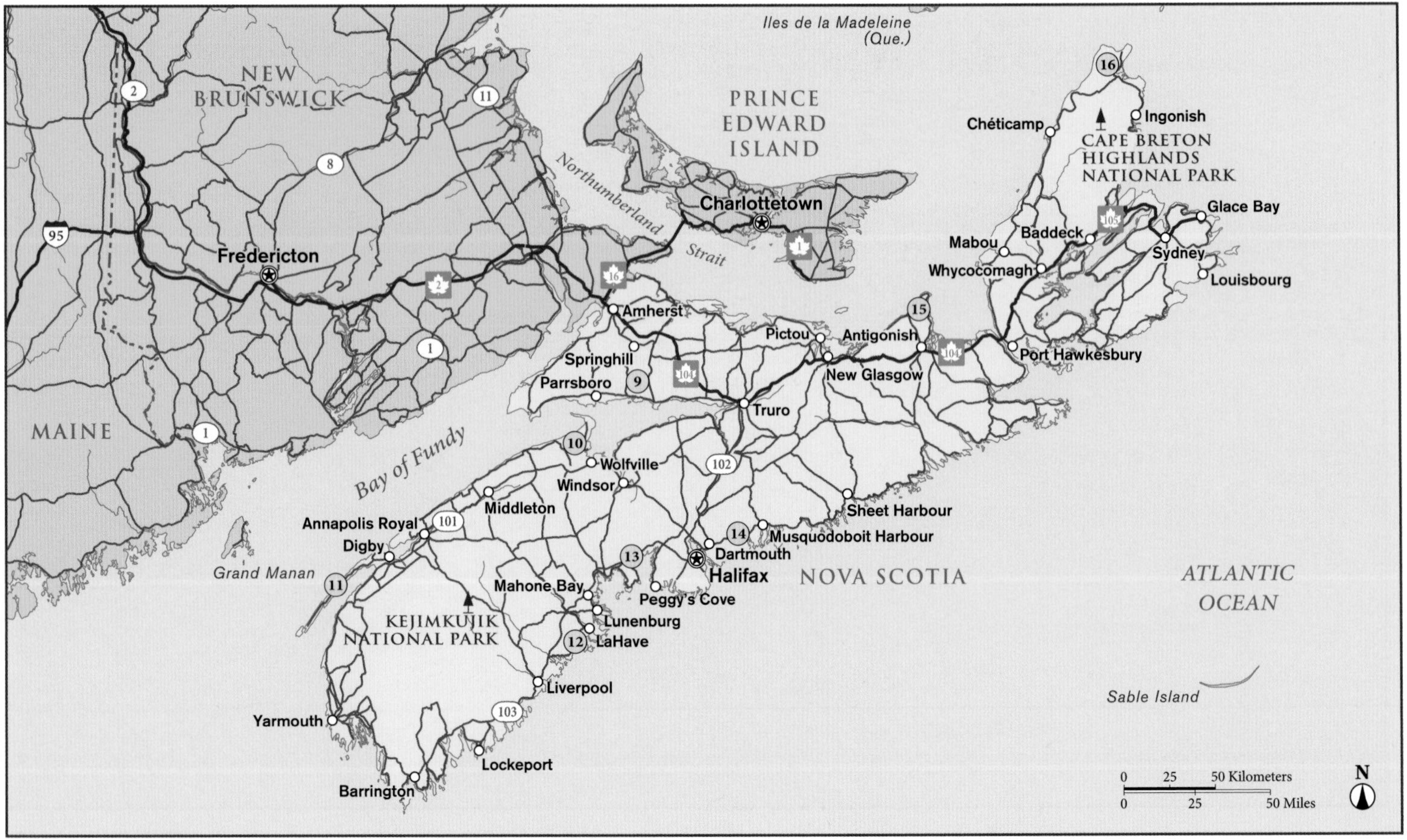

ATLANTIC OCEAN

Sable Island

| 0 | 25 | 50 Kilometers |
| 0 | 25 | 50 Miles |

NOVA SCOTIA

PRINCE EDWARD ISLAND

Charlottetown

Iles de la Madeleine (Que.)

NEW BRUNSWICK

MAINE

Fredericton

Bay of Fundy

Grand Manan

Northumberland Strait

Yarmouth

Barrington

Lockeport

Liverpool

KEJIMKUJIK NATIONAL PARK

LaHave

Lunenburg

Mahone Bay

Middleton

Windsor

Wolfville

Annapolis Royal

Digby

Peggy's Cove

Halifax

Dartmouth

Musquodoboit Harbour

Sheet Harbour

Truro

New Glasgow

Pictou

Antigonish

Parrsboro

Springhill

Amherst

Port Hawkesbury

Whycocomagh

Mabou

Baddeck

Chéticamp

CAPE BRETON HIGHLANDS NATIONAL PARK

Ingonish

Sydney

Glace Bay

Louisbourg

Prince Edward Island

Newfoundland & Labrador

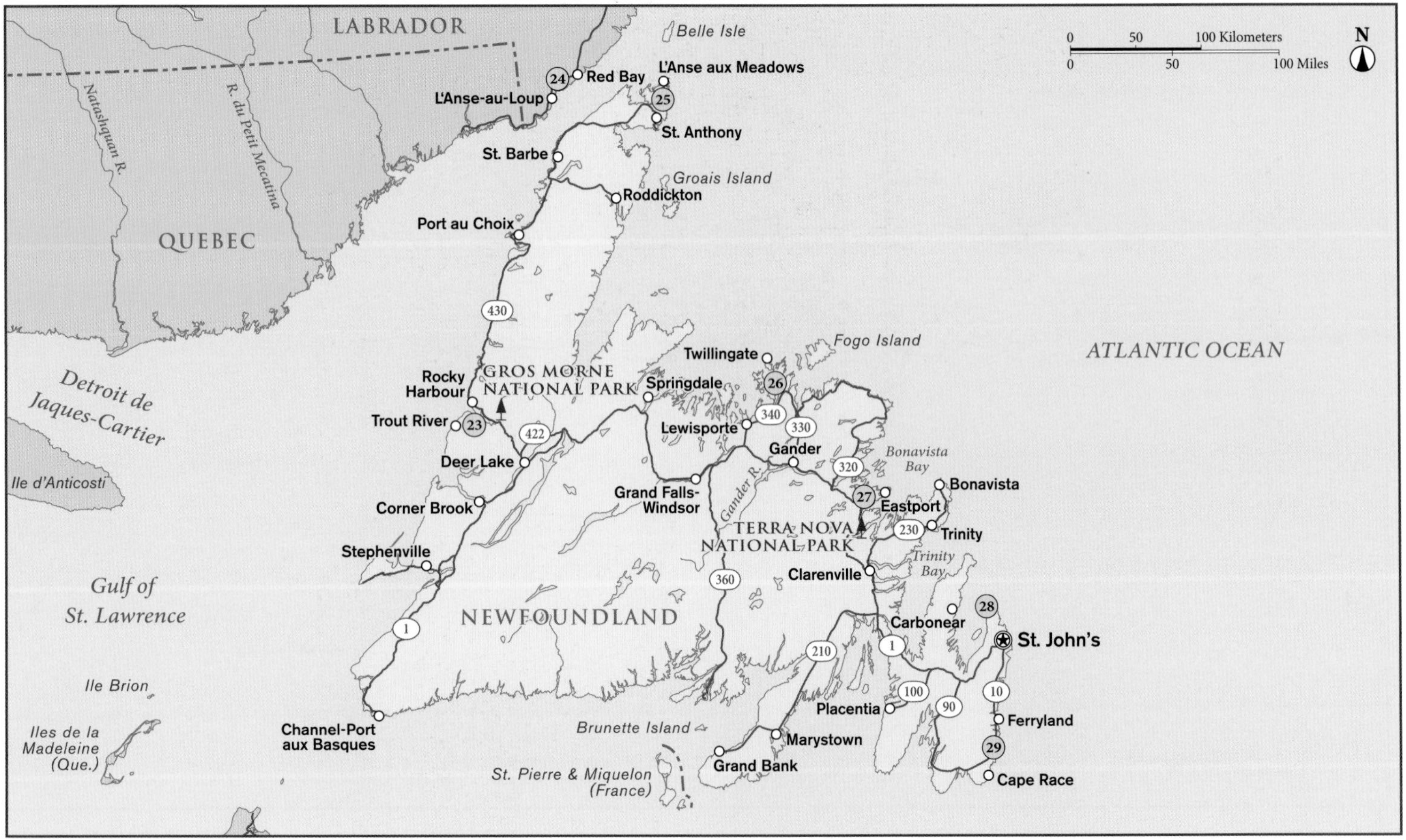

NEW BRUNSWICK

Fundy Island–Hopping

Campobello Island to Deer Island

General Description: This 55-kilometer (34-mile) island drive teases with water views, winding roads, and ferry rides. The attractions number only a few on Campobello and Deer Islands, but they are excellent ones: a former president's 34-room summer cottage, an island lighthouse, and a tidal whirlpool. Shorebirds and whales frequent the coast, drawn by a rich ecosystem freshened daily by the Bay of Fundy's powerful tides. Watch for this wildlife from the isolated beaches, hiking trails, or on a boat tour.

Special Features: Roosevelt Campobello International Park, Herring Cove Provincial Park, Head Harbour Lightstation (East Quoddy Lighthouse), Old Sow Whirlpool, free Deer Island–L'Etete ferry, bird watching, hiking, golfing, beaches, whale watching, sailing.

Location: The Fundy Islands lie near the Maine–New Brunswick border at the mouth of Passamaquoddy Bay. The Lubec, Maine–Campobello, New Brunswick, border crossing is about 85 kilometers (52.8 miles) from St. Stephen, New Brunswick.

Driving Route Numbers & Names: Route 774, Herring Cove Road, Route 772.

Travel Season: The summer season, with its warmer ocean temperatures and whale sightings, has been a favorite for centuries. Part of the Atlantic Flyway, the islands welcome migratory birds like sandpipers and endangered piping plovers in August. Late spring (May and June) and early autumn

(September and October) are considered shoulder seasons but are still lovely in the Maritimes, bringing slightly cooler days and mostly clear skies. The ferry from Campobello Island to Deer Island runs only mid-June through September—call ahead to confirm the route is running.

Camping: Campsites close to a beach and hiking trails are tucked in Herring Cove Provincial Park on Campobello Island. Full-service sites for RVs as well as no frills tent sites mean the campground easily accommodates a range of campers. The amenities stack up: laundry facilities, water, washrooms, showers, and even a 9-hole golf course and restaurant. Deer Island has a private campground on the southern point.

Services: As both of these Fundy Islands have small populations, you won't find many services on either Campobello Island or Deer Island. Campobello offers the better services, including a grocery store, restaurants, library, and post office. But there is no gas station, so you'll have to fill up across the border in Lubec, Maine, or continue on to Deer Island and the gas station in Fairhaven. For accommodations, you have the pick of a heritage inn or vacation cottages.

Nearby Points of Interest: St. George Gorge, Canal Beach, Canal Covered Bridge, Grand Manan Island and ferry.

Time Zone: Atlantic time zone (GMT minus 4 hours).

The Drive

This 55-kilometer (34-mile) scenic drive slots into a few different itineraries. It can be part of a loop around Passamaquoddy Bay, an out-and-back ferry trip from

Fundy Island-Hopping

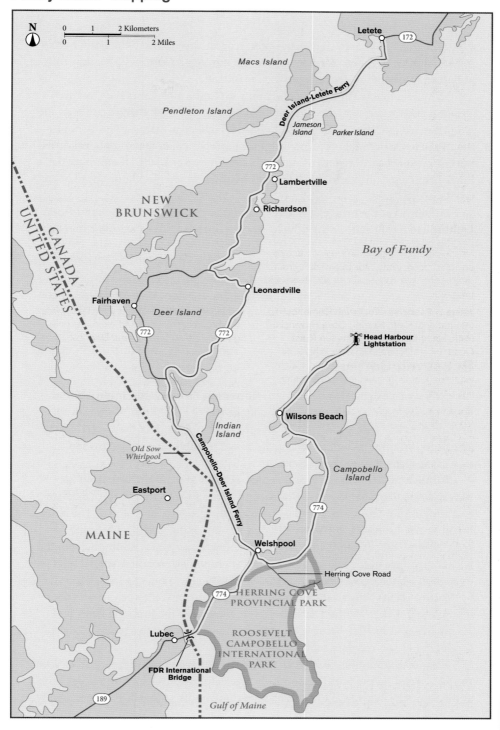

Letete (thereby staying in Canadian waters), or an alternative to the border crossing at Calais–St. Stephen. We treat it here as a through-trip from the border crossing at **Lubec, Maine,** to the New Brunswick mainland.

In Maine, follow US 1 to the junction with Route 189. Cross the river at Whiting and head east to the international border. The **FDR Bridge** connects the US peninsula to Canada's Campobello Island. Dubbed a "friendly" border crossing in the tourism brochures, you'll still need proper documentation (a valid passport or passport card) to enter Canada. In addition to crossing an international border, you also move into the Atlantic time zone, which is an hour ahead of Eastern Standard Time.

Driving over the bridge, watch for the classic red-capped **Mulholland Point Lighthouse** on the left. To visit the lighthouse, turn left after the bridge on Narrows Road.

About 1.5 kilometers (0.9 mile) past the border on Route 774, make a left turn to head down to the shore at **Friars Head.** Trails, a picnic area, and observation deck provide access to and views of the shoreline at **Friars Bay.** Stop here, or continue on to **Roosevelt Cottage** less than a kilometer farther along Route 774 for similar views and more shoreline access.

Roosevelt Cottage

A clearly sign-posted, left-hand turn to **Roosevelt Campobello International Park** leads to the rust-red, three-story cottage where Franklin D. Roosevelt spent his summers as a boy, young father, and the 32nd president of the United States. Thirty-four rooms, including 18 bedrooms and 6 bathrooms, make the house more than a small summer getaway.

Admission is free to the visitor center, cottage, and park where, from late May to Canadian Thanksgiving (the second Monday of October), the Canadian and American interpreters give the history of the property and family. The house is run as an international historic site, as a symbol of the Canada-US friendship. Rooms still contain the Roosevelts' furniture in pristine condition, from the wicker furniture in the living room to the toys in the playroom. A special treat is Tea with Eleanor, served on fine china, daily at 11 a.m.

Roosevelt first visited the island with his parents in 1883 when he was only one year old. FDR's mother, Sara Roosevelt, purchased the property from Mrs. Hartman Kuhn in 1909 because it neighbored her own. When she died, Sara Roosevelt left her son the then much-smaller cottage.

Eleanor and Franklin Roosevelt visited the cottage in the summers from 1909 to 1921, spending the warm season without electricity or telephone. Besides hiking and visiting the beach, the Roosevelts spent long hours sailing in Passamaquoddy

Roosevelt Cottage on Campobello Island is where Franklin D. Roosevelt spent his summers.

Bay on their schooner *Half-Moon*. Roosevelt added a wing to the cottage in 1915 to accommodate his growing family. He returned to the cottage only briefly during his presidency, from 1933 to 1945.

Large grounds include gardens, an icehouse, the foundation of the Roosevelts' old family cottage, and a beach on Friars Bay. A highlight is seeing the Roosevelt master bedroom. In this pretty room, which has a rather small-looking bed by today's standards, Franklin Roosevelt Jr. was born in 1914; it is also where FDR became ill with polio in 1921.

Campobello Island

Roosevelt Cottage was just one part of a vast summer industry on the island. In the late 1880s, a group of businessmen from New York and Boston built large hotels here and promoted **Campobello Island** as a summer destination. Summer cottages followed, and the vacation buzz lasted for about 30 years before taking full-summer holidays became impossible for the wealthy. Only a few of these summer cottages, and none of the large hotels, are left.

With the construction of the FDR Bridge in 1962, Campobello has again become a popular summer destination.

Historically the Passamaquoddy First Nation was the first to live in the area. Prior to foreign influx, they hunted and fished in the bay.

French and then British settlers began arriving in the mid-1700s, and the island population grew steadily after Captain William Owen's arrival in 1770. Crops and local fisheries sustained communities in Welshpool and Wilsons Beach.

To continue the scenic drive and explore these historic communities, drive northeast on Route 774. The road heads through the forested island to a three-way intersection. The left route takes you directly to Welshpool, but for now continue exploring Campobello by turning right toward Herring Cove and Wilsons Beach.

Shortly after the intersection, make a right on Herring Cove Road and follow signs for the provincial park. At **Herring Cove Provincial Park,** a 1.6-kilometer (1-mile) dark-sand-and-pebble beach looks out on **Grand Manan Island.** Watch for ferries making the passage from Blacks Harbour on the New Brunswick mainland to the largest of the Fundy Islands. A 9-hole golf course, restaurant, and campground at the park revive the feel of Campobello as a summer destination.

Back on Route 774 head northeast again for a forest drive that cuts through the middle of the island. Occasionally the trees break to reveal rocky coves and fishing wharves. Across from Schooner Cove Road, the views improve. The harbor mouth features cragged cliffs, slender island profiles, abandoned boats, aquaculture ponds, and the older wooden homes of **Wilsons Beach.**

The road turns here to follow a narrow peninsula. To the right is Head Harbour, and to the left is Head Harbour Passage. The land signals an end near East Quoddy Head as it narrows enough to allow water views on both sides.

At the northern end of Lighthouse Road, the photogenic **Head Harbour Lightstation** sits on its own island. Also known as **East Quoddy Lighthouse,** it is the second oldest in the province, dating to 1829, and you can walk out to the island at low tide. The Friends of Head Harbour Lightstation maintain the lighthouse, charging a fee to visit the island or climb the lighthouse tower. If you only have time for a quick stop, the no-charge observation area provides a panoramic shot but limited views of the actual lighthouse. You'll see the keeper's quarters but not the iconic lighthouse—its white tower flashed with a bold red cross. The best view of the lighthouse is from the water—by way of a whale watching tour.

Return on Route 774 past the provincial park, this time bearing right to **Welshpool.** The small village lanes include a historic bed-and-breakfast as well as a public library built in 1898. The library is also a museum, and introduces Campobello history with exhibits including photos, quilts, and even a carriage.

The **Campobello–Deer Island ferry** runs from Welshpool to Deer Island, hourly during the daytime from mid-June through September. The 2018 season

You can only walk out to Head Harbour Lightstation at low tide.

was delayed and later canceled, but service is expected to be running in 2019 and beyond. Contact **East Coast Ferries** (eastcoastferries.nb.ca) for updates. If you take the 20-minute crossing from Campobello to Deer Island, keep an ear out for island gossip and an eye out for whale pods. Great views of **Eastport, Maine,** a small city on Moose Island, are another highlight, including grand old brick buildings lining the waterfront and a church spire rising above the town that once thrived on its sardine canning factories.

About three hours before high tide, the **Old Sow Whirlpool** forms off Eastport as the largest tidal whirlpool in the Western Hemisphere. Taking different forms, the roiling turbulent waters sometimes form a large funnel as the rising tide pushes around Indian Island and over the ocean floor. There's even a certificate available from the Old Sow Whirlpool Survivors' Association for those who pass through the whirlpool and—tongue in cheek—live.

Deer Island

If the Campobello–Deer Island ferry is running on your visit, it's easy to connect the Campobello Island route with **Deer Island.** Touring the latter Fundy island is

The Deer Island Ferry provides great views of a tidal whirlpool, Passamaquoddy Bay, and occasionally whales.

more about the drive than any single destination. At the southern tip of the island, **Deer Island Campground at Deer Island Point** provides great views of the tidal whirlpool, Passamaquoddy Bay, and occasionally whales. There's also a small navigation light on the end of the grassy point.

Then follow Deer Island Point Road to Route 772, which splits left to Fairhaven or right to Chocolate Cove and Leonardville. While Fairhaven has restaurants and a gas station, I prefer the more coastal route around the eastern shore of the island. Turning right toward Chocolate Cove, follow Route 772 as it passes narrow inlets and fishing wharves. At low tide the fishing weirs appear as a tangle of nets, lines, and posts. Used to catch herring, the weirs make for great coastal photos at low water. Also along the shore, see the aquaculture ponds used to raise Atlantic salmon and lobster pounds that store live lobsters before they are shipped or processed.

At **Leonardville** more fishing weirs, wharves, historic homes, and the Leonardville Light show the working community's connection to the saltwater. Fishing boats and floats dot the shoreline, and piled nets edge the road.

The road climbs back up from the shoreline toward the head of Northwest Harbour. Here the road branches left to Fairhaven or right to the ferry to L'Etete. Marshlands, hilly terrain, and historic buildings trim the drive.

The road twists sharply through the communities of **Richardson, Lords Cove,** and **Stuart Town,** feeling more like a country lane as it winds around veranda-fronted houses. To the east the **Bay of Fundy** is clogged with rocky islands.

Just before Richardson you cross the 45th parallel—halfway between the equator and the North Pole. At the ferry terminal to L'Etete on the New Brunswick mainland, a small cafe/diner serves snacks and sells gift items. Running year-round, the free 20-minute crossing weaves through a dozen islands before docking on the far shore.

There are more than two dozen Fundy Islands, of which Campobello and Deer are the second and third largest.

Via Letete, Route 172 connects to Highway 1 to continue a coastal drive along the Bay of Fundy.

Side Trip: Grand Manan

Grand Manan, the largest of the Fundy Islands, is not accessible directly from Campobello or Deer Islands.

The island is a rugged spot, with small fishing communities, coastal trails, and excellent bird watching. Artists—both locals and visiting—take inspiration from the offshore whale pods and tidal-carved rock formations.

Perhaps the most unique island attraction, however, is the **Grand Manan Whale and Seabird Research Station.** Scientists and volunteers get hands-on with observations and research projects on common terns, right whales, and harbor porpoises.

Besides fishing, dulse is picked and processed on the island. The Atlantic seaweed is collected at low tide, sun dried, and then packaged as a salty snack.

2

Drive the Ocean Floor

St. Andrews to Covenhoven via Bar Road

General Description: The book's shortest drive, covering just 8 kilometers (5 miles) round-trip, it is also the most unique: A road accessible only at low tide leads to an abandoned summerhouse that looks more like a English country estate than the former home of a railway man. Walk the grounds of Covenhoven to see the windmill, bathhouse, and tidal swimming pool. It's the perfect vantage over Chamcook Harbour and the island-studded expanse of Passamaquoddy Bay.

Special Features: Wild Salmon Nature Centre, Ministers Island Historic Site—Covenhoven summerhouse, bathhouse, windmill, barns, carriage house, livestock, year-round walking trails, clam digging.

Location: Southwestern New Brunswick, on the Fundy coast. St. Andrews lies across the St. Croix River from Maine; the closest border crossing is about 30 kilometers (18.6 miles) away at St. Stephen.

Driving Route Numbers & Names: Bar Road, Carriage Road.

Travel Season: Visit the summerhouse in its best season, when lawn picnics and clam digging are possible. The attraction retains a longer season than most local attractions. Tours run from May through mid-October,

although visitors should contact the island for the exact, tide-dictated schedule.

Camping: Perhaps the prettiest location for a campground I've seen, the Kiwanis Oceanfront Camping sits at the tip of St. Andrews overlooking Passamaquoddy Bay. The oceanfront sites are geared toward RVs, and tent sites are tucked to the back of the campground. Facilities include showers, washrooms, Internet, laundry, a playground, and a kitchen shelter.

Services: St. Andrews offers the basics plus a lovely selection of historic inns, waterfront restaurants, and adorable shops. The town's Water Street is a heritage district and a picturesque spot to enjoy an afternoon on a patio. There are grocery stores, public washrooms, and a gas station to serve the community and visitors. While there are medical clinics in St. Andrews, the closest hospital is in St. Stephen.

Nearby Points of Interest: Kingsbrae Garden, Ross Memorial Museum, Algonquin Resort and golf course, St. Andrews Blockhouse National Historic Site, St. Croix Island International Historic Site.

Time Zone: Atlantic time zone (GMT minus 4 hours).

The Drive

An adventurous drive, this 8-kilometer (5-mile) loop heads off the paved road and over a low-tide sandbar to arrive at an uninhabited summerhouse. The island lies to the northeast of the holiday haven of **St. Andrews,** once a railway resort town.

Off Highway 1, take exit 39 to follow Route 127 toward St. Andrews. A same-numbered route also cuts down from Highway 1, exit 25, and arrives on the west side of town. If that is your route, cross the peninsula on Ghost Road, Clarke Road, or Cornelia Street, and then follow Route 127 south to Bar Road.

Drive the Ocean Floor

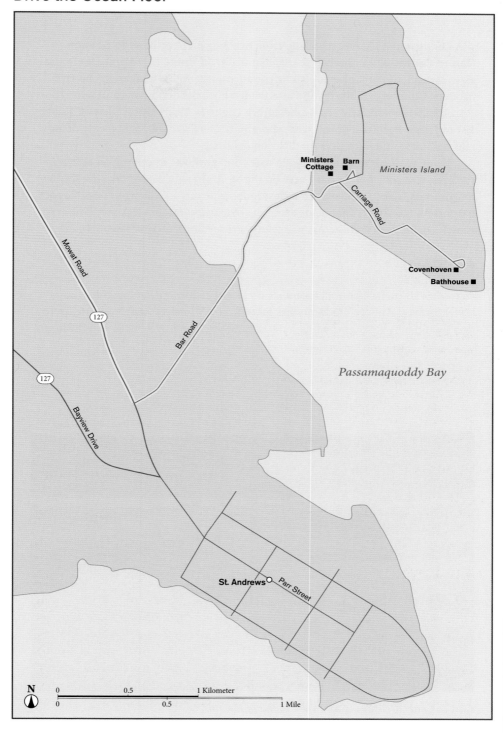

Ministers Cottage

Barn

Ministers Island

Carriage Road

Covenhoven

Bathhouse

Mowat Road

127

Bar Road

127

Bayview Drive

Passamaquoddy Bay

St. Andrews

Parr Street

N

0   0.5   1 Kilometer

0   0.5   1 Mile

On the way to Ministers Island from exit 39, you pass the **Wild Salmon Nature Centre,** at 24 Chamcook Lake No. 1 Rd. off Route 127. Nature trails and an in-stream salmon aquarium allow you to interact with the riparian and river habitats. Cultural exhibits tell the intertwined histories of humans and salmon.

About 17 kilometers (10.6 miles) from Highway 1 exit 39, turn left off Route 127 to follow Bar Road down to the shoreline. This drive will yield plenty of animal sightings; watch for deer on this wooded road.

If you're uncomfortable dodging rocks and potholes or driving on uneven surfaces, it may be best to park here on the St. Andrews side and take the shuttle to Ministers Island. While you'll be less independent, you will avoid possible rock hazards on Bar Road. That being said, on any given summer weekend, dozens of vehicles of all sizes drive across to explore. Proceeding slowly is essential.

Bar Road

Across a 750-meter (0.5-mile) sandbar that is accessible only at low tide, you travel from St. Andrews to **Ministers Island.** The Ministers Island website (ministersisland.net) posts a schedule for accessing the island by vehicle, and the hours

Cars can only drive out to Ministers Island at low tide.

change daily with the tides. Allow plenty of time to explore the island; otherwise, subject to the rush of the Bay of Fundy's high tides, you could be stranded for hours.

There's no single route across the sandbar. Marked in part with large stones, the shaley ground offers a number of paths that change as the water scours the surface. Clam diggers may be parked along the sandbar, fishing for bivalve mollusks in the thick mud.

As the road approaches Ministers Island, there's a gatehouse where you'll pay a worthwhile admission fee. Leading up from the shore a steep gravel road forks left to the barn and right to the summerhouse, Covenhoven.

Most of the island is a mix of forest and bucolic farm fields. Taking the right fork, follow the gravel road—Carriage Road—through an idyllic English countryside. Stone walls, grazing sheep, and mature hardwoods transport visitors to a British landscape. Look out over the green pastures to see llamas, cows, horses, and goats all grazing.

Covenhoven House

The towers, wings, and windmill of **Covenhoven** cut impressive silhouettes on Ministers Island. Sir William Van Horne was a railroad baron who rose from a telegraph operator in Illinois to president of the Canadian Pacific Railway as it built its coast-to-coast railway. Van Horne watched as the last spike was hammered into the ground in Craigellachie, British Columbia, thus finishing the railway five years ahead of schedule.

Built in the 1890s and designed by architect Edward Maxwell with heavy input from Van Horne, Covenhoven has 50 rooms, including 11 bathrooms, and 11 fireplaces. Banquet-sized dining rooms, endless bedrooms, playrooms, kitchens, and drawing rooms were all elegantly furnished in Van Horne's time.

A painter, amateur architect, and livestock breeder, Van Horne incorporated his many interests into this summerhouse. Adding wings and completing renovations to the mansion, the most treasured, perhaps, was the nursery he added for his only grandchild, William. In his grandchild's room, Van Horne painted a scene of Dutch boys and girls playing that still livens the nursery walls.

After the deaths of Van Horne in 1915 and his wife Lady Van Horne in 1929, the property was left to their unmarried daughter Adaline. In 1941, upon Adaline's death, the property was bequeathed to a niece and later sold. It became a provincial historic site in 1977, the start of its long road to protection and restoration.

Featuring a wooden-shingle style slightly reminiscent of the great national park lodges in the US, the multiwing house now sits empty. Explore the house independently or with a guided tour. Walking through the rooms, you'll note that some are partially furnished while others have nothing but peeling wallpaper and crumbling plaster. Simple exhibits pale in comparison to the empty upstairs rooms, which have so many doors and bathrooms one can quickly get lost.

At the back of the house, you'll see the windmill that pumped water into the house and a small building where carbide gas was produced and piped into the house for lighting.

From the front porch, where there are patio tables with a panoramic view, walk down to the round bathhouse on the shore. A handsome circular stone tower overlooks **Passamaquoddy Bay.** Van Horne used the bathhouse as a painting studio and displayed his fossil collection in the glassed-in top floor. A curved staircase leads down to a changing area and then out to the shoreline where a tidal swimming pool is sunken into the rock.

Looking out over blue water and verdant hills, it's easy to imagine why first the Passamaquoddy First Nation and later Van Horne were enchanted into taking up residence here.

A network of hiking and biking trails surrounds the property, and the large grassy lawns are dappled with fruit trees and historic monuments.

The Barn and Ministers Cottage

Return on the gravel road to the main fork, just uphill from the junction with Bar Road. This time turn right toward the barn.

Built by unemployed shipbuilders, with each floor covering 771 square meters (8,300 square feet), the finely smoothed curves, shingled grain silos, and huge footprint of the barn stand out. It towers larger than the house.

Admire the ribbons awarded to Van Horne's prized Clydesdale horses and herds of Dutch Belted cattle.

Beyond a retreat and artistic haven for Van Horne, the property was very much a working farm. Crops, livestock, heated greenhouses, and a creamery meant the island boasted great self-sufficiency. Van Horne had milk, produce, and other farm foods couriered by train from Covenhoven to his winter residence in Montreal.

Near the barn you'll spot the blue-trimmed stone cottage built by Rev. Samuel Andrews in 1790. Andrews was the island's namesake minister, although the Passamaquoddy called the island Qonasqamqi Monihkuk, meaning "sand point island." A Loyalist Anglican minister, Andrews came to the area from Connecticut in 1786.

Ministers Island also features a windmill, beautiful barn, and historic cottage.

From the cottage, drive down the gravel hill, over Bar Road, and to the mainland. Route 127 and then Reed Street lead south into St. Andrews and to a junction at Harriet Street. There is a nearby visitor information center that can direct you to the attractions, but the pretty railway-resort town is also small enough to explore impromptu.

Side Trip: St. Andrews and St. Croix

Better explored on foot than in a vehicle, **St. Andrews** is a quintessentially cute seaside town. The national historic district includes the thoroughfare of Water Street where large inns, fine restaurants, and lush gardens line the main route. Around the town lies a seeming week's worth of attractions.

At 188 Montague St. in the heart of the historic district, the **Ross Memorial Museum** features a decorative art collection in a heritage house. The almost-palatial brick home was constructed in 1824 for Loyalist Harry Hatch, his wife, and 11 children. An art collection donated by Henry and Juliette Ross can be viewed throughout the two-story mansion.

Nearby on Frederick Street, visit the **Old Gaol** with its grim 1832 conditions, and the **Charlotte County Courthouse,** which is still used for trials. The **Sheriff Andrews House** at 63 King St. continues the locked-down theme. Sheriff Elisha Andrews owned the house, built in 1820. He was the son of Rev. Samuel Andrews of Ministers Island.

Concerned over their proximity to the American border during the War of 1812, when Great Britain and the United States were at arms, local residents raised funds to construct the fortification at **St. Andrews Blockhouse National Historic Site.** The blockhouse surveys the St. Croix River, and, in summer, guides revive those nervous days of the border watch.

Close to the grand Algonquin Resort, **Kingsbrae Garden** provides a day of botanical explorations for gardeners. Trim flower borders, neatly pruned bushes, and labyrinth-like paths have earned it a nod as one of the best public gardens in Canada. More than 50,000 trees, shrubs, and flowers are carefully planted over 11 hectares (27 acres).

West of St. Andrews, follow Route 127 along the St. Croix River to a viewing point for **St. Croix Island International Historic Site.** Located on the international border and inaccessible for visitors, the island was the site of North America's first attempted French settlement. The French explorer Pierre Dugua, with Samuel de Champlain aboard, arrived here in 1604. The site was later abandoned in favor of Port Royal, Nova Scotia (see Drive 11).

3

Fundy Trail Parkway

St. Martins to Seely Beach

General Description: In this 38-kilometer (23.6-mile) scenic drive, sea caves and two covered bridges in St. Martins preface the developed lookouts of the paved scenic drive: Fundy Trail Parkway. Along the parkway itself, the viewpoints and observation decks number three dozen. Cross a suspension bridge, learn about shipbuilding, find an old foundation of a long-gone community, visit a sea captain's burial ground, and hike to waterfalls. A haven for walkers, runners, and cyclists, the wooded coastal trail parallels the smoothly paved roadway, and then splits from the road to connect through to Fundy National Park farther northeast.

Special Features: Two covered bridges, St. Martins sea caves, Quaco Museum, 21 lookouts, 15 observation decks, guided hikes, a tide-carved pillar or "flowerpot" rock, suspension bridge, Melvin Beach, Pangburn Beach, Big Salmon River, Long Beach, Seely Beach, walking, running, hiking, and cycling.

Location: On the Fundy coast, south-central New Brunswick.

Driving Route Numbers & Names: Main Street, Big Salmon River Road, Little Beach Road, Melvin Beach Road, Fundy Trail Parkway.

Travel Season: Summer brings the clearest days for a drive, but the sea caves and lookouts along this coast are interesting and make for stunning photographs year-round. In autumn, the leaves turn glowing fall colors, giving the drive new life at the end of its season. The Fundy Trail Parkway is open Victoria Day weekend (May) through Canadian Thanksgiving (second Monday in October).

Camping: While there is no camping available along the Fundy Trail Parkway, find family-oriented campgrounds in St. Martins.

Services: St. Martins has gas stations, craft shops, and restaurants. For medical services, Saint John lies less than an hour to the southwest along Route 111. The selection of ocean-side accommodations includes cottages and bed-and-breakfasts.

Nearby Points of Interest: Quaco Head Lighthouse, covered bridges; in Saint John: Reversing Falls, Carleton Martello Tower National Historic Site, Irving Nature Park, Rockwood Park, City Market, museums, and galleries.

Time Zone: Atlantic time zone (GMT minus 4 hours).

The Drive

Hairpin bends, tidal beaches, and forest trails make the **Fundy Trail Parkway** a delightful journey along the Bay of Fundy coast. The first phase of the roadway opened in 1998, and the full scenic portion of the route opened in 2018. A connector road through to Fundy National Park is expected to open in 2021. A multiuse trail—the **Fundy Footpath**—parallels the road and connects to **Fundy National Park** along the coast.

Fundy Trail Parkway

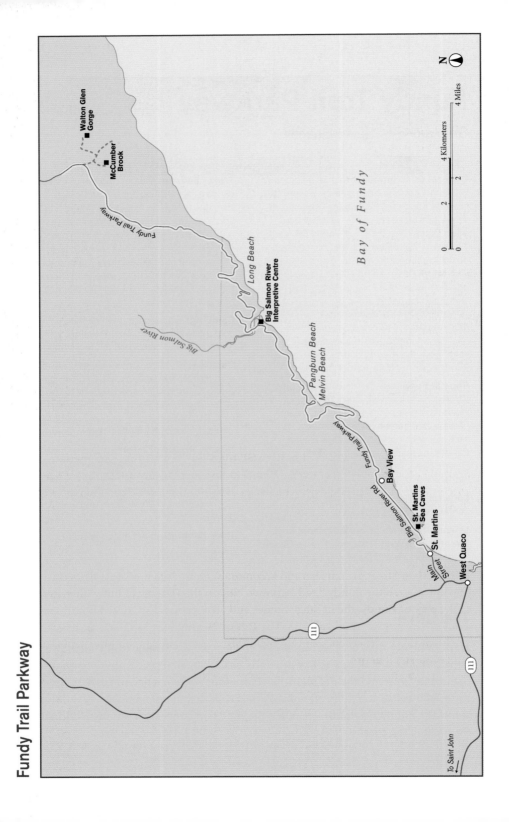

A covered bridge near St. Martins, New Brunswick crosses the Irish River.

To reach the parkway, first head to **St. Martins.** From Saint John, follow Route 111 for about 40 kilometers (25 miles) east past the airport. From Moncton and other areas, drive Highway 1 to Sussex before taking exit 198 to connect with Route 111.

St. Martins

A busy Main Street of canteens and accommodations leads northeast from **St. Martins** toward the Fundy Trail Parkway. Not on the waterfront but with views of the **Bay of Fundy,** the heritage homes and an occasional shuttered house stand alongside craft shops and galleries. The **Quaco Museum** at 236 Main St. has a small selection of excellent exhibits, including a feature on shipbuilding and a hand-cranked foghorn.

The Mi'kmaq were the area's first settlers and named the locale Goolwagagek, meaning "haunt of the hooded seal."

Loyalist soldiers from New York founded the town in 1783, and St. Martins was once a center for shipbuilding with hundreds of ships being launched from the slipways here. But, like many places in Atlantic Canada, with the advent of metal-hulled ships, the demand for wooden sailing boats disappeared and the town lost its economic driver.

The town hosts its annual **St. Martins Old Home Week Festival** in July—welcoming new visitors and old-timers for a weekend celebration with a parade plus theater, music, and tours.

Drive northeast on Main Street toward the Fundy Trail Parkway. As the road follows a cove it captures views of a covered bridge. The bridge, built in 1935, crosses the Irish River. Fishing boats tied up to a wharf and a lighthouse-style tourism information center add to the lovely Atlantic Canadian scene. Continue left up the river along Main Street to cross on a second covered bridge dating to 1946, or keep right to head to the parkway (the road by-passes the covered bridge).

Big Salmon River Road follows the coastline to an impressive frame: the **St. Martins Sea Caves,** surrounded by beach, forest, and ocean. Often at low tide

These sea caves are across Macs Beach, near St. Martins, New Brunswick.

people will be exploring the mouths of the gaping caves, giving a sense of their great size even from a distance. The sea caves are carved into the red cliffs by the tide and are accessible around low tide—just walk across Macs Beach after checking the tide table with the visitor information center.

From the sea caves, the road cuts through farmland and past homes for about 6.5 kilometers (4 miles), becoming Little Beach Road and then Melvin Beach Road, which reaches the parkway admission gate.

Fundy Trail Parkway

The paved **Fundy Trail Parkway** provides a low-speed way to see the Bay of Fundy coastline. Ultimately the route will connect to Fundy National Park, farther east along the coast, but until then it is an out-and-back scenic drive.

Along the way dozens of lookouts, observation decks, and beaches feature as scenic stopping places. Day-use parking lots allow walkers, runners, and cyclists to explore the coastal multiuse trail independently and safely. For hikers, a by-reservation shuttle bus provides options to travel further by foot: You can walk ahead then catch a shuttle back to your vehicle.

It's possible, but not necessary, to stop at all the lookouts. In fact, stopping at every one can be tiring. I recommend picking four to six that are located near beaches, hikes, waterfalls, and services that suit your interests and needs. Two absolute musts to add to your list are the Big Salmon River Interpretive Centre and Long Beach.

The first lookout **Fox Rock** gives views of the coastline to the west, out to **Quaco Head Lighthouse.** But I prefer the second observation area **Fownes Head,** where a short trail leads to views of a "flowerpot" rock—a tree-topped pillar of rock, sliced from the coastline by the tides. Look northeast to the dramatic bluffs and cliffs of the Fundy coast. Inland a walk to the **Sea Captain's Burial Ground** will reveal the area's shipbuilding history. Other marked hiking trails go to the old community schoolhouse, Hearst Lodge, and Fundy National Park—a distance of 41 kilometers (25.5 miles).

The next stop at **Melvin Beach** provides more great views as well as staircase access to the pebbly shore. At low tide only, walk to the sandier **Pangburn Beach.** At high tide, explore inland to **Fuller Falls**—a pretty waterfall where cable stairs (which are similar to a rope ladder, although less steep) lead down to an observation deck. Both beaches and Fuller Falls connect to a parking area and **Bradshaw Lookout** via a multiuse trail.

At **Black Point Lookout,** spectacular views include Pangburn Beach, Melvin Beach, and cliffs that separate the two at high tide. **Hearst Lookout** gives big ocean views across the Bay of Fundy to Nova Scotia from its high altitude.

The Fundy Trail Parkway is a low-speed way to see the Bay of Fundy coastline.

Pejebescot Lookout also provides a nice perspective of the coastline. At **Davidson Lookout,** which has picnic tables, look east on a clear day to see Nova Scotia and the small Isle Haute off Cape Chignecto.

After Davidson Lookout the road descends a hill, and your gaze will widen over tidal flats, river, and forest.

Big Salmon River

At the stop sign, turn right to the **Big Salmon River Interpretive Centre,** or continue straight on the Fundy Parkway drive. If you're returning to St. Martins, my recommendation is to complete the scenic drive, then return to Big Salmon River to walk the trails, see the remains of the old community, and cross the suspension bridge.

At the **Big Salmon River Interpretive Centre,** which shows a short film in French and English about the area, browse the photos and exhibits on display. Primarily covering the history of the community at Big Salmon River, the exhibits tell how the logging-company town developed over a century from the mid-1800s to the 1940s.

More than 20 families lived here in the 1920s. The men worked for the sawmill, which provided electricity. The children attended classes at the schoolhouse; in 1910 the teacher at the school was just 16 years old. And the community would gather at the local hall for social functions.

But when the sawmill burnt down in 1933, the loss crippled the town's industry. Walking down from the large parking lot to the interpretive center takes you past the old foundation of the schoolhouse—one of the few remaining signs of the community.

Explore further from the interpretive center and walk along **Big Salmon River** to watch for birds and water life. Then follow the river upstream to where the 84-meter (276-foot) suspension footbridge spans the banks and provides a fun diversion.

The interpretive center is also the departure point for the 2.7-kilometer (1.7-mile) hike to **Hearst Lodge,** built by newspaperman William Randolph Hearst.

Long Beach and Beyond

Continuing past the stop sign, drive over Big Salmon River on **Mitchell Franklin Bridge**. Look left to see the suspension footbridge. Talus slopes and quarry-like cliffs flank the roadway, which has been cut into the bedrock, and the rock strata reveal a tumbled ancient creation—the grays, browns, reds, and purples forming a geological mosaic.

While **Cranberry Brook Lookout** provides views of the interpretive center as well as secluded picnic tables, I prefer to continue to the **Interpretive Centre Lookout** where you can look out on broad **Big Salmon River** and the suspension footbridge. **Big Salmon River Lookout** delivers majestic views of the river delta and the ocean it feeds.

Stop briefly at **Hairpin Lookout** to see the turn you're about to make: a tight bend around a point that has been sliced flat to make way for the road. Driving slowly around the turn, keep your eyes on the road and let your passengers enjoy the views. It's then just meters to **Long Beach Lookout.**

Long Beach, about 150 meters (492 feet) below the cliffs, stretches out to Tufts Point. Smooth, golden sands edge the coastline, made all the sweeter by its inaccessibility. Admission to the parkway is good until evening (check exact times with parkway staff), making it tempting to stay here to watch the tides turn. The road itself takes the long way around, but it does eventually curve around to the beach turn off. At the shoreline there are washrooms and an observation deck.

From Long Beach the drive continues another 10 kilometers (6.2 miles) through to a turn-around at McCumber Brook, and so the next string of scenic lookouts are the last.

A trail at **Tufts' Point Lookout** leads to the viewpoint. **Quaco Lookout** is a west-facing *yin* to the east-facing *yang* of **Martin Head Lookout.** Both provide views of the dramatic coastal cliffs. Named for the first explorer who mapped the area, **Champlain Lookout** provides another panorama—as do the following stopping points at **Seely Beach Lookout, Isle Haute Lookout,** and **Fundy Lookout.** All have picnic tables.

The scenic drive then takes an inland jog. At the time of publication, the road continued to a launching point for trails to **McCumber Brook Wetlands, McLeod Brook Falls,** and **Walton Glen Gorge,** but the route through to Fundy National Park was still in-progress.

Side Trip: Saint John

With large industrial factories within its limits, New Brunswick's second largest city might not make the best first impression. But park along the sometimes roughly paved city streets and explore the **Saint John** downtown district on foot

Saint John has the oldest market in Canada—and still rings a bell to start the market day.

to discover the combination of grit, creativity, and history that make a truly interesting city.

First browse the vendors at Canada's oldest market, the **Saint John City Market** in its historic location on Charlotte Street—bonus points if you're there to hear the Market Bell as it's rung to mark opening and closing of the market day. Near the marina-side market square, find quality museums such as the **New Brunswick Museum** with its collections of art and geology exhibits, or the **Loyalist House,** which hosts tea with the city's mayor during summer.

Within a short drive of downtown, view natural tidal-bore rapids at the **Reversing Falls** viewpoint at Wolastoq Park off Bridge Road, observe seabirds while walking the ocean-side trails in the 243-hectare (600-acre) **Irving Nature Park,** or explore a campground and canoe lakes in **Rockwood Park.**

To get a better sense of these contradicting forces of nature and industry in Saint John, head up to **Carleton Martello Tower National Historic Site** on Whipple Street and survey the landscape from the city's best viewpoint.

4

Hopewell Rocks

Hillsborough to Fundy National Park

General Description: Connecting the Fundy coast's iconic attractions, this scenic drive visits the flowerpot-shaped Hopewell Rocks, the rocky point at Cape Enrage, and the ocean-side playground of Fundy National Park. Over just 80 kilometers (49.7 miles), the road covers a diverse landscape that includes forest, river, marsh, and ocean. Opportunities for bird spotting on the mud-flat beaches are a highlight, as is watching the tide come in.

Special Features: Steeves House Museum, New Brunswick Railway Museum, Albert County Museum, Hopewell Rocks, Sawmill Creek Bridge, Bank of New Brunswick Museum, Shepody National Wildlife Area, Cape Enrage Interpretive Centre, Fundy National Park, bird watching, golfing, saltwater swimming pool, hiking.

Location: Southeastern New Brunswick, near Moncton, on the Fundy coast.

Driving Route Numbers & Names: Route 114, Route 915, Cape Enrage Road, Point Wolfe Road, Hastings Road.

Travel Season: The tides run in every season, but spring through autumn is the most pleasant time to kayak the high tide, hike wooded trails, or walk the muddy ocean floor. Spring and fall bring migratory birds

such as the sandpiper to the tidal beaches. In summer, undoubtedly the busiest season, room rates increase while availability decreases. It is also when the national park is most crowded. If you plan to spend time outdoors, black flies are vicious May through mid-June, while mosquitoes hone in for most of the warm season. Most attractions stay open summer long.

Camping: Camp at the end destination, Fundy National Park, where a campground at Point Wolfe is secluded and equipped with showers, washrooms, and fire pits. RV sites with hookups are available at park headquarters and Chignecto North. Beyond the basics, these also have kitchen shelters, playgrounds, dump stations, and laundry.

Services: Stock up on gas and snacks in Moncton, Alma, or Sussex. On the scenic drive, Alma and Hopewell both feature dozens of motel rooms and seafood restaurants. More overnight options include bed-and-breakfasts, independent vacation homes, and beachside cottages.

Nearby Points of Interest: Magnetic Hill, heritage museums, local galleries, and shopping—all in Moncton.

Time Zone: Atlantic time zone (GMT minus 4 hours).

The Drive

This 80-kilometer (49.7-mile) scenic drive never strays far from the water—first following the Petitcodiac River and then the Bay of Fundy coastline. Museums, natural oddities, bird-watching beaches, and plenty of outdoor activities from golfing to boating all make the trip stand out.

From downtown **Moncton,** cross the Gunningsville Bridge to Route 114 and follow the busy route as it heads downsteam with the Petitcodiac River. Heading

Hopewell Rocks

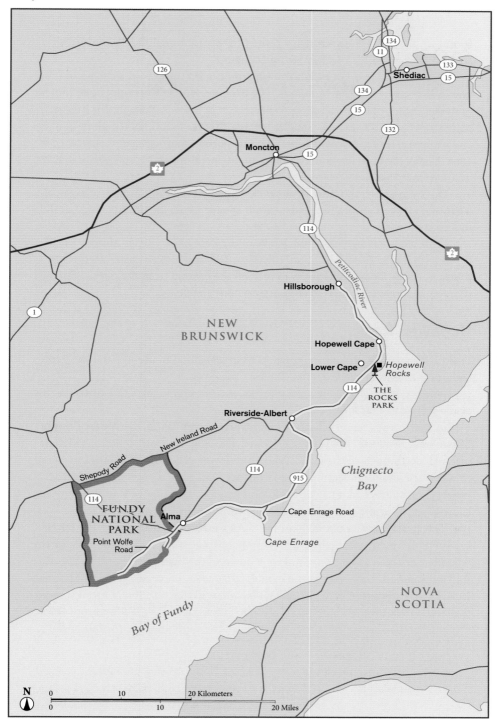

southeast, the route runs through a residential area through to Hillsborough, about 25 kilometers (15.5 miles) from Moncton.

The riverside town of **Hillsborough** tempts a first stop with a cluster of museums and restored heritage buildings. The **Steeves House Museum,** at 40 Mill St., honors a Father of Confederation, William Henry Steeves. Born in this historic mansion when it was a much smaller cottage, Steeves found his wealth in lumber and shipping. He represented Albert County at the Charlottetown Conference in 1864. Today the heritage house shows antique furniture and gorgeously detailed quilts sewn by Steeves's relatives.

On Main Street, the **New Brunswick Railway Museum** displays a large collection of artifacts and railway cars. Climb aboard to see the interiors or visit the replica station.

From Hillsborough along the banks of the Petitcodiac River, meadows lead down to marshes. From 1700 until the Great Deportation, Acadians farmed the pretty riverside lands, using dikes to reclaim the ground from the tides. German immigrants arrived in 1766 to continue farming the fields.

Hopewell Rocks

From Hillsborough, drive 13 kilometers (8 miles) along Route 114 and the Petitcodiac River toward the Hopewell Rocks.

Before you reach the Flowerpot Rocks, the Memramcook and Petitcodiac Rivers converge around Fort Folly Point.

In this former center of Albert County, **Hopewell Cape,** the **Albert County Museum** at 3940 Rte. 114 is an overlooked gem. Eight historic buildings in their original locations retell the tales of this shire town, or county seat. From murders to war stories, you can learn the area's history with guided visits to the records office, courthouse, and jail. The exhibition hall tells the story of R.B. Bennett, Canada's 11th prime minister, who hailed from Albert County.

Toward Lower Cape, watch for the signs for **Hopewell Rocks** at 131 Discovery Rd. Pull into the vast parking lot—probably one of the largest you'll see at any Atlantic Canadian attraction—and walk down to the interpretive center. There, find a restaurant, washrooms, and exhibits that cover the area's geology, Mi'kmaq legends, and wildlife. Check the tide tables and walk the 10-minute forest trail to the famed rock towers topped with greenery, also known as the **Flowerpot Rocks.** The interpretive center can provide details on the shuttle service for those who have limited mobility.

Walk on the muddy ocean floor of the Bay of Fundy
when the tide recedes at Hopewell Rocks.

Although it's nice to see the tidal-carved pillars at both high and low tide, don't miss the chance to walk among the curious shapes when the tide is out. This window of opportunity starts three hours before low water and ends three hours after. Aliens and animals all make great photos. A photo tip: While the scenery looks beautiful empty of other visitors, be sure to take a few pictures with people next to the Hopewell Rocks to capture the scale. Throughout the park discover lookouts, hiking trails, and beaches to enjoy on a longer visit.

From Hopewell Cape continue west along **Shepody Bay.** The spit of land across the water is Cape Maringouin, New Brunswick, with the Joggins fossil coast of Nova Scotia behind (Drive 9). This shoreline features marshy meadows that fill twice daily with tidal saltwater, only to be completely drained six hours and thirteen minutes later. This scenery changes vastly between tides with the water's range at the Hopewell Rocks measuring about 14 meters (46 feet).

At Hopewell Hill take an easy detour along "Old Route 114" to the now decommissioned 1908 **Sawmill Creek Covered Bridge.**

Cape Enrage

Follow Route 114 for 5 kilometers (3.1 miles) to **Riverside-Albert.** The enchanting riverside farming community features the old **Bank of New Brunswick Museum.** The town hosts the mid-September weekend **Albert County Exhibition** with a pageant, draft horses, and entertainment.

At Riverside-Albert there are also two options to continue the scenic drive and reach Fundy National Park. As the road bends at Crooked Creek, Route 915 spurs toward the coast and Cape Enrage, while Route 114 continues inland. Either route is lovely.

A shorter, faster option, Route 114 passes through **Shepody National Wildlife Area.** With marshland surrounded by rolling hills and the **Shepody River No. 3 covered bridge** (also called Germantown Lake) at Midway Road, it is an equally scenic alternative but with no must-stop attractions.

Along Route 915, the road draws closer to the coast through Harvey, New Horton, and Little Ridge. At Cape Enrage Road, make the left turn and follow signs to Cape Enrage. You're now alongside **Barn Marsh Island**—faintly separated from the mainland by Barn Marsh Creek. Follow the road to its end, where the light station at **Cape Enrage** has been beaming since the 1840s. Besides the views across Chignecto Bay, enjoy rappelling and ziplining or just browse the art and crafts gallery.

The light station at Cape Enrage has been beaming since the 1840s.

Fundy National Park

From Cape Enrage, Route 915 rounds Rocher Bay on the way to Fundy National Park. Along the way **Waterside Farms Cottage Winery** at 2008 Rte. 915 offers fruit-wine tastings as well as tours.

At **Alma,** flat tidal beaches are feeding grounds for seabirds such as migratory semipalmated sandpipers and endangered piping plovers. Restaurants advertising fresh lobster and seafood line the main street. When you arrive in town, an information and activity center in the town building can provide accommodation suggestions and brochures.

Just through town, visit the **Fundy National Park** visitor center and park headquarters on Upper Salmon River for trail maps. Point Wolfe Road leads into

Point Wolfe Road provides access to the covered bridge, golf, a pool, and waterfall hikes in Fundy National Park.

the park, providing access to the golf course, saltwater swimming pool, and waterfall hikes. The road is not a coastal one, rather heading through thick forests and over **Point Wolfe covered bridge** to reach dozens of hiking trails. The Fundy Circuit links seven of these trails to form a 48-kilometer (30-mile) loop. For a shorter challenge, try the 0.6-kilometer (0.4-mile) boardwalk trail to Point Wolfe Beach, with its telescope and wildlife interpretive panels, or the 1.5-kilometer (0.9-mile) loop to Dickson Falls, where a tiered waterfall tumbles over mossy rocks.

Fundy National Park, which was designated in 1948, is now a haven for the once-endangered peregrine falcon. The bird of prey was reintroduced to the park after being displaced. Populations have since rebounded—the bird is no longer considered endangered. Other wildlife species to watch for in the park include bears, moose, raccoons, deer, and coyotes.

From the park headquarters, Route 114 cuts inland through the forest, passing a boat rental at **Bennett Lake** and another visitor center at **Wolfe Lake.** In the center of the park, **Hastings Road** provides an option to leave the paved surface and see the forest from your vehicle. It's a one-way drive through to Point Wolfe Road.

From the park boundary, it's about 22 kilometers (14 miles) to Highway 1 for journeys east to Moncton or west to Sussex and Saint John. For a spectacular September event, visit Sussex during the **Atlantic Balloon Fiesta**—during which dozens of hot-air balloons float like Christmas ornaments in the sky.

5

Saint John River

Grand Bay to Fredericton to Lower Prince William

General Description: One of Canada's prettiest riverside drives, this journey along the Saint John River includes small cable ferries, a military base, and a power-generating dam. Escape the well-traveled Fundy coast to head inland and discover historical districts, art galleries, and the provincial capital. Covering 190 kilometers (118 miles) along the Saint John River, the scenic drive travels from coastal to pastoral.

Special Features: Cable ferries on Saint John River, Queens County Court House Museum, Tilley House, Grand Lake Meadows, New Brunswick Military History Museum, Canadian Military Engineers Museum, Kings Landing, Mactaquac Provincial Park, Mactaquac Dam. In Fredericton: Historic Garrison District, Fredericton Region Museum, School Days Museums, New Brunswick Sports Hall of Fame, Beaverbrook Art Gallery, Legislative Assembly of New Brunswick, Government House.

Location: From New Brunswick's largest city (Saint John) to its capital (Fredericton), this drive travels through the province's south-central region.

Driving Route Numbers & Names: Route 177, Route 102, Highway 2, Route 105.

Travel Season: In spring, watch the river as it swells with snowmelt. Summer brings boating, swimming, fishing, and other outdoor activities for a languid vacation. The fall foliage of the Acadian forest along the Saint John River makes the area an autumn favorite.

Camping: Camp at Mactaquac Provincial Park at the northern end of this drive, where a golf course and beach add interest to the basic amenities. Both tent sites and pull-through RV sites are available.

Services: The major centers of Saint John and Fredericton lack no services. En route, find gas stations and basic supplies in Grand Bay, Gagetown, and Oromocto. For heritage inns and quality restaurants, Fredericton tops my list as the best in the province. Plus you can check in with the city's visitor center to obtain a free parking pass.

Nearby Points of Interest: In Saint John: Reversing Falls, Carleton Martello Tower National Historic Site, Irving Nature Park, Rockwood Park, City Market, museums, and galleries. Farther northwest along the Saint John River: Crabbe Mountain ski area, Grand Falls Gorge, Hartland covered bridge (the longest in the world), and Covered Bridge Potato Chip Company in Waterville.

Time Zone: Atlantic time zone (GMT minus 4 hours).

The Drive

Known as the **River Valley Scenic Drive** and signposted with a fiddlehead—fiddleheads being the spring shoots of the ostrich fern that are readily foraged, cooked, and eaten in the Maritimes—this 190-kilometer (118-mile) scenic route follows the beautiful banks of the **Saint John River.**

Take Highway 7 to exit 90, then follow Route 177 to Grand Bay-Westfield. The first of the endangered cable ferries on this scenic drive runs from Westfield

Saint John River

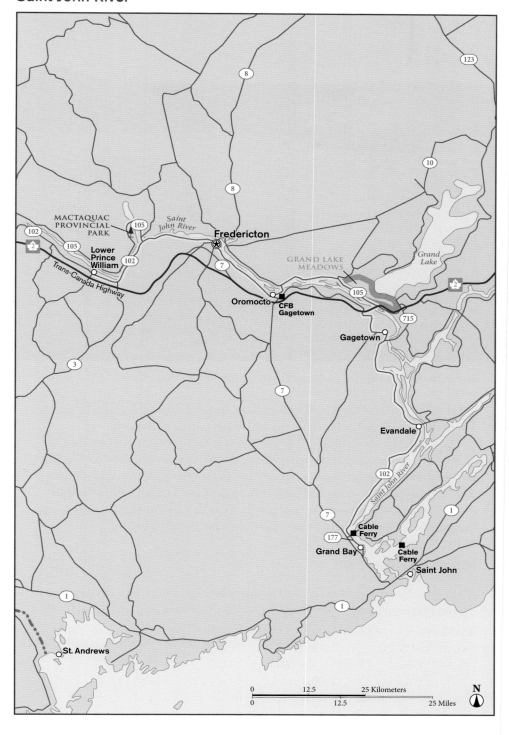

Part of the highway system, the cable ferries charge no toll to vehicles.

to Hardings Point on the Kingston Peninsula. But while the ferry ride is short, the labyrinth of roads on the far shore can add hours to your exploration.

Route 102 heads northeast in Grand Bay-Westfield. The road traces the west bank of the river toward Fredericton. Along the way, marshlands and rolling hills surround the Saint John River. Keeping close to the riverbank you can see where mid-river islands and sandy beaches break up the flow. The large **Kiwanis Oak Point Campground** provides a clear panorama at its pull-through RV sites. Here, the gorgeous wide views end as the tangle of river tributaries begins.

Historic Gagetown

A second cable ferry crosses the river at **Evandale.** Part of the New Brunswick highway system, the cable ferries charge no toll to vehicles. Feel free to take one across, explore some riverside roads, and return again to the scenic drive route.

Spoon Island, Long Island, and Upper Musquash Island change the path of the river as it takes varied paths. Passing Queenstown and Otnabog Lake, the road curves inland to Pleasant Villa.

Until 2016, a third cable ferry ran from Route 102 over to Lower Jemseg. While it's still possible to reach the east side of the river by road on Highway 2, the cancellation cuts off easy access. You may see signs about the loss of the ferry as you reach the historic village of **Gagetown**.

The seat of Queens County, Gagetown offers provincial historic buildings and well-preserved homes. The 1836 **Queens County Court House Museum** at 16 Court House Rd. is one of the oldest justice buildings in the province. Having meted verdicts into the 1960s, today the building is filled with antique decor and a genealogy research center.

Tilley House at 69 Front St. was home to a former premier and Father of Confederation Samuel Tilley; it now houses the **Queens County Museum** and the visitor information centre. Historical fashions and furnished rooms bring life to the 1786 home. Born in the wooden Gagetown house, Tilley attended the Charlottetown, Quebec, and London conferences. It is said he offered the suggestion for calling the newly created nation the Dominion of Canada.

Along Front Street, find a bustling pub and river views. Artisan galleries and a picturesque church build on the village's historic appeal.

Farm stands give the true rural feel of this scenic drive.

But Gagetown wasn't always so mild. Acadians settled here in the 1700s alongside the native Maliseet. In 1758, a British raid saw the village burned and Acadians scalped. In 1783, Loyalists founded Gagetown and laid out the village in grid-like streets.

From Gagetown, continue along Route 102, and as it meets the Trans-Canada Highway 2 you have a choice of routes.

The first is to continue on the west side of the river on Route 102 through Upper Gagetown and Burton.

The second is to pick up the main highway for one exit, crossing to the east bank of the Saint John River. On this lesser-populated east side, abandoned houses and fallow fields give a vacant feel. Farmlands cover the hills, and there are large meadows of Queen Anne's lace and goldenrod.

This second option takes Route 105 along the river toward Fredericton. Through **Grand Lake Meadows,** the landscape of marsh and riverfront grows only more beautiful. The land protects the massive **Grand Lake,** which retains so much of the summer heat that it increases the region's number of frost-free days. Watch for cows grazing on the mid-river islands—contained in a unique pasture without a fence. The meadow between Jemseg and McGowans Corner is the province's largest wetland, so be sure to watch for wildlife amid this rich ecosystem.

Route 105 leads through the sparsely populated **McGowans Corner** and **Sheffield.** At Maugerville, about 25 kilometers (15.5 miles) after crossing, the Burton Bridge returns over the Saint John River to Oromocto.

Oromocto

For those not intrigued by one of Canada's largest military bases—which covers 1,100 square kilometers (425 square miles), or about the size of Hong Kong—continue the 20 kilometers (12.4 miles) to Fredericton along the quieter Route 105. My preference is to explore the base's military museums.

Oromocto centers on the **Canadian Forces Base Gagetown,** named for the vastly different historic village visited earlier in the drive. Follow Route 102 to the North Gate, entering the base on Ganong Street. Alternately, turn onto Tilley Avenue or continue to the South Gate at Cumberland Street.

Driving through the base you'll see troops jog past in their camouflage fatigues. Tiny churches of differing denominations and coffee shops create a feeling of the base as its own community.

Through the maze of buildings, follow the signs for MUSEUM, which will take you to the **New Brunswick Military History Museum.** WWII-era tanks, jeeps, and guns sit alongside picnic tables and a parking lot. Inside the museum, barrack and weapon displays provide insight into military routines, as well as historical figures such as General Gage who was Commander-in-Chief of the British forces in North America at the outset of the American Revolution. Gage received a grant of land on the Saint John River. The base also has the **Canadian Military Engineers Museum,** with exhibits ranging in topic from World War I trenches to the United Nations.

On the way to Fredericton, stop in at the **Oromocto Visitor Centre** at the corner of Restigouche and Wassis Roads, which can point you to the trails and the bird reserve at the riverside Deer Park.

Fredericton

Leaving Oromocto on Route 102, or Lincoln Road, you pass **Fredericton International Airport**. Residential areas blend with the outskirts of **Fredericton.** Large and beautiful historic homes can be ogled from Waterloo Row, which leads directly along the river to downtown. If stopping in Fredericton, head first to the visitor center at City Hall where you can obtain a free parking pass (valid for three days for out-of-province visitors).

See outdoor sculptures at the Beaverbrook Art Gallery, Fredericton, New Brunswick.

Since parking is so convenient, walk through Fredericton's **Historic Garrison District,** where family-friendly museums and events create a dynamic visit. The handsome stone **Fredericton Region Museum** at 571 Queen St. is located in former officers' quarters and delves into the history of the capital. Nearby, the **School Days Museum** sits pupils in front of a slate to learn lessons about early science and see retro toys. Find more historical interpretation with costumed guides at the **Guard House** at 15 Carleton St. and watch the changing of the Guard in **Officers' Square**.

Tour the athletic galleries of the **New Brunswick Sports Hall of Fame** at 503 Queen St., or the sculptures and paintings at the exceptional **Beaverbrook Art Gallery,** 703 Queen St., which owns the dominating Salvador Dali work, *Santiago*

Bike paths trim the Saint John River in the New Brunswick capital.

Fredericton stands out for its footpaths and bicycle trails.

El Grande (although the work is often loaned out as part of touring exhibitions—check ahead if you're set on seeing the work).

Across the street from the gallery, take a free tour of the **Legislative Assembly of New Brunswick** at 706 Queen St. when the legislature is not sitting.

Beyond its historic and artistic treasures, Fredericton stands out for its footpaths and bicycle trails. Rent a bicycle to cycle across the **Bill Thorpe Walking Bridge,** or walk up the hill to tour the brick buildings of the **University of New Brunswick** campus.

Festivals and live music rate as Fredericton highlights. In July the **New Brunswick Highland Games Festival** brings ceilidhs, pipe bands, Highland sports, and dancing to the capital. In cooler September, the **Harvest Jazz and Blues Festival** welcomes world-class musicians for free shows and other events.

Mactaquac and Kings Landing

After exploring Fredericton, continue the scenic drive along Route 102 by following Queen Street through the historic district, keeping left on Northumberland, and right onto King Street through to Woodstock Road. At 51 Woodstock Rd.

you'll pass **Government House,** the current lieutenant governor's residence that dates to 1828. Summer tours of the main and second floors are available, while the gallery is open year-round.

Continuing along a narrow stretch of the Saint John River on Route 102, you soon approach **Mactaquac Dam**, about 18 kilometers (11 miles) from Fredericton. Exit onto Mactaquac Road.

There is a parking lot to stop for photos before crossing the dam, which produces about one-eighth of the province's power with its six turbines. Although, according to news reports, the dam has experienced problems with concrete expansion and is slated for extensive repairs to have it hold until 2068—its planned lifespan.

To visit **Mactaquac Provincial Park** at 1265 Rte. 105, follow the road as it crosses back over the Mactaquac Stream Basin. At the park a golf course, sand beach, and campground provide a weekend escape.

Alternately, skip the Mactaquac trip to continue on Route 102 along the Saint John River to where it parallels Highway 2. At exit 253, find **Kings Landing** where costumed interpreters re-create rural 19th-century life. When the Mactaquac Dam was built in the 1960s, historical buildings had to be moved due to the rising water levels and were set up to create an idyllic village here in Lower Prince William.

Farms, churches, a sawmill, a gristmill, and gardens spread out over the site, and interpreters revive the Loyalist history.

6

Miramichi River

Miramichi to Boiestown

General Description: Along the banks of the Miramichi River and into the center of New Brunswick, this 127-kilometer (79-mile) drive strays from coastal scenery to experience salmon pools and evergreen forests. The Atlantic salmon is the region's darling, having drawn royalty and celebrities to cast a fly-fishing line here. But explore further and find a millennia-old First Nations community, island excursions, and haunted woods.

Special Features: Boishébert and Beaubears Island Shipbuilding National Historic Sites, Beaverbrook House, Metepenagiag Heritage Park, Doak Historic Site, Atlantic Salmon Museum, Central New Brunswick Woodmen's Museum, TBM Avenger Air Tanker #14, salmon fishing.

Location: From the eastern coast of New Brunswick to the geographic center of the province.

Driving Route Numbers & Names: Water Street, St. Patrick's Drive, Highway 8, King George Highway, Route 425, Route 420, Route 415.

Travel Season: When the ice leaves the river, the Atlantic salmon season begins. The early mid-May catches are the salmon that have wintered in the river since the

fall spawn. The first salmon run stretches from mid-June to mid-August, and a second spawning runs from mid-August to mid-October. Even if you are not fishing, it's fascinating to watch the anglers cast their fly-fishing lines in lasso-like swoops. In autumn, add the spectacular allure of the Acadian forest foliage.

Camping: Find a number of private campgrounds close to the river on the outskirts of Miramichi, offering sites for tents and RVs. Enclosure Campground at Wilsons Point has a restaurant, a beach nearby, and the closest location to the city of Miramichi.

Services: At the start of the journey, Miramichi provides a full complement of services including gas, groceries, restaurant meals, hotel rooms, and medical care. En route, fuel up in Blackville, Doaktown, or Boiestown. Find overnight accommodations by driving beyond the end of this scenic route, following Highway 8 to Fredericton. The provincial capital has charming historic inns and a lively university-fueled nightlife.

Nearby Points of Interest: Kouchibouguac National Park, fishing, boat tours.

Time Zone: Atlantic time zone (GMT minus 4 hours).

The Drive

Famed for its Atlantic salmon runs, the "mighty" Miramichi draws anglers to its riverbanks year after year. You'll see folks out fishing from mid-May through the end of the spawning run in mid-October. The pretty river charms visitors with its ambling curves and unique attractions.

If traveling down from the north, follow Highway 8 from Bathurst or on Highway 11 from Caraquet. From Moncton or Shediac, take Highway 11. This 127-kilometer (79-mile) scenic drive is an attractive alternative route to reach

Miramichi River

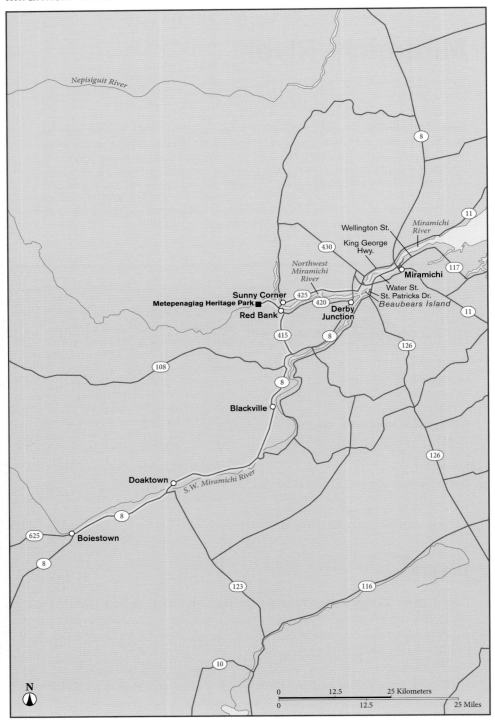

Nepisiguit River

8

11

117

Miramichi River

Wellington St.

King George Hwy.

430

Northwest Miramichi River

425

Sunny Corner

Metepenagiag Heritage Park

Red Bank

420

Derby Junction

Water St.

St. Patricks Dr.

Miramichi

Beaubears Island

11

415

8

126

108

8

126

Blackville

Doaktown

S.W. Miramichi River

8

625

Boiestown

8

123

116

10

N

| 0 | 12.5 | 25 Kilometers |
| 0 | 12.5 | 25 Miles |

Fredericton, the provincial capital, which lies about 65 kilometers (40 miles) beyond Boiestown.

Miramichi

The city of **Miramichi** amalgamated a number of communities in 1996 and each still very much retains its own identity. The city also hosts an impressively large number of cultural festivals—the mostly summertime events celebrate First Nations, Acadian, Irish, and Scottish heritage.

Begin exploring in **Chatham** on the south riverbank, and amble through the historic waterfront district of Water Street, where shipbuilders and lumber barons once built homes that demonstrated their wealth.

Miramichi, astride its namesake river, is a city of bridges.

The Miramichi River is famous for its salmon runs.

The northwest and southwest branches of the Miramichi River converge around **Beaubears Island,** which was first a meeting place for the Mi'kmaq. In 1755 many Acadians fled here when faced with an English deportation order. The 1800s brought a thriving shipbuilding industry—the slips, wharves, and foundations of which are still visible. Visits to the forest island begin at an interpretive center on St. Patrick's Drive. By ferry, boat tour, or canoe, visitors can then head out on the water to reach **Boishébert National Historic Site** and **Beaubears Island Shipbuilding National Historic Site**. The evening tour also visits **Wilsons Point**, a historic Scottish settlement where trails now visit a church and old cemetery.

From the Beaubears interpretive centre head to Highway 8 and the **Miramichi Bridge**. This is one of two vehicle bridges that span the river: the Miramichi Bridge, completed in 1995 to replace the iron-truss Morrissey Bridge, and the **Centennial Bridge** that replaced a ferry service in 1967.

On this left-hand side of the river in Newcastle, **Beaverbrook House** at 518 King George Hwy. was the childhood home of William Maxwell Aitken, who became Lord Beaverbrook—a multimillionaire, press baron, and British cabinet member.

Either from the museum or Highway 8, follow King George Highway as it becomes Route 425 toward Sunny Corner and starts the rural portion of this scenic drive.

Metepenagiag First Nation

A 16-kilometer (10-mile) stretch of Route 425 follows the Northwest Miramichi River toward **Metepenagiag First Nation.** With the river on the left, the road climbs through forest and passes through **Eel Ground First Nation.** It's a simple country scene, and at Sunny Corner a bridge crosses the river to **Red Bank.** Small islands sit in the river flow, and tributaries feed into the watery giant, the "Mighty Miramichi", as it gathers power.

Follow signs that direct right to the **Metepenagiag Heritage Park** at 2156 MicMac Rd., part of the Metepenagiag First Nation. Winding through a pine and spruce forest, you come to a beautiful stone-and-beam heritage center. Museum exhibits provide background to the park's two national historic sites: the **Augustine Mound burial ground** and the **Oxbow Site,** which was used as a fishing site for 2,500 years before Europeans arrived. Walking trails lead through the park to explore the grounds of New Brunswick's oldest village, dating back three millennia. Inside the center, admire the crafts and gallery.

From Red Bank, two routes reconnect with Highway 8. Take the shorter Route 415 through a thick forest of maple, spruce, and silver birch to the junction with Highway 8. Or, take the longer trip along the river for 18 kilometers (11.2 miles) on Route 420 back toward Miramichi and Derby Junction, then follow the quiet and rural Route 108 through Lower Derby, Derby, and Quarryville. In Quarryville, options for the slow road continue with Route 118 through to Blackville.

Center of New Brunswick

Highway 8 becomes monotonous at times, with one stretch of forest blending into the next. For many who travel only New Brunswick's highways, this is often their first impression of the province: trees. When the speed limit slows in **Blackville,** refresh with a quick stop at the municipal park, gardens, and picnic area. Due to its fishing pools, the village is often touted as the salmon capital of the Miramichi River. Along the main street, part of Highway 8, watch for a giant fishing fly, a massive replica of those used to fly fish on the rivers here (although—remarkably—it is *not* the world's largest).

As Highway 8 journeys south, survey the scenery as you crest the area's larger hills—you'll likely glimpse the snaking river, elusive in its beauty.

Highway 8 passes directly through **Doaktown.** At the **Doak Historic Site,** 386 Main St., learn about the daily chores, be it from the spinners making thread from flax or the weavers shuttling the spun fiber through the loom. Robert Doak, a Scot, originally settled the village in 1825 and established grist-, saw- and carding mills in the community.

Also in town, the **Atlantic Salmon Museum** at 263 Main St. provides a great stop for families. See the flash of salmon scales or meet the turtles in the aquarium, and walk down to the riverbanks with an ice cream or a picnic.

Continuing south on Highway 8, you'll likely see cars stopped along the shoulder in late July and August. During blueberry season, the highway slopes swell with ripe berries. Again, watch for views of the Southwest Miramichi River from the hills in the 25-kilometer (15.5-mile) stretch from Doaktown to Boiestown—the center of New Brunswick.

Arriving in small **Boiestown,** the few attractions are conveniently clustered together on Highway 8. A giant logger and even larger log-shaped buildings give away the **Central New Brunswick Woodmen's Museum** at 6342 Hwy. 8. Venture into the grounds to see the trapper's cabin and the blacksmith's shop. As a

Atlantic Salmon Museum in Doaktown shows the art of fishing in fine detail.

bonus, if you're under 6 or over 96, admission is free! Across the road, admire the grounded **TBM Avenger Air Tanker #14** that serves as a memorial to lost pilots.

From Boiestown, the forested heart of New Brunswick, it's a 70-kilometer (43.5-mile) drive to Fredericton, which is covered fully in Drive 5. Along the way, the route's scenery is—you guessed it—more river and forest.

Acadian Peninsula

Grande-Anse and Caraquet to Miscou Island

General Description: From painted lobster traps to deck furniture, you'll lose count of how many times you see the Acadian flag—the blue, white, and red flag with the gold star—as you travel this 120-kilometer (75-mile) scenic drive along Chaleur Bay. A historic Acadian Village and large churches show the region's ties to the French language and Roman Catholic faith, while an aquarium, ecological park, and peat bogs ground it to the natural environment.

Special Features: Chaleur Bay, Founding Cultures Museum, Village Historique Acadien, Éco-musée de l'Huître (Oyster Museum), Musée Acadien de Caraquet (Acadian Museum), Inkerman Migratory Bird Sanctuary, New Brunswick Aquarium and Marine Centre, Ecological Park of the Acadian Peninsula, Sainte-Cécile Church, Miscou Island Lighthouse.

Location: Northeastern New Brunswick, on the Acadian Peninsula between Chaleur Bay and the Gulf of St. Lawrence.

Driving Route Numbers & Names: Highway 11, Route 303, Route 145, Route 335, Route 345, Route 113, Route 313.

Travel Season: June through October offers pleasant weather, but fog can roll in even in the height of summer. During the first two weeks of August, celebrate Acadian pride with the Festival Acadien de Caraquet. Most houses don colorful strings of flags, and the ever-present Acadian pride intensifies. The weeks lead up to the Acadian National Holiday on August 15 with the noisy Tintamarre—a parade of thousands in costumes with noisemakers.

Camping: Although there are no provincial park campgrounds in the area, Caraquet, Shippagan, and Miscou Island all have private campgrounds with full camping and RV services.

Services: Caraquet has all the essentials including medical care, gas stations, and grocery stores. For heritage bed-and-breakfasts, inns, and chain motels, the large town also has ample options. In Shippagan, you'll easily find gas stations, accommodations, and restaurants.

Nearby Points of Interest: Bathurst Heritage Museum, Tracadie Historical Museum.

Time Zone: Atlantic time zone (GMT minus 4 hours).

The Drive

French greetings, Acadian flags, and cultural festivals delight on this 120-kilometer (75-mile) scenic drive to the Acadian Peninsula. Ocean-side churches and old convents show the force of Roman Catholicism here. But there are also marshland trails, a monstrous lighthouse, and an aquarium to create a lovely balance of attractions.

Linking to the closest cities, Miramichi and Bathurst, Highway 11 is the main artery to the peninsula. Heed the moose warning signs on the mostly two-lane highway.

Acadian Peninsula

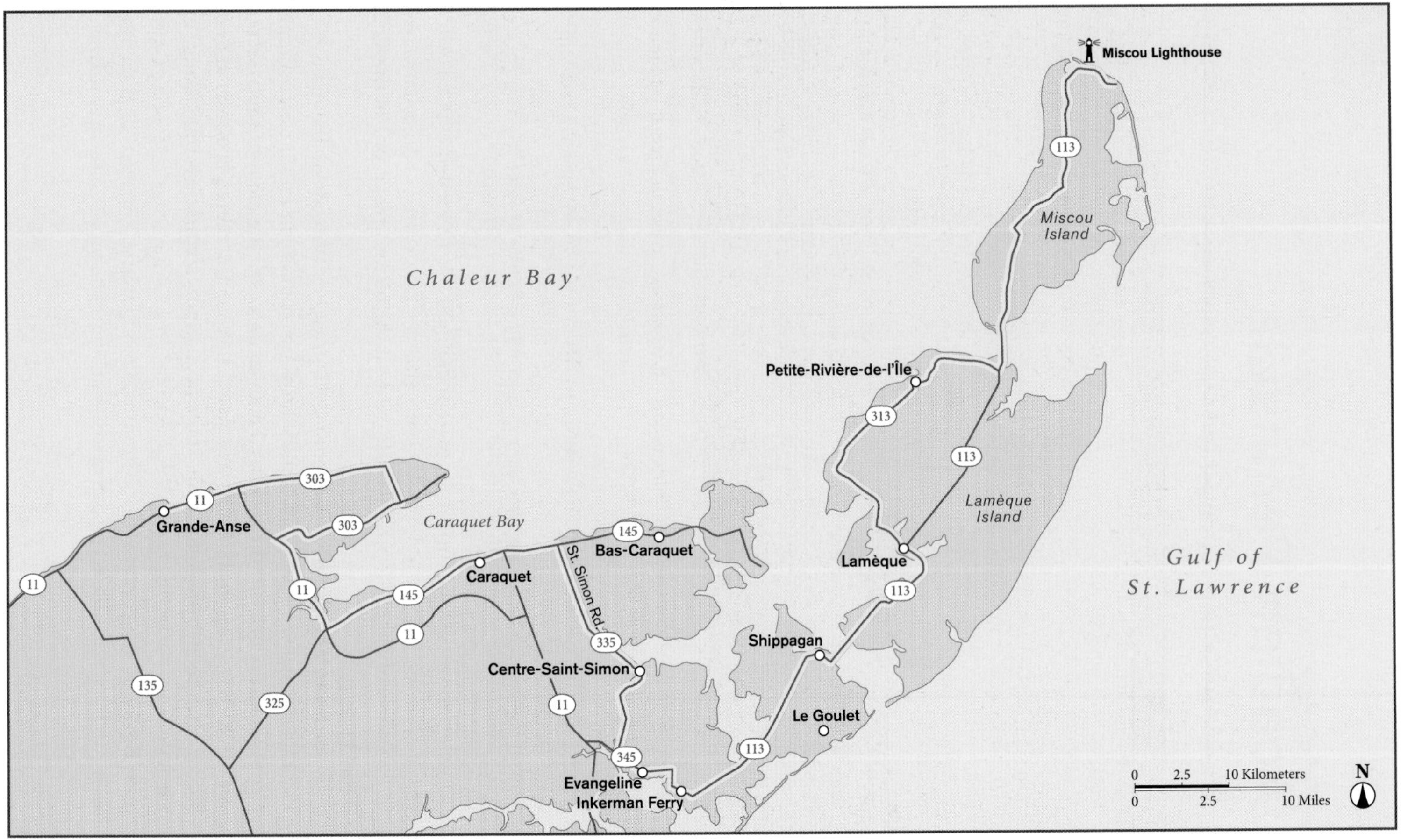

Miscou Lighthouse

Miscou Island

Lamèque Island

Gulf of St. Lawrence

113

113

113

Lamèque

113

Shippagan

Le Goulet

113

Petite-Rivière-de-l'Île

313

Chaleur Bay

145

Bas-Caraquet

St. Simon Rd.

335

Caraquet Bay

Caraquet

Centre-Saint-Simon

345

Evangeline

Inkerman Ferry

11

145

11

11

303

303

325

11

Grande-Anse

135

11

N

10 Kilometers

10 Miles

0   2.5

0   2.5

In Grande-Anse, the salty smell of the ocean—anse means "cove" in French—enhances the appeal of stopping at a local beach.

At the shoreline, follow Highway 11 to **Grande-Anse.** (If you are arriving from Miramichi, take Highway 8 to Bathurst and then cut east.) Fog can roll in quickly and thickly in **Chaleur Bay,** but with good visibility the coastline allows views out to the Quebec shore.

The Grande-Anse tourist information lighthouse is decorated with an eye-catching Acadian-flag paint job. The salty smell of the ocean—*anse* means "cove" in French—enhances the appeal of stopping at the picnic area or one of the local beaches.

The **Founding Cultures Museum** at 184 Acadie St. stands on the main route and introduces the many settlers in the area. It was once the rather unique Popes' Museum, but as visitor tastes changed over time, so did the focus of the museum.

Continuing east on Highway 11 toward Caraquet, a fishing boat marks Route 303 to Anse-Bleue. While the main route bears right, continue straight along the Chaleur coast. Following the point of land out, round the other side along **Caraquet Bay**.

Caraquet

Back on Highway 11, drive through forest and marshlands to visit the **Village Historique Acadien** near **Bertrand.** Just west of Caraquet, the historical re-creation is a full-day affair. Bake bread, hook rugs, eat a typical Acadian meal, and watch dinner theater. Those lacking French can enjoy the music, costumed actors, and historically restored buildings.

Passing through the **Bertrand Marshes** and crossing the **Caraquet River,** take the Caraquet turn (Route 145) on the roundabout. This is a junction with Highway 11 and Route 325. Here, west of town, **Éco-musée de l'Huître (Oyster Museum)** at 675 West St-Pierre Blvd. digs into all-things oysters in its quirky building. Mollusks are raised at aquaculture sites in the bay.

Known as the **capital of L'Acadie,** busy **Caraquet** shadows the road, making local services all easy to find. A visitor information center is well appointed at 39 West St-Pierre Blvd. Inside, get tips for viewing seabirds and whales in Caraquet Bay as well as the standard brochures and advice.

Rue du Portage heads south to Miramichi, but continue straight along the bay on Route 145 toward Bas-Caraquet. The waterfront complex on Caraquet

Éco-musée de l'Huître in Caraquet digs into all-things oysters in its quirky building.

Harbour—**Carrefour de la Mer**—features a cultural center, minigolf course, restaurants, and accommodations. The French-only exhibits at the nearby **Musée Acadien de Caraquet (Acadian Museum),** 15 East St-Pierre Blvd., tell important histories of local Acadian families through original documents and photos.

About 3 kilometers (2 miles) past the visitor center, turn right at St. Simon Road (Route 335) to follow the route inland. The treed thruway catches occasional water views as it passes North Saint-Simon Bay. At a junction turn left onto Route 345 to drive through **Evangeline,** then a second left onto Route 113 at **Inkerman Ferry.** On nearby **Pokemouche Bay,** the **Inkerman Migratory Bird Sanctuary** is part of the Pointe aux Rats Musques heronry—home to the largest colony of black-crowned night herons in the Maritimes.

Route 113 cuts an economical distance inland from a meandering coastline, bypassing the South Saint-Simon and Petit-Pokemouche Bays. At Pokemouche Road, find a detour down to **Le Goulet,** where there is a beach with washrooms, showers, and a picnic area.

Shippagan

Shippagan, located about 35 kilometers (22 miles) from Caraquet, is an industrial area and a hub port for fishing boats. The Shippagan campus of the **Université de Moncton** features the **New Brunswick Aquarium and Marine Centre.** Bright blue signs painted on the pavement direct you to the aquarium at 100 Aquarium St., where you can touch lobsters and sea cucumbers or watch playful harbor seals as they eat herring for dinner. You can also start an exploration along the waterfront boardwalk here.

On J. D. Gauthier Boulevard, part of Route 113, the small **St. John's United Church** indicates the region's small Anglophone community. It holds service just once a year in August.

A causeway and lift bridge connect Shippagan to Savoy Landing on Lamèque Island. Near the causeway, commercial fishing boats line up in a large boatyard and there's

A blue lobster is in the touch tank at the New Brunswick Aquarium and Marine Centre in Shippagan.

Near the causeway in Shippagan, commercial fishing boats line up in a large boatyard.

a waterfront park where you can watch for boat traffic before crossing the narrow passage to **Lamèque Island**.

Follow Route 113—which draws a line through the center of the island—before turning left on Route 313 as it branches left into **Lamèque.**

More road paint, this time in green, leads to another excellent attraction: the **Ecological Park of the Acadian Peninsula** at 65 Du Ruisseau St. A boardwalk leads out across the marshes from the visitor center to explore the park's ecosystems: forest, river estuary, beach, wetland, and peat bog.

The peat industry, along with fishing, is a significant business on the island and is celebrated with the annual **Provincial Peat Moss Festival** in Lamèque during July. Peat is amazing stuff: its uses ranging from absorbing oil spills to adding a smoky hint to whiskey.

Ask directions to **Petite-Rivière-de-l'Île,** also on Route 313, where the vibrantly painted **Sainte-Cécile Church** is home to the midsummer **Lamèque International Baroque Music Festival.** The church's dizzying pastel paint job weaves a motif of swirls, stars, bells, music notes, and crosses.

Miscou Island

Follow Route 313 until it rejoins the main road at a junction. Turn left to continue north to **Miscou Island.**

The smell of low tide may welcome you to the island, where fishing for herring and lobster is still the main industry. The Miscou Island Bridge crosses the Miscou Channel. It replaced a ferry that ran here until 1996.

A visitor information center can give directions, but with just one long main road that again slices through the center of the island, it is difficult to get lost. Follow Route 113 north as it passes through marshes and the **Miscou Plains.** While not achingly scenic at first, consider the bird and bug life these wetlands sustain. Walking trails explore this precious ecosystem, like the bird observation trail over the **St. Pierre peat bog.**

At the end of Route 113, **Miscou Island Lighthouse** is close to being the northernmost point in New Brunswick (a spot near Dalhousie edges it out). Climb to the top of this 1856 lighthouse once powered by seal oil. The octagonal wooden lighthouse has one of the stoutest profiles of any Maritime navigational beacon, plus wires to lash it down.

Along the shores of Miscou Island find a sheltered beach with soft sand, snack canteen, washrooms, and picnic tables—all inviting a longer visit to this tip of the Acadian Peninsula.

Acadian Shore

Shediac to Bouctouche to Kouchibouguac National Park

General Description: A 140-kilometer (87-mile) coastal trip through fishing villages out to a Dark Sky Preserve, this drive is about discovery. En route visit a 12-kilometer (7.5-mile) sand dune, craft workshops, and a village pulled from the Acadian fiction of Antonine Maillet. Go bird watching for migratory shorebirds, see seafood aquaculture sites, or watch for twinkling stars and lighthouses on the Acadian coast.

Special Features: Parlee Beach Provincial Park, Pascal-Poirier Historic House, world's largest lobster, Musée des Pionniers de Grande-Digue (Pioneer Museum), Bouctouche Dune, Le Pays de la Sagouine, Irving Arboretum, Irving Eco-Centre, Olivier Soapery, Bonar Law Historic Site, Richibucto River Museum, Kouchibouguac National Park (Dark Sky Preserve), swimming, walking, biking, beaches, camping.

Location: Southeastern coast of New Brunswick along the Northumberland Strait.

Driving Route Numbers & Names: Route 133, Route 134, Route 530, Route 535, Route 475, Route 505.

Travel Season: Time a spring or fall visit to catch the migratory birds, including plovers

and sandpipers, feeding along the shoreline. In summer, the swimming at Kouchibouguac National Park is some of the best in Atlantic Canada, and New Brunswick ocean temperatures are renowned for their summer warmth—reaching up to 29 degrees Celsius (84 degrees Fahrenheit)!

Camping: Parlee Beach Provincial Park and a host of private campgrounds offer full services near Shediac. Kouchibouguac National Park, at the northern end of this drive, provides the greatest number of camping options with more than 300 sites for tents and RVs.

Services: Fuel up in Shediac or Bouctouche, or in Saint-Louis-de-Kent outside the national park. This scenic drive is close to Moncton at its southern start and Miramichi to the north. Both cities have hospitals.

Nearby Points of Interest: Magnetic Hill, heritage museums, local galleries, and shopping—all in Moncton.

Time Zone: Atlantic time zone (GMT minus 4 hours).

The Drive

This 140-kilometer (87-mile) coastal amble truly shows the personality and pride of the local residents, and is part of the provincially marked **Acadian Coastal Drive** (look for the starfish highway signs throughout). Following the coast along the Northumberland Strait, various rural roads link fishing wharves, bird-watching beaches, viewpoints, and lighthouses. The scenery is quiet but ever moving, as the tides sweep in or out, birds flock and fly south, and fishing boats pull into the harbor.

Acadian Shore

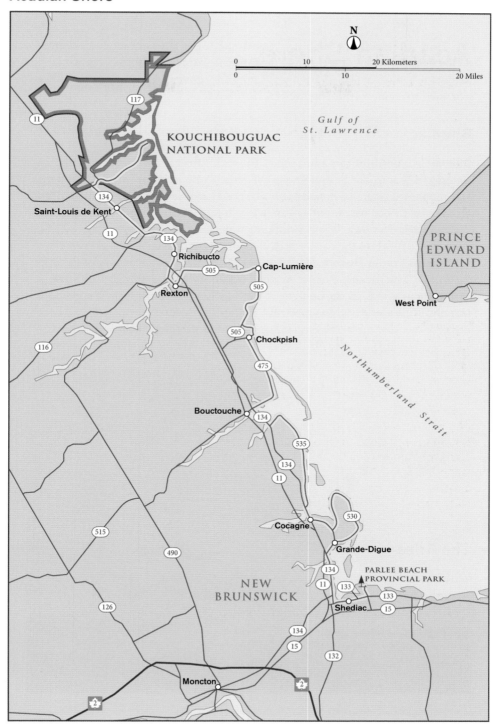

From Moncton, take Highway 15 or Route 134 to Shediac (about 25 kilometers [15.5 miles] from downtown to downtown). If traveling from Nova Scotia, follow the Trans-Canada or Highway 2 from the provincial border and then take exit 467B to connect with Highway 15.

Shediac

Shediac is a bustle of cars and people. The main street is not so scenic, despite its waterfront setting, but businesses pack in closely to offer great variety for dining and shopping. To grab a breath of sea air, head to **Parlee Beach Provincial Park,** on the eastern side of town at 45 Parlee Beach Rd., which has a campground and beach on **Shediac Bay.** Warm swimming waters, summer festivities, and sunshine draw large crowds to the park, which charges a day-use fee.

Pascal Poirier Historic House at 399 Main St. traces the history of Pascal Poirier, who became the first Acadian senator in 1885, and is also a hive of crafting activity—from rug hooking to carving. But the town's biggest attraction, literally, is the world's largest lobster at the head of Shediac Harbour. You'll not miss the speckled mass of legs, giant claws, and protruding antennae as crowds

The giant speckled lobster in Shediac is the world's largest.

climb up for a photo next to the giant crustacean. Neighboring visitor services can answer questions and provide brochures. Shediac hosts an annual **Lobster Festival,** complete with lobster-eating contests and entertainment.

Passing the giant lobster, follow Route 133 out of Shediac and head north at Chapman Corner. The road quickly becomes Route 134 along the coast.

On your right, look out to Shediac Island and the much smaller Skull Island. At Shediac Bridge, a one-lane crossing signals the backroad nature of the drive.

Leaving Westmorland County and entering Kent County, turn right on Route 530 through **Grande-Digue.**

Grande-Digue's Musée des Pionniers (Pioneer Museum), at 468 B Rte. 530, shows the coast's pioneer life with historic wooden buildings that include a barn, chapel, school, lighthouse, and the Gagnon family house. There's a vistor center here too. From the museum follow the indirect Route 530 as it traces the coast through Caissie Cape and Cap-de-Cocagne. Amid hay fields and marshlands, an occasional rusty tractor signals the area's mostly bygone farming industry, although a few organic and small-scale farms remain. At Grande Digue Road, turn right toward **Cocagne.**

Large tidal beaches draw seabirds to the plentiful feeding grounds, but the shoreline also shows erosion. On the water's edge, some cabins appear to have the earth washed out from underneath or be sinking into the marshes. The fairly flat landscape has sparse, immature forest. Look for the five-point stars on homes and the bright Acadian flags flying from poles.

Coming into wide Cocagne Harbour, turn right to rejoin Route 134. Just across the Cocagne River, turn right on Route 535 as it trims the coast inside Cocagne Island. Although the attractions are minimal from here to Bouctouche, shorebird sightings and possible views of Prince Edward Island in the distance will fill in the scenery until you catch sight of the stunning Bouctouche Dune.

Bouctouche

Near **Saint-Thomas-de-Kent,** 14 kilometers (8.7 miles) past Cocagne, look right to see the tip of the 12-kilometer (7.5-mile) **Bouctouche Dune** with a lighthouse on the very end. Rows of aquaculture buoys sit in the well-protected **Buctouche Bay**—which retains the older spelling of Bouctouche. Although the dune sits no more than 4 kilometers (2.5 miles) offshore at the farthest, its lone connection to the land is a 10-minute drive north near Saint-Èdouard-de-Kent.

Crossing the Buctouche River on Acadie Street, look left to see the tiny fictional Acadian village of **Le Pays de la Sagouine** on a river island. Walk the boardwalk to **l'Île-aux-Puces** where the village throbs with costumed actors, kitchen musicians, and the daily gossip. Pulled from the imagination of

The Acadian Shore shows the personality and pride of the local residents.

Bouctouche writer **Antonine Maillet,** the village recreates Acadian life with a bootlegger, traditional cuisine, and the house of **La Sagouine**—a washerwoman and Maillet's best-known character.

Acadie Street leads across the Buctouche River to an intersection. Take Irving Boulevard east through Bouctouche as it becomes Chemin du Couvent (Route 475) and heads toward the dune.

The large **Irving Arboretum** lies hidden behind a stone wall here. The garden is not well marked, but the trails and thousands of trees are worth finding. Continuing northeast, you'll pass the 1880 white **Convent of the Immaculate Conception,** which now houses the **Kent Museum.** Then at 1554 Route 475 comes the strange sight of three masts of a Spanish galleon, part of a fantastical waterfront property created by a local carver.

Off the coast, the Bouctouche Dune tapers in to the mainland at the **Irving Eco-Centre,** 1932 Rte. 475. Climb the observation tower. Visit the interpretive center, and then walk along the snaking 800-meter (0.5-mile) boardwalk— designed with its pleasing curves to withstand tidal surges and ice. Watch for birds

The boardwalk at the Bouctouche Dune snakes out over the saltmarsh and beach.

in the dune grasses and along the shoreline, which is said to be 2,000 years old and yet changes shape with each large storm. It's possible to enjoy a beach walk along the 12-kilometer (7.5-mile) dune out to the lighthouse, but this fragile habitat is best left alone.

From Bouctouche the road heads north to Kouchibouguac National Park along a scenic coastline with limited attractions. At low tide you may see clammers digging for the bivalve mollusks in the tidal flats.

At **Chockpish** you can choose between two routes. Either turn left on Route 475 then right on Route 505 to visit the **Olivier Soapery**—an economuseum that demonstrates the craft of natural soap making and gives tours. Alternately, follow the starfish scenic drive signs right on Côte-Ste-Anne Road and continue through to the junction with Route 505. Here, opt to follow the coast with a right turn, and then another right to keep on Route 505. The northward drive heads over a one-lane bridge before cutting the point short at **Cap-Lumière.**

Kouchibouguac National Park

Following Route 505 from Cap-Lumière, the scenery fills with forest as it nears the national park. Join Route 134 again and follow the rural route through Rexton, Richibucto, and Saint-Louis-de-Kent. You'll pass a few historical museums and attractions on the way to the national park.

The **Richibucto River Museum** shares a location with the birthplace of British prime minister, Andrew Bonar Law, at the **Bonar Law Historic Site** at 31 Bonar Law Ave. in **Rexton.**

Just up the Richibucto River, the **Elsipogtog First Nation** holds an annual Powwow on Labour Day weekend with drumming, dancing, and food. In Richibucto, indulge your love of seafood at the **July Scallop Festival.**

A number of roads thread into **Kouchibouguac National Park.** An extension of the Acadian Coastal Drive, Route 117 pulls clear through to the Pointe-Sapin. Follow this main road to signs for the national park and Kelly Beach.

A treed 11-kilometer (6.8-mile) road leads into the national park and to the beaches, salt marshes, and largest campgrounds. Long barrier dunes protect warm swimming lagoons along the **Gulf of St. Lawrence** exposure.

Created in 1969, Kouchibouguac protects an environment of Acadian forest, peat bogs, lagoons, salt marshes, and barrier islands. Its name means "river of the long tides" in the Mi'kmaq language. Some of the estuary channels in the park even dip meters below sea level.

Walk out over the salt marsh boardwalk to bird watch for migratory species along the shore. If camping, you'll trace the constellations in the national park, which is a designated Dark Sky Preserve.

Quiet roads lead toward Kouchibouguac National Park.

Side Trip: Moncton

Close to the starting point for this drive lies the city of **Moncton.** One of the fastest growing areas of the province, Moncton is also the most metropolitan, with shopping, spas, amusement parks, and golf courses to add to the attractions list.

It sits inland from the Bay of Fundy, although it still experiences the tidal action along the Petitcodiac River—and scenery takes second seat to urban entertainment. Theaters and galleries complement the historical homes and museums.

Magnetic Hill is the city's most trumpeted attraction. It's an unusual phenomenon that will see your car, when put in neutral gear, seemingly travel uphill on Mountain Road.

NOVA SCOTIA

9

Glooscap Trail

Truro to Parrsboro to Cape Chignecto

General Description: This is a 175-kilometer (109-mile) shoreline scenic drive, where the Fundy tides sweep in and out of Cobequid Bay and the Minas Basin. But it's also a land of dinosaur fossils, the summer home of a former prime minister, and a World War II observation point. Sample locally made pie, practice your shipbuilding skills, and catch a live theater show as you journey out to the protected end of the peninsula, Cape Chignecto.

Special Features: Truro Tidal Bore Viewing Visitor Centre, Bass River Heritage Museum, That Dutchman's Farm, Thomas' Cove Coastal Reserve, Cobequid Interpretative Centre, Five Islands Provincial Park, Fundy Geological Museum, Ottawa House, Ship's Company Theatre, Age of Sail Heritage Centre, Cape d'Or Lighthouse, Cape Chignecto Provincial Park, hiking, camping, kayaking, running, clam digging, tidal zones.

Location: Northern Nova Scotia, south of the Cobequid Mountains.

Driving Route Numbers & Names: Highway 4, Highway 2, Soley Cove Road, Bentley Branch Road, Main Street, Two Islands Road, Whitehall Road, Route 209, Cape Dor Road.

Travel Season: Summer beaches bring clammers and campers to Five Islands

Provincial Park. Many of the attractions on this drive can also be explored in the shoulder season during the months of May, June, September, and October.

Camping: Five Islands Provincial Park makes a lovely family camping destination with its beach and good facilities. At Cape Chignecto Provincial Park—a wilderness park with a coastal hiking trail—there are no drive-in campsites, but the walk-in sites at New Yarmouth campground can be found just off Eatonville Road. For avid backpackers, secluded campsites are spaced out around the peninsula.

Services: Get any essentials in Truro before setting out. For heritage accommodations, theater, and seafood, stop in Parrsboro. You can fuel up along the scenic drive route in Great Village, Parrsboro, or Advocate Harbour.

Nearby Points of Interest: Colchester Museum, Little White Schoolhouse Museum, Truro Raceway (harness racing), Debert Military Museum, Joggins Fossil Cliffs, Anne Murray Centre, Springhill Miners' Museum.

Time Zone: Atlantic time zone (GMT minus 4 hours).

The Drive

When the busy Highways 102 and 104 meet in Truro, it's a relief to escape the tangle of exits and take a quiet country drive along Cobequid Bay and Minas Basin. The scenic drive begins in what is now a commercial hub in Nova Scotia—Truro—and journeys out along a coast shaped by the Bay of Fundy tides to Parrsboro, which was an economic powerhouse back in 1900, at that time being second in tonnage shipped only to Halifax.

Glooscap Trail

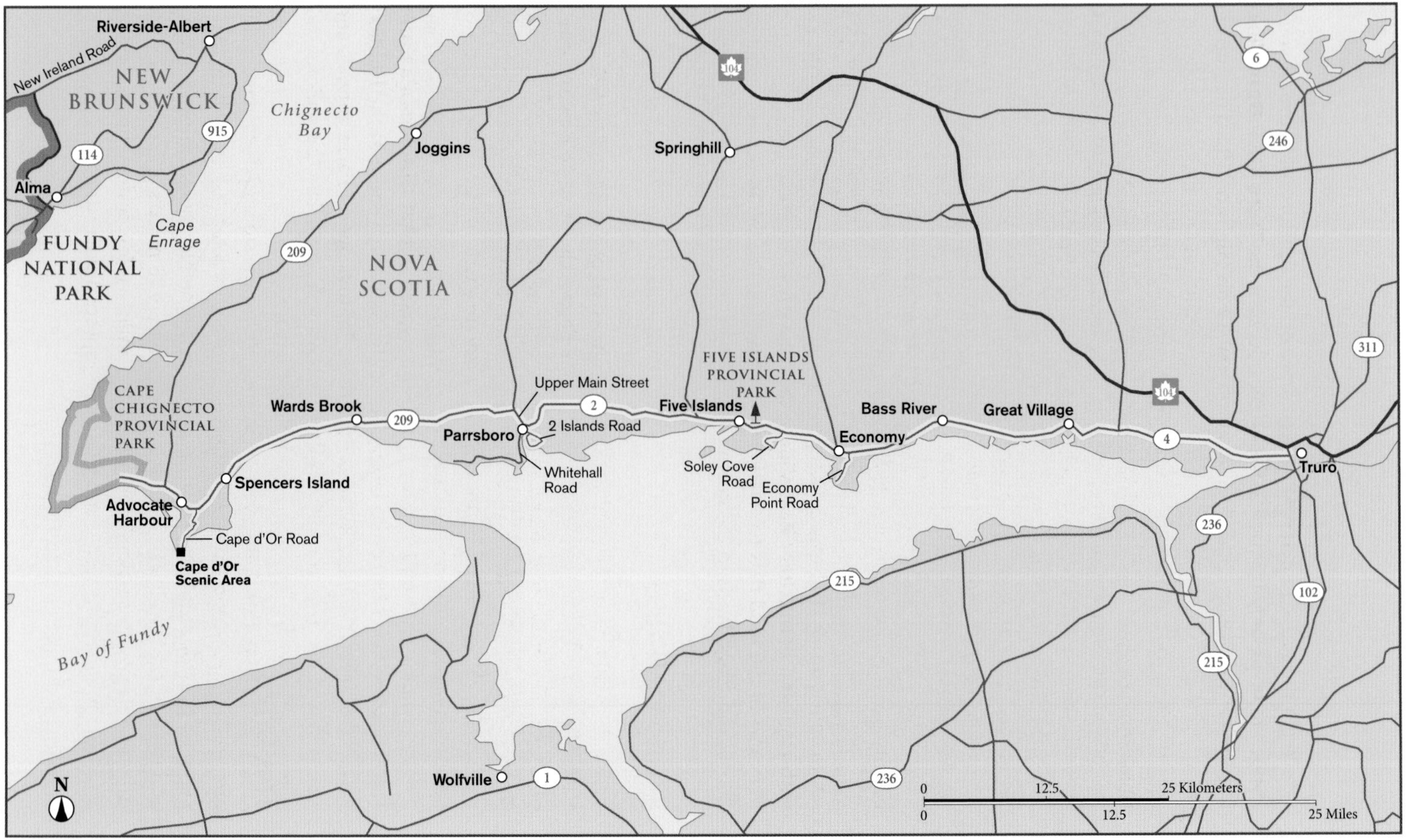

NEW BRUNSWICK

Riverside-Albert

New Ireland Road

915

114

Alma

FUNDY NATIONAL PARK

Chignecto Bay

Cape Enrage

CAPE CHIGNECTO PROVINCIAL PARK

Advocate Harbour

Cape d'Or Scenic Area

Cape d'Or Road

Spencers Island

Wards Brook

209

209

Joggins

NOVA SCOTIA

Parrsboro

Upper Main Street

2 Islands Road

Whitehall Road

2

Five Islands

FIVE ISLANDS PROVINCIAL PARK

Soley Cove Road

Economy Point Road

Economy

Bass River

Great Village

4

Springhill

246

6

311

Truro

102

236

215

236

215

1

Wolfville

Bay of Fundy

N

25 Miles

25 Kilometers

0   12.5   25

0   12.5   25

Begin the 175-kilometer (109-mile) drive on the outskirts of Truro. If you happen to be passing through at the rising tide, visit the **Truro Tidal Bore Viewing Visitor Centre** on Tidal Bore Road off exit 14 on Highway 102. The info center can give exact times to watch for the rush of saltwater up the Salmon River.

To begin the scenic drive, however, take exit 14A off Highway 102 and follow posted signs for Highway 4 West and Highway 2 North to Parrsboro. Signposted as both Highway 4 and Highway 2, the route heads west from the highway, through the residential areas of Central Onslow and Masstown. The route is also called the **Glooscap Trail,** named for the hero from Mi'kmaq and other First Nation legends—more on this later in the drive.

Set in from the shore, the road provides occasional glimpses out to the purple-red tidal flats of Cobequid Bay. Crossing the Debert River, note how the arable land yields thick crop fields. The **Masstown Market** has a selection of this bounty—and is also where you keep on Highway 4 at the roundabout.

At Glenholme, about 17 kilometers (10.6 miles) from the highway exit, turn left to continue on Highway 2. (Keeping straight on Highway 4 would reconnect with Highway 104.) After Great Village the road draws closer to the shoreline, giving views of the mud flats (or watery bay at high tide) to the south, and coniferous forests and marshlands to the north.

Economy Shore

Through small towns, the road winds along the coast of the **Economy Shore.** In **Bass River,** a relocated church on Highway 2 houses the **Bass River Heritage Museum.** The museum explores local genealogy and history, including that of the **Dominion Chair Company,** whose factories once shipped Bass River furniture worldwide. Although a 1989 fire ceased factory production, the company still operates a general store with a furniture gallery in town.

Continuing west on Highway 2, stop for a snack at **That Dutchman's Farm,** at 132 Brown Rd. in Upper Economy. A regular Saturday vendor at the Halifax Farmers' Market, the farm declares itself to be "always open." Farm animals and a petting area are great for kids, while grownups will appreciate the walking trails and subtleties of the Dragon's Breath blue cheese.

At **Economy Point,** turn left on Economy Point Road and then make a right turn to **Thomas' Cove Coastal Reserve.** Two 4-kilometer (2.5-mile) loop hiking trails provide coastal views from Economy Point. Nearly matching the greatest height of the Fundy tides, the tidal range here is 16 meters (52.5 feet) and the Atlantic retreats more than 2 kilometers (1.2 miles) at low water—but given that distance the incoming tide is merciless in its speed: Take caution.

Explore the tidal flats of Cobequid Bay and Minas Basin, but return to shore before the tide rises.

In nearby Economy, you'll easily find the **Cobequid Interpretive Centre** on the highway with its World War II observation tower. Climb the three steep sets of stairs to the tar-paper roof, stopping to admire newspapers and historical artifacts on the levels in between. Ask at the information center about walking trails along the Economy River.

Also in the small community, buy a few souvenirs at the **Glooscap Country Bazaar.** The local cooperative sells homemade pies, garden vegetables, mustard pickles, handmade baby items, and jewelry. Prices are very reasonable, and the quality is excellent.

From Economy, views to the left at high tide are impressive but far more dramatic when the bay is drained. For a quick detour, turn left and drive 1.5 kilometers (0.9 mile) on Soley Cove Road in **Lower Economy.** The **flowerpot rock** here is lesser known (and a little less enchanting) than its Fundy cousins at Hopewell Rocks, New Brunswick. Still, the curious tidal-carved pillar crowded with trees makes for lovely photos of the bay.

The Cobequid Interpretive Centre is a World War II observation tower.

Venture down side roads for extra exploring.

Just past Lower Economy, turn onto Bentley Branch Road to **Five Islands Provincial Park.** The park offers hiking trails, a campground, and a clam-digger's delight. At low tide one can just about walk out to the dumpling islands that give the park its name.

First Nation legends tell of a beaver that flooded the garden of Mi'kmaq hero Glooscap. Unhappy with the animal and its destruction, Glooscap threw clumps of earth at the beaver. The mud pats landed on the ocean floor of the Bay of Fundy, creating the Five Islands, and in breaking the beaver's dam, Glooscap also caused a rush of water that created the tides.

And the tides really do move with the quickness of a flood—more quickly in parts than some can run. Know the tide table and do not venture too far out. Walk on the bottom of the bay, get muddy, and find some beach treasures. Then, before the tide rises, return in plenty of time to walk the park trails, look out from the viewpoints, and barbecue in the campground.

The **Not Since Moses Race** provides unique 5- and 10-kilometer (3- and 6.2-mile) courses over the drained basin. Happening in summer, the muddy running course crosses the tidal zone. A good incentive to run faster!

Parrsboro

Heading west from Five Islands, the Glooscap Trail twists and turns, losing the shore to venture between forested hills. At **Parrsboro,** Highway 2 cuts sharply north on Upper Main Street—but as this is one of the prettiest main streets in Atlantic Canada, take some quality time to explore.

At the junction with Highway 2, turn left on Main Street and cross **Parrsboro Aboiteau** on Two Islands Road. The aboiteau is an unusual and human-made feature. For years holding water to create a recreational area and habitat for wildlife, it is now a drained basin that leads to Parrsboro Harbour.

Visit the **Fundy Geological Museum** at 162 Two Islands Rd., where dinosaur exhibits easily engage kids. Dinosaur footprints were discovered in the area in 1984, leading to the discovery of thousands more fossils. The museum also hosts the August **Nova Scotia Gem and Mineral Show,** known as the "Rockhound Roundup." Two Islands Road leads to a wharf with a beach, small canteen, and lighthouse view.

Back on Main Street, the MV *Kipawo* is firmly beached as **Ship's Company Theatre.** A summer season delights with plays and camps.

A storied history docks along with the *Kipawo*. Launched in 1924, the steel ship was a passenger ferry shuttling between Kingsport, Parrsboro, and Wolfville in the Minas Basin (the name is derived from the first two letters of each town name). In the 1940s, the *Kipawo* tended antisubmarine nets in Conception Bay and went on to become a Bell Island Ferry (see Drive 28) and later provided tours in Newfoundland's Terra Nova National Park (Drive 27) before finally returning to its first homeport.

For a different historical bent, continue on Main Street as it becomes Whitehall Road and visit **Ottawa House** at number 1155. The waterfront house, built in the 1780s, was once a summer home to Sir Charles Tupper, Canada's sixth and shortest-serving prime minister. Tupper held the political position for barely two months (May 1 to July 8, 1896) before Wilfred Laurier, the longest-serving prime minister, came to power. Historical furnishings fill the 21-room mansion, while trails explore nearby Partridge Island, a stop on Samuel de Champlain's 1607 voyage.

Backtrack through Parrsboro and along Highway 2 to where it intersects Route 209, or the Parrsboro Shore Road, to Cape Chignecto. (Western Avenue also connects with Route 209.)

About 15 kilometers (9 miles) from Parrsboro along Route 209, the road draws close to the shoreline again at Fox River and explores the hilly treed area along Greville Bay. Near Port Greville, turn left on Cochrane Road and drive down to the beach for views of Nova Scotia's **Cape Split**—a hook-shaped peninsula where a hiking trail leads out to cragged cliffs. For more in that area, see Drive 10 covering the Annapolis Valley.

The surprising **Age of Sail Heritage Centre** provides a lovely stop with a cafe and hands-on activities in North Greville. A 1908 lighthouse and boathouse add to the heritage appeal of the converted 1854 church. Kids can use a wood plane to smooth out a plank for the ship works or hear a mother's story about a son lost to the sea.

Cape Chignecto

Take a quick detour on Spencers Island Road for lunch or beach and lighthouse views in **Spencers Island**—a favorite spot for camping and kayaking.

Continuing southwest on Route 209 to East Advocate, follow well-posted signs that direct you down a 6-kilometer (3.7-mile) gravel road to **Cape d'Or Scenic Area.** Continue in from the lighthouse at the parking area, to find the

Cape d'Or is on a rocky point overlooking the Bay of Fundy with wrap-around views from Cape Split to Cape Chignecto.

restaurant, accommodations, and red-and-white lighthouse on a rocky point with wrap-around views from Cape Split to Cape Chignecto.

End the scenic drive here. Or, if you have more time in the area, backtrack to Route 209 and continue through fishing villages toward the large wilderness area of **Cape Chignecto Provincial Park.** Ask at the park's interpretive center about hikes to the abandoned village of Eatonville or Red Rocks Beach—both of which are much shorter options than the full 51-kilometer (32-mile) wilderness hike around Cape Chignecto.

Side Trip: Joggins Fossil Cliffs

From the Cape Chignecto area, Route 209 cuts north across the peninsula toward **Joggins.** It's 56 kilometers (34.7 miles) to the **Joggins Fossil Cliffs,** a UNESCO World Heritage Site on Chignecto Bay. A large interpretive center and guided hikes will help you identify the fossils that dot the shoreline. New finds are continually being reported, so keep your eyes open.

While this section is less scenic than the route along Cobequid Bay and Minas Basin, for many the prospect of finding your own piece of ancient history is a weighty enough draw to make the drive.

Rockhounds hunt for fossils at the Joggins Fossil Cliffs, Nova Scotia.

10

Annapolis Valley to Fundy Tides

Windsor to Grand Pré to Wolfville to Halls Harbour

General Description: This 80-kilometer (50-mile) route heads through Annapolis Valley farmlands to Nova Scotia's Bay of Fundy coast. Starting in Windsor—with its hockey museum, oldest Canadian block-house, and giant pumpkins—the journey ventures across rivers, dike lands, and heritage districts. Be lured by freshly roasted coffee, touched by the tragic history of deported Acadian people in the mid-1700s, and arrested with the views from the Lookoff. Finally, savor a sunset and a lobster supper on the wharf at Halls Harbour, while you view Nova Scotia's version of the world's highest tides.

Special Features: West Hants Historical Society Museum, Fort Edward National Historic Site, Windsor Hockey Heritage Centre, Haliburton House, Shand House Museum, Howard Dill Enterprises, Grand Pré National Historic Site, Evangeline Beach, Randall House Museum, Acadia University, Robie Tufts Nature Centre, Fox Hill Cheese House, the Lookoff, Halls Harbour Lobster Pound, eagle watching, tidal zone, lobster suppers, beach walks, beachcombing.

Location: Bay of Fundy coast, Western Nova Scotia.

Driving Route Numbers & Names: Highway 1 (Evangeline Trail), Bluff Road, Highway 101, Grand Pré Road, Route 358, Church Street, Gospel Woods Road, Route 359, West Halls Harbour Road.

Travel Season: From the spring apple blossoms to the fall harvest to winter eagle watching, this is close to an all-season drive. Private gardens are at their peak in June and July while the monster pumpkins fatten up for the autumn harvest. Just west of Canning, in Sheffield Mills, January and early February bring the best bald eagle watching. Although July and August are most popular with visitors, avoiding these months can be recommended, as the Annapolis Valley records some of the hottest temperatures in the province. Summer days often top 30 degrees Centigrade (86 degrees Fahrenheit) plus humidity.

Camping: Drive-in campsites are available in Blomidon Provincial Park, north of Canning. Near Windsor, Smileys Provincial Park has sites plus a dump station, toilets, and water. Reservations are taken for both sites at (888) 544-3434 or parks.novascotia.ca. Find additional private campgrounds near Grand Pré.

Services: This drive passes through a number of small towns, all with gas stations, restaurants, and accommodations. Most of the places to stay are heritage-home bed-and-breakfasts or inns. Hospitals are in Windsor and Kentville.

Nearby Points of Interest: Blomidon Provincial Park, Cape Split, hiking.

Time Zone: Atlantic time zone (GMT minus 4 hours).

The Drive

This 80-kilometer (50-mile) drive connects a string of historic and scenic towns in Nova Scotia's agricultural heartland, the Annapolis Valley. From the once-grand

Annapolis Valley to Fundy Tides

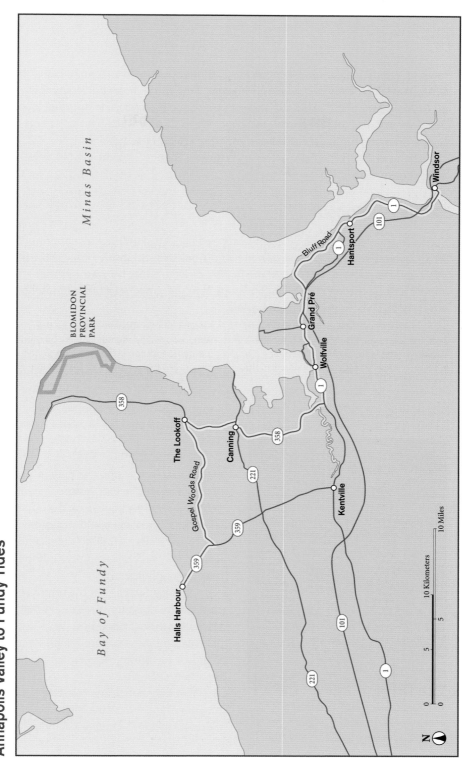

town of Windsor, now most famous for giant pumpkins and a claim to being the **Birthplace of Hockey,** follow the Evangeline Trail through the university town of Wolfville and make a side trip for an eagle-watching session or stunning lookouts—often called look offs in Nova Scotia. Wrap the day watching the Bay of Fundy tides and dining at the lobster pound in Halls Harbour.

Highway 101 is the main artery to Windsor, about 65 kilometers (40 miles) from downtown Halifax.

Heritage Windsor

Start the drive in **Windsor,** where it's easy and delightful to lose the main route when arriving in town. The town's one-time opulence still shows in the gabled roofs and ornate wooden trim on the buildings. Depending on your interests choose a route through the town that stops in at the varied selection of museums, covering bicycles to pumpkins to hockey.

The first settlers, the Mi'kmaq, named the place Pesaquid, meaning "junction of waters." The French later settled the area in 1685, followed by the British in 1749. And it is the British that have left one of the most indelible marks on the town. On Fort Edward Street off King, **Fort Edward National Historic Site** sits on a prominent hill overlooking the junction of the St. Croix and Avon Rivers. Both rivers flow into the Bay of Fundy, famous for its tides that rise and fall as much as 16 meters (52.5 feet) twice daily.

Fort Edward Blockhouse, the oldest blockhouse in Canada, was built as part of an elaborate English defense system. With another blockhouse on the opposite hill, the garrison could survey the two rivers. Today, climb to the second-level of the blockhouse to peer out the cannon loopholes.

On King Street, visit the impressive community museum run by the **West Hants Historical Society** at 281 King St. Wedding dresses, photographs, and Windsor furniture pieces crowd the by-donation museum.

You may notice a public-relations plug for Windsor as "the Birthplace of Hockey." Thomas Chandler

The Annapolis Valley is famed for many crops—including grapes from its local vineyards.

Haliburton—whom I'll get to next—wrote about students at King's College, Canada's oldest independent school, playing "hurley" on Long Pond. West of the downtown, follow Albert Street and then Clifton Avenue to stop in at **Haliburton House,** the 1837 estate of Judge Thomas Chandler Haliburton, and also the location of the **Windsor Hockey Heritage Centre**.

Apple orchards, lush lawns, and a sprawling white house named Clifton feature in the estate. Haliburton is known for penning the humor tales of Sam Slick. Today we know less his name and more his famous turns of phrase turned clichés, which included: "It's raining cats and dogs", "The early bird gets the worm", and "You can't get blood out of a stone".

Make a loop up past King's-Edgehill School and stop in at its odd neighbor: **Howard Dill Enterprises** at 400 College Rd. There, farmer Howard Dill grew world-record-size pumpkins fit for a Cinderella coach. The Dill family continues the tradition, and the friendly farm sells seeds to start your own pumpkin patch and welcomes visitors to see the valley giants growing. You can also drive through the property on a hockey pilgrimage to see **Long Pond,** direct from the writings of Haliburton.

The Dill Farm welcomes visitors to see giant pumpkins growing.

Windsor's heritage-home-lined streets tend to slope down toward Water Street and the river. Overlooking the Avon, **Shand House Museum** at 389 Avon St. has a beautiful vantage that belies the wealth of some families of Windsor; however, the museum only opens for special events and by appointment.

To leave town, pick up Highway 1 and the Evangeline Trail on Water Street, as a bridge spans a narrow tentacle of the Avon River. Avoid the controlled-access Highway 101, and opt instead for the meander of Highway 1 toward Hantsport.

After 11 kilometers (6.8 miles), Highway 1 follows Hantsport's Main Street. Pass through town and turn right to drive along Bluff Road. The two-lane road with a narrow shoulder sneaks lovely river views in with the roadside wildflowers like goldenrod and Queen Anne's lace. Hay fields in various stages of cutting, drying, and baling abut apple orchards and animal-feed cornfields. Roads are sliced with railroad tracks leading to the now-closed Hantsport gypsum plant.

Bluff Road meets Highway 1 and Highway 101 after 8 kilometers (5 miles) in order to cross the Gaspereau River. To reach Grand Pré, hop on Highway 101 for one exit (from 9 to 10).

Grand Pré Acadians

Take exit 10 and your nose will lead you to **Just Us! Coffee Roasters,** at 11865 Hwy. 1. Maybe not a planned stop, the invading smell of freshly roasted coffee seems to turn the signal indicator light on all by itself. Pull in for fair-traded, organic coffee. While you wait for your brew, look through the varied displays in the fair trade museum.

Continue on Highway 1 toward Grand Pré, making a right turn at Grand Pré Road to follow signs for **Grand Pré National Historic Site.** The admission building looks like a train station (the land was once owned by Dominion Atlantic Railway), but venture through to discover postcard-worthy scenery: the iconic memorial church, statue of Evangeline—poet Henry Wadsworth Longfellow's fictional Acadian heroine sculpted by artist **Louis-Philippe Hébert**—and pretty grounds filled with flowering arbors, rambunctious ducks, and even an archaeological dig.

In the interpretive center view the film, excavated artifacts, and scale models that help piece together the Acadian story. As they settled in the Maritimes, Acadians reclaimed marshes from the sea. When they refused to pledge allegiance to the English, who had most recently gained control of the territory, Acadians were deported starting in 1755. About 10,000 were uprooted between 1755 and 1763

Grand Pré National Historic Site has postcard-worthy scenery:
the iconic memorial church and a statue of Evangeline.

in the Great Upheaval—*Le grand dérangement* in French—and thousands died en route to exile in France and the United States.

End the visit with a drive through historic Acadian farmlands, traveling along Grand Pré Road (about 3 kilometers [2 miles] each way) as it cuts across the dike lands. This particular agricultural area covers 1,219 hectares (3,013 acres) that are below sea level. Bald eagles may be perched on utility poles above the flats, waiting for small prey to scurry across the fields.

Grand Pré Road climbs back above sea level and ends above **Evangeline Beach,** with views of the Minas Basin and Blomidon Ridge. On the red-sand shore, flocks of endangered semipalmated sandpipers feed on the rich tidal flats, fattening up for their migration. For those whose lunch doesn't include invertebrates from the mud flats, there is a small canteen at the beach.

Wolfville's Lovely Main Street

Return on Grand Pré Road to Highway 1 and continue west about 5 kilometers (3 miles) to **Wolfville.** You'll pass the lovely **Domaine de Grand Pré** winery at 11611 Hwy. 1, which welcomes guests for wine tasting, a walk through the grapevines and simple museum, or a fine dinner under the patio arbor. A little farther along the road at 11143 Hwy. 1 is **Lightfoot & Wolfville,** which has a tasting room open daily. A trusted source recommends their Blanc de Blancs Brut.

Wolfville's Main Street, which is also Highway 1, confirms why the town is one of the most desirable and artistic communities in the province. Wolfville hosts the **Apple Blossom Festival** in May when spring flowers are budding in the valley, and the **Deep Roots Music Festival** each September.

Wrought-iron-style lampposts, flower boxes, and pub patios, create a historical but lived-in feel. The town revolves around **Acadia University**—the students of which double the town population during the school year. Established in 1838, the Acadia University grounds sit west of downtown and are lovely for a stroll as the pretty architecture features ornate clock towers and regal columns.

In Wolfville, which was originally (and far less appealingly!) named Mud Creek, stop in at the Dijon-colored **Randall House Museum,** 259 Main St., or the lovely gardens at **Blomidon Inn,** 195 Main St., just one of the historic inns and heritage homes that offer accommodation choices in the town.

If it's near dusk, wait around at the **Robie Tufts Nature Centre** (Front Street and Elm Avenue) for the chimney swifts that reportedly swoop into the chimney as the sun sets.

If not, depart from Wolfville along Highway 1 (which heads west to traffic-clogged New Minas and Kentville) before you cut toward the Bay of Fundy through cow pastures and cornfields.

From Greenwich, Route 358 leads across the Cornwallis River toward Canning and the Bay of Fundy coast. After about 4.5 kilometers (2.8 miles) Church Street intersects the route for an easterly detour to **Fox Hill Cheese House** at 1678 Church St. Taste aged cheddars and smoked Goudas at the farm and store, which raises the cattle on-site. The shop area includes a glassed-in production facility with a few interpretive displays.

Returning on Church Street to Route 358, the road continues north to **Canning.** The tiny town features a rather unique memorial—a monument honoring Harold Borden, who died in the Boer War. Harold Borden was the son of Sir Frederick Borden, a government minister. (Another relation, Robert Borden, was born in nearby Grand Pré and served as prime minister during the First World War.)

Sheffield Mills, west of Canning, lures in the Audubon crowd with its winter **Eagle Watch Festival.** Eagles are fed most mornings in January and early February, and the birds of prey flock by the dozens to the local fields for the snack.

Although Route 358 continues to Scots Bay and a wonderful hike to **Cape Split** (about 12 kilometers [7.5 miles] return over easy-to-moderate terrain) as well as **Blomidon Provincial Park,** with its 180-meter (591-feet) cliffs, this drive turns around after a steep climb to a viewpoint.

Known as **the Lookoff,** a parking area along the right side of the road places you in perfect position to enjoy stunning views from 200 meters (656 feet) up. The hill plummets down to near sea level before flattening out into grassy fields, straight hedgerows, white farmhouses, domed pigsties, and red barns. The scene ripples out to Minas Basin.

Farms in the area produce rich fruit and vegetable harvests, from strawberries to cucumbers and broccoli. Try to identify the crops as you drive past the many local farms. Agricultural festivals abound here, from the spring Apple Blossom Festival in Wolfville to the **Windsor Pumpkin Festival and Regatta.**

Tidal Zone in Halls Harbour

From the Lookoff, take a local-worthy shortcut through Arlington and Glenmont (when returning from the Lookoff, it's the right turn at the sharp bend). Not so much a scenic route as a means to reach a scenic destination, the 18-kilometer (11.2-mile) route along Gospel Woods Road climbs and descends the terrain of **North Mountain.**

The road connects with Route 359, which cuts a more direct route to **Halls Harbour** from Kentville. After a couple of tight turns, you're on West Halls Harbour Road—the only road through town. Park near the town wharf, where fishing boats sit at the mercy of the tides, or near the beach and **Halls Harbour Lobster**

Fishing boats sit at the mercy of the tides in Halls Harbour, Nova Scotia.

Pound. The restaurant serves lobster suppers on a wharf patio, sometimes with blueberry shortcake for dessert.

Before or after a meal, wander down to the beach for views across the Bay of Fundy to Cape d'Or and Cape Chignecto (Drive 9). Facing west, you're in the perfect location to catch the sunset.

11

Brier Island

Annapolis Royal to Digby Neck to Brier Island

General Description: Over a favorite, 135-kilometer (84-mile) scenic drive, follow the ferries and views out to Nova Scotia's most westerly point. Lush gardens and Acadian history define Annapolis Royal, while scallops and sea captains are at home on the wharf in Digby. The trip along Digby Neck is a remote venture west: Hike to the precarious-looking Balancing Rock, watch sea birds and whales, and learn about the first solo round-the-world sailor, Joshua Slocum.

Special Features: Annapolis Royal Historic Gardens, Fort Anne National Historic Site, Sinclair Inn Museum, O'Dell House Museum, Annapolis Tidal Station, Melanson Settlement National Historic Site, Port-Royal National Historic Site, Upper Clements Parks, Annapolis Basin Look-off Provincial Park, Digby scallops, Admiral Digby Museum, Balancing Rock, Joshua Slocum Monument, Grand Passage Lighthouse, Brier Island Lighthouse, whale watching.

Location: Western Nova Scotia, along the Bay of Fundy coast.

Driving Route Numbers & Names: Highway 8, St. George Street, Highway 1, Granville Road, Highway 101, Route 303, Shore Road, Route 217, Petite Passage Ferry, Grand Passage Ferry, Water Street, Lighthouse Road.

Travel Season: Whales feed in these waters starting in the spring, but July through fall is the best time for viewing humpbacks, dolphins, porpoises, minkes, finbacks, and the endangered right whales.

Camping: Private campgrounds in Digby and Annapolis Royal offer complete facilities for tents and RVs, while Whale Cove Campground has the only facilities on Digby Neck. Inland, about 50 kilometers (31 miles) from Annapolis Royal along Highway 8, Kejimkujik National Park has forested campsites close to canoeing lakes, swimming beaches, boat rentals, and hiking trails.

Services: Digby Neck has cottages and other summer-vacation comforts, while Annapolis Royal and Digby offer the essentials: medical services as well as gas stations and supplies. As Nova Scotia's dock for the Saint John–Digby ferry, the scallop-famous town of Digby offers many basic accommodations. For heritage charm, book a stay at one of the many large Victorian homes-turned-B&Bs in Annapolis Royal.

Nearby Points of Interest: Yarmouth-area Acadian shore, Bear River Heritage Museum, Mi'kmaq Heritage and Cultural Centre.

Time Zone: Atlantic time zone (GMT minus 4 hours).

The Drive

Starting at a military stronghold that flipped from French to British control, this 135-kilometer (84-mile) scenic drive travels out to the westernmost tip of the province and packs in some of Nova Scotia's best attractions. Whale watch or hike; take tea in the garden or eat a scallop dinner; learn about Acadian settlers or ride a roller coaster—the options are bountiful.

Brier Island

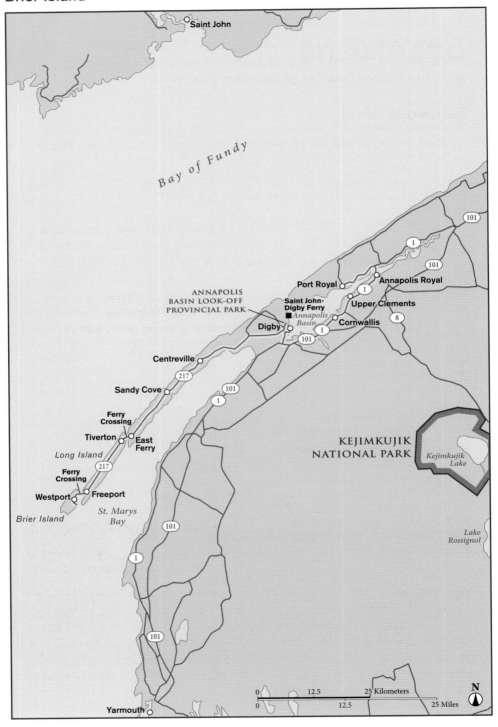

Drive Highway 101 to exit 22, taking Highway 8 into Annapolis Royal. Alternately, arrive on Highway 8 via Kejimkujik National Park (see the side trip at the end of this drive), cutting through the center of the province.

Annapolis Royal

Tucked between the wide Annapolis River and the small Allains River, **Annapolis Royal** boasts a compact and lovely heritage district of Victorian homes and museums. Highway 8 intersects the Evangeline Trail (Highway 1) and St. George Street in the town center. From there, quickly access the town's delightful historic attractions.

At 441 St. George St. (Highway 8), the **Annapolis Royal Historic Gardens** offer lush summer blooms over 6.9 hectares (17 acres). Lovely features include a rose garden, aquatic plants, and dike land trail. A thatched Acadian cottage is a special treat as it shows life before the 1755 deportation. The garden is open May to Oct, with spring blossoms and fall foliage in the shoulder seasons.

Fort Anne National Historic Site, also on St. George Street, sits on watch over the river. Three blocky white chimneys and steep grassy slopes give away its

Fort Anne was Canada's first national historic site.

fortified position. Fort Anne was Canada's first national historic site and has been the scene of much upheaval as groups struggled for control of the region. For more historic exploration, stop in at the the fascinating **Sinclair Inn Museum,** 230 St. George St., or the **O'Dell House Museum,** 136 St. George St.

Before traveling southwest on the scenic drive along the Annapolis Basin, take a detour—crossing to the North Mountain side. On the causeway, the **Annapolis Tidal Station** turns the energy of the Fundy tides into electricity, and is also the location of a summer visitor center.

In Granville Ferry, turn left on Granville Road. Here, there are lovely views of Annapolis Royal as you make the 9-kilometer (5.6-mile) drive to **Melanson Settlement National Historic Site,** the location of an Acadian settlement prior to

Port-Royal National Historic Site reconstructs Samuel de Champlain's original 1605 fur-trading post.

deportation. Only a few mounds and depressions remain in sight, showing where Charles Melanson dit La Ramée and Marie Dugas settled in 1664.

Continue along the coast to **Port-Royal National Historic Site.** The site reconstructs Samuel de Champlain's original 1605 fur-trading post, and costumed actors bring the historical figures to life. The site also revives Canada's first social club, **the Order of Good Cheer**—a club-like tradition of feasting that got men through winter.

Cross the Annapolis River causeway back to Annapolis Royal, following Highway 1 west along the coast. Amid rolling forested hills find **Upper Clements Parks**, one of the few places to ride a roller coaster or zipline in the province.

Although HMCS/CFB Cornwallis closed in 1994, Cornwallis Park still has the look of a military base with barracks-style housing. About 4 kilometers (2.5 miles) after Cornwallis Park, join Highway 101 as it bridges Bear River.

Follow signs to Digby at exit 26.

Digby

Route 303 connects the controlled-access highway to the **Digby** town center. Scallop dinners and wharf cats define the waterfront district of this slightly rough-edged community. Walk down to the fishing wharf where the scallop boats are moored, or stop by the **Admiral Digby Museum** at 95 Montague St. to learn about the region's fishing history as well as the Loyalist settlers.

Digby Scallop Days celebrates the famous local seafood in August, while thousands of motorcycles gather for the **Wharf Rat Rally** over Labour Day weekend.

The MV *Fundy Rose* departs Digby making one or two trips daily to Saint John, New Brunswick (Drive 3). Before continuing on the drive, head north of town past **Digby Pines Resort** to admire the view from **Annapolis Basin Lookoff Provincial Park** on Shore Road.

Digby Neck

Over a 70-kilometer (43.5-mile) stretch of the Digby Neck and Islands Scenic Drive, Route 217 travels southwest across islands connected by two ferries. Mostly forested but with the feel of the sea close by, the drive arrives in ever-smaller communities. Pass through Seabrook, then Centreville. At **Sandy Cove** see what the ocean has washed ashore on the sheltered east-facing beach, and cross the peninsula to see the differences on the Fundy-facing coast. Near **Little River,** a wind turbine rises above the forest landscape.

About 45 kilometers (28 miles) from Digby, the road switchbacks down to wharves and a ferry dock. Gulls circle above the shore. Cross Petite Passage by ferry from East Ferry to Tiverton. Ferries generally depart East Ferry on the half hour, and at press time the fare was $7 per crossing (info: 902-839-2882). (For the way home: There is no return fee collected and ferries depart Tiverton on the hour.)

The 5-minute ferry ride provides a quick opportunity to take in the coastal scenery. At **Tiverton,** disembark and drive 4 kilometers (2.5 miles) to a large parking area and trailhead for the walk to the **Balancing Rock**—the highlight of Long Island. A 1.5-kilometer (0.9-mile) hike through marshland and forest leads to a staircase and viewing platform. Admire the basalt-rock coastline and the seemingly set-in-place Balancing Rock, which weighs about 20 tonnes.

Further on, you reach **Central Grove Provincial Park,** which provides a basic picnic spot and 800-meter (0.5-mile) walk out to the Fundy coast.

Time your stops well to continue along Route 217 to Freeport, and not miss the second ferry.

Brier Island

The Grand Passage ferry connects Long Island to **Brier Island.** The fare is again $7, and the journey takes about 10 minutes and leaves Freeport on the hour (info: 902-839-2302). (For the way home from Brier Island: ferries depart Westport at 25 minutes past the hour.)

The community of **Westport** is a fair size for being the end of the road, and fishing and tourism are important sources of income for residents. All four corners of the island are worth a visit.

Turn left off the ferry to follow Water Street around to a small park that pays tribute to **Joshua Slocum,** who lived on Brier Island as a boy and was the first man to solo circumnavigate the world in his boat the *Spray*. Slocum wrote *Sailing Alone Around the World* about the experience. Today, the **Joshua Slocum Monument** stands next to a small park area. Hike over a rocky, fireweed-covered bluff to view the basalt coastline. Binoculars are handy to observe the birds out on Peter Island in Grand Passage. **The Peter Island Light** was constructed in 1851.

Whale-watching cruises leave from Brier Island to observe the huge marine mammals that feed offshore. Local species visiting the Bay of Fundy during summer include minkes, finbacks, humpbacks, and endangered right whales. The latter also mate in these waters.

Check that the basalt Balancing Rock is still hanging in, on Long Island, Nova Scotia.

Basalt rock, seabirds, and a lighthouse form a picturesque complement off Brier Island, Nova Scotia.

Driving back along Water Street from the Slocum Monument, pass the ferry dock and follow the gravel road to its northern end at **Grand Passage Lighthouse.** A guest book is a fun place to record your observations—be it about seabirds, whales, or fishing boats. The Grand Passage Lighthouse is also the island's newest, having been built in 1901.

Other island lighthouses include one at the southwest point of the island, located on Lighthouse Road and built in 1809.

To reach the fourth and final corner of Brier Island, take Gull Rock Road to wide and wind-swept Big Pond Cove.

Side Trip: Kejimkujik National Park

The inland **Kejimkujik National Park** is a starkly different ecosystem and it protects a forest and network of lakes in the heart of Nova Scotia, near Maitland Bridge. The park is a cultural site for the Mi'kmaq people with petroglyphs and traditional camps that pay testament to the indigenous people's long history in the area.

Kejimkujik National Park protects a forest and network of lakes in the heart of Nova Scotia.

Hike forest trails, swim off the beaches, and watch for loons and other bird life. The park rents canoes and kayaks at **Jakes Landing.** More than 300 camp-sites are located at **Jeremys Bay campground,** but those paddling a canoe can access backcountry sites, including some situated on lake islands and riverbanks. These allow for a remote escape into the quiet of the park as well as incomparable stargazing.

12

LaHave River

Lunenburg to LaHave to Rissers Beach

General Description: Along the banks of the LaHave River and out to some of Nova Scotia's loveliest beaches, this 65-kilometer (40-mile) scenic route combines hidden history with a river crossing and coastal scenery. Travel on a cable ferry before eating lunch at a local bakery. Visit Mi'kmaq wigwams, a mission cemetery, and lighthouse at Fort Point Museum, or walk beaches and a boardwalk at Rissers Beach Provincial Park.

Special Features: Halifax & Southwestern Railway Museum, Masons Beach, the Ovens Natural Park, Hirtles Beach, LaHave River cable ferry, Fort Point Museum, Crescent Beach, LaHave Islands Marine Museum, Rissers Beach Provincial Park.

Location: Southwestern Nova Scotia, Lunenburg County.

Driving Route Numbers & Names: Falkland Street, Victoria Road, Highway 3, Route 332, Feltzen South Road, Ovens Road, Kingsburg Road, Hirtle Beach Road, LaHave River cable ferry, Route 331, Fort Point Road, Crescent Beach Road, LaHave Islands Road.

Travel Season: In the summer, hit the beaches—Hirtles, Crescent, and Rissers on this route—to enjoy the warm days and fresh Atlantic air. The shoulder seasons, June and September, are particularly lovely on Nova Scotia's South Shore.

Camping: Camp at Rissers Beach Provincial Park, where more than 90 sites offer options for RVs and tents. Showers, washrooms, and a playground add comfort to the camping experience. Plus, you'll be at the beach!

Services: Lunenburg, at the start of this drive, and Bridgewater, which lies inland along the LaHave River, both offer a good selection of services. Groceries, gas, and medical attention are available in both towns. Lunenburg offers superb heritage bed-and-breakfasts amongst the hilly streets, but on busy festival weekends, motels and inns in Bridgewater may have greater availability.

Nearby Points of Interest: DesBrisay Museum, Wile Carding Mill Museum, Miller Point Peace Park, Petite Riviere Vineyards.

Time Zone: Atlantic time zone (GMT minus 4 hours).

The Drive

Covering over 65 kilometers (40 miles), this coastal and riverbank drive visits some of the province's loveliest and—often times—emptiest beaches. Find perfect crescents of sand near coastal hikes, island museums, and provincial campgrounds. Plus you cross the LaHave River on a cable ferry to visit the first capital of New France, established on these banks in 1632.

Begin the drive in the iconic waterfront town of **Lunenburg,** where diverse museums and heritage accommodations line the hilly streets (covered in Drive 13,

LaHave River

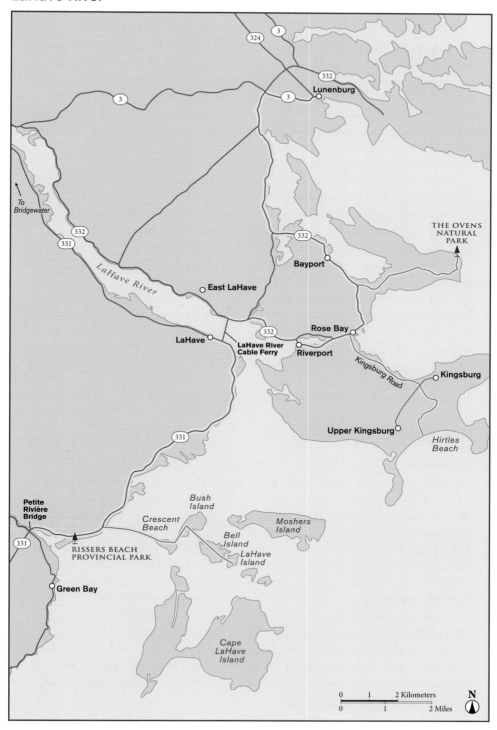

the Lighthouse Route). Leave downtown driving west following Falkland Street and then take Victoria Road as it becomes Highway 3 inland toward Bridgewater.

You'll pass the **Halifax & Southwestern Railway Museum** on Victoria Road (Highway 3), which recalls the long-past days of steam engines in the area. An intensely detailed scale model shows the route of the train, with buildings recreating the Lunenburg waterfront and Bridgewater rail yard. Tracks torn up, the railway beds around the province have now been converted to a trail system.

At the junction with Route 332, turn left toward Riverport.

Route 332 follows the water through First South, where a left turn on Masons Beach Road leads to **Masons Beach** on Puffeycup Cove.

Pass through Bayport on the shore of Lower South Cove, and about 12 kilometers (7.5 miles) from Lunenburg, turn left to follow Feltzen South Road out onto a hooked peninsula. Take a right on Ovens Road to find the 77-hectare (190-acre) **Ovens Natural Park** where gold panners once swirled the sand looking for riches.

The Nova Scotia gold rush started in 1861, and the frenzy grew enough to sustain a local community of more than 1,000 miners. You can still pan for gold on Cunards Beach and hike coastal trails. The park's namesakes, the Ovens sea caves, are perhaps the most dramatic attraction: Descend a boardwalk to hear the waves boom in Cannon Cave. Kayak tours are another way to view the sea caves at the park, which also boasts a campground, eatery, and cabins.

Leave the park and rejoin Route 332.

Rose Bay

From Feltzen South Road, follow a 2-kilometer (1.2-mile) less-coastal stretch toward Rose Bay. The lesser-known **Sand Dollar Beach** on Rose Bay is more sheltered than the shores that lie ahead. Exposed only at low tide, the sandbar offers the delight of beachcombing. Live sand dollars are brown, while the dead ones (and the ones okay to collect) are white.

In the small community of Rose Bay, a left heads to Upper Kingsburg. (Route 332 continues straight on to Riverport and East LaHave). Here, turn left on Kingsburg Road and follow the road for 4 kilometers (2.5 miles) and then make a right on Hirtle Beach Road.

With about 3 kilometers (2 miles) of tide-washed sand on Hartling Bay, **Hirtles Beach** is popular for dog walking, surfing, picnicking, and beachcombing. It's a magically changing beach, and one of my family's favorites. Out to the west (right when looking offshore), the protected Gaff Point offers an excellent 6.5-kilometer (4-mile) hike to hidden coves. View the remote and wave-washed **West Ironbound Island** that sits off the point.

Hirtles Beach is popular for dog walking, surfing, picnicking, and beachcombing.

Follow Hirtle Beach and Kingsburg Roads back to Rose Bay to head west on Route 332 toward the LaHave cable ferry. Pass through Riverport, where the large wooden homes are a reminder of the area's shipbuilding history and good natural harbor.

The **LaHave River cable ferry** crosses near the rivermouth, connecting East LaHave and Riverport with LaHave on the far shore. The 10–15 minute crossing costs $7 or less if purchasing tickets by the book (info: 902-527-7632). Fishing boats, wharves, and heritage commercial buildings edge the river.

To bypass the ferry, or if it's not running, follow Route 332 for about 18 kilometers (11 miles) up the river to the bridge crossings in Bridgewater. You'll pass the wooded trails at **Miller Point Peace Park** on the way.

LaHave

When the ferry docks in **LaHave,** stop in at the **LaHave Bakery** in the heritage LaHave Outfitting Company building. Treats and breads stock the shelves, while a small cafe serves simple lunch fare. My favorite? The fresh herb-and-cheese rolls, which can be eaten unaccompanied, straight from the bag.

Fishing boats, wharves, and heritage commercial buildings edge the river, where the LaHave River cable ferry crosses.

Less than a kilometer past the ferry dock, watch for Fort Point Road on the left. Make a left turn, and continue out on the point to visit **Fort Point Museum and Lighthouse,** the place where Lieutenant General Isaac de Razilly settled to establish the first capital of New France in 1632.

Long before de Razilly's arrival, however, the Mi'kmaq people lived along the **LaHave River**, calling it Pijenooiskak—meaning "having long joints". In the fort grounds, a cemetery and garden offer more to explore and a Mi'kmaq interpretive village has canvas wigwams and hosts festivities and activities.

The LaHave River was first mapped by Samuel de Champlain in 1604. Champlain moved on to establish a colony first on St. Croix Island (see side trip for Drive 2) and later at Port Royal (see Drive 11). When de Razilly's New France settlers arrived in 1632, they started the local lumber industry, clearing land for agriculture near Petite Riviere. To protect itself, the fort had 40 cannons, and Capuchin monks started a chapel and mission here.

The fort was abandoned in 1636, after de Razilly had died, but the story survives through the lighthouse and museum. The face of the river is continually

Lieutenant General Isaac de Razilly settled to establish the first capital of New France in 1632 at Fort Point.

changing: Since the 1600s this point has eroded, and the original location of Fort Sainte Marie de Grace is now out in the low-tide zone.

As British and other Europeans settled the area in the 1700s, the forests of mature lumber begat sawmills and shipyards.

Today, the LaHave's salmon runs draw anglers to the riverbanks, and many use the river for recreational boating.

Crescent Beach & Bush Island

Follow Route 331 southwest. You're passing islands and coves tucked in behind the shelter of the LaHave Islands. In fact the spot is so protected there's even a place called **Snug Harbour.** At Crescent Beach Road, turn left to explore a beach that is also the road to Bush, Bell, and LaHave Islands.

The 2-kilometer (1.2-mile) sand bar of Crescent Beach was once the only route to the LaHave Islands. Now a road connects to the mainland, but cars are still permitted to drive along the compact sand area of the beach. There are access points at both ends of the beach. If you choose that route, drive slowly and watch for pedestrians. My preference, however, is to keep to the road.

Continue over a one-lane bridge to Bush Island and then on to Jenkins and Bell islands. The **LaHave Islands Marine Museum** at 100 LaHave Islands Rd. shows exhibits in a heritage United Church. Outside, the double-ender *Vera Mae* is a preserved Bush Island boat that was built on adjacent Bell Island.

Rissers Beach

Back on Route 331 from Crescent Beach Road, you'll soon enter **Rissers Beach Provincial Park.** One of the few provincial campgrounds in the area, it quickly fills up in summer with beachgoers. Walk the boardwalk over the marshlands, relax on the sands, and learn about the local wildlife species.

To the west, look out along the Lunenburg County coast. To the east lies the wide, H-shaped Cape LaHave Island.

Inland from Petite Riviere Bridge, Italy Cross Road tours past **Petite Riviere Vineyards.** The winery uses local grapes and features an art gallery, reviving a wine-making tradition that de Razilly and the French started with their settlement in the 1600s.

13

Lighthouse Route

Peggy's Cove to Oak Island to Mahone Bay to Lunenburg

General Description: This is an iconic 195-kilometer (121-mile) coastal drive featuring shipwrecks, lighthouses, and buried treasure. At its full length the Lighthouse Route continues south to Yarmouth. But this first stretch from Halifax to Lunenburg holds the weightiest bounty. Watch the ocean spray at Peggy's Cove, take the ferry to Tancook Island, mull over Oak Island theories, reach into a touch tank at the Lunenburg Fishermen's Museum, or sail on the *Bluenose II*.

Special Features: SS *Atlantic* Memorial, Peggy's Cove Lighthouse, William E. deGarthe Memorial, Swissair Memorial, Cleveland Beach Provincial Park, Queensland Beach Provincial Park, Bayswater Beach Provincial Park, Graves Island Provincial Park, Chester Playhouse, Oak Island, Mahone Bay Museum, Amos Pewter, Second Peninsula Provincial Park, Lunenburg Academy, *Bluenose II*, Fisheries Museum of the Atlantic, Knaut-Rhuland House Museum, St. John's Church, UNESCO World Heritage Site, seafood.

Location: Southwest Nova Scotia, from the Halifax Regional Municipality to Lunenburg County.

Driving Route Numbers & Names: Route 333, Terence Bay Road, Highway 3, Fox Point Road, Route 329, Duke Street, Water Street, Crandall Point Road.

Travel Season: Summer festivals draw many to Chester, Mahone Bay, and Lunenburg, and the sunny weather attracts all to the beaches and coastline. But this drive can be completed close to year-round, save in bad winter conditions. September and October are particularly lovely months to visit the South Shore, when the attractions and restaurants are still open but crowds have lessened.

Camping: Graves Island Provincial Park, mid route near Chester, offers waterside camping with full services for tents and RVs. Campgrounds in Lunenburg and Martins River offer additional options. Rissers Beach Provincial Park is featured in Drive 12 and lies about 24 kilometers (15 miles) from Lunenburg via the LaHave River cable ferry.

Services: Halifax, near the start of the drive, offers the greatest array of services (including medical). Find a hospital in Lunenburg. You'll locate gas stations regularly along the route in Chester, Mahone Bay, and Lunenburg—towns that also tempt with heritage inns and homey bed-and-breakfasts. Call a few and book based on the friendliness of the host.

Nearby Points of Interest: Tancook Island, Ross Farm Museum, as well as Drive 12 attractions along the LaHave River.

Time Zone: Atlantic time zone (GMT minus 4 hours).

The Drive

Trace the Nova Scotia coastline with this drive to shipwrecks, lighthouses, and islands. The 195-kilometer (121-mile) route meanders around hidden coves, past

Lighthouse Route

fishing wharves, and into friendly small towns to follow heartbreak and mystery—including tales from the legendary Oak Island.

Begin this scenic drive at exit 2, traveling east-bound on Highway 103.

If coming from Halifax, follow St. Margarets Bay Road from the Armdale roundabout (Highway 3 from Halifax), or take exit 2B if traveling west-bound on Highway 103.

Both connect with Route 333 and head toward the coast. The first stretch of the drive passes through unscenic commercial and residential buildings. But think instead about the fishing schooners, shipwrecks, and seafaring history ahead—considering the perseverance needed to live on the coast.

At Terence Bay Road in **Whites Lake,** turn left and follow the route for about 8 kilometers (5 miles). Turn left to Sandy Bay (right goes to Lower Prospect) and follow signs for the **SS *Atlantic* Memorial** at 178 Sandy Cove Rd. Instead of sandy beaches, this coastline is edged with granite shores. The fairly flat but uneven landscape is pitted with boulders left by the last ice age. Lobster traps, fishing wharves, and docked boats show the local heritage.

On April 1, 1873, a storm battered the SS *Atlantic,* a White Star Line ship, as it headed to Halifax to refuel for its crossing from New York to Liverpool. The ship, carrying 954 people, smashed against Mars Rock. In the largest shipwreck before the *Titanic,* 562 people died. Of those, 277 are buried at the memorial site.

Walk the pretty trail down to the shoreline memorial. A seawall protects a mass grave from the ocean's force, while a boardwalk leads to the community cemetery. An interpretive site records the details of the shipwreck, including a report from the captain, James A. Williams.

Nearby, the old foundation of St. Paul's Church, which was struck by lightning and burnt down in 1942, is near a newer church. This reflective note of the day will continue, as you return to Route 333 and head toward memorials for an airplane crash and lost fishermen.

Peggy's Cove

Past Blind Bay, the landscape empties. **Peggy's Cove Preservation Area** treasures both the icons and the environment of the Chebucto Peninsula. Scant trees are rooted in this boulder-dotted landscape. The verdant green contrasts the fog-gray granite with its vitality.

Make a left turn at Peggy's Point Road and drive through the active fishing village, clustered with shingled buildings and wharves. Park at the information center (there's another large lot at the end of the road, near the lighthouse), and then explore the village on foot—it's a 5-minute stroll to the lighthouse. Cafes and

Peggy's Cove is both a working fishing village and a tourist attraction.

restaurants will be busy with tourists, perhaps escaping the chill of the Atlantic fog.

Across from the info center at 96 Peggys Point Road, the **William E. deGarthe Memorial Monument** is a 30-meter (98-foot) granite sculpture and fishermen's monument. Chiseled into the outcropping behind the artist's house, the granite features 32 fishermen, their families, and Saint Elmo, the patron saint of sailors.

Red-and-white **Peggy's Cove Lighthouse** sits at the far end of the road, cemented firmly to its granite bluff. Be cautious of the strong Atlantic swells that roll in: They make for fantastic photos but can be extremely dangerous.

The trip to Peggy's Cove is a popular route for tour buses—try not to get stuck behind one when leaving, as you return to Route 333.

Follow the road to the quiet vantage of the **Swissair Memorial Site** at Whalesback. On September 2, 1998, local fishermen and emergency workers helped with rescue and then recovery efforts for Swissair Flight 111, which crashed off the Nova Scotia coast. There were no survivors; 229 people died.

Be cautious of the strong Atlantic swells that roll in at Peggy's Cove: They make for fantastic photos but can be extremely dangerous.

Driving toward the head of **St. Margarets Bay,** for which Peggy's Cove Lighthouse marks the entrance, look out for sailboats in the Atlantic waters and craft galleries along the shore. The homes along this stretch show more heritage style than previous sections of Route 333. Islands parallel the coast—as the route passes waterfront scenes of timber fishing wharves, moored sailboats, and leaning boatsheds—to reconnect with Highway 3 in Upper Tantallon. Here, turn left on Highway 3 to travel west toward Hubbards and Chester.

Through to Hubbards, the snaking coastline is defined by almost-white-sand beaches—first **Black Point Beach,** then two provincial parks at **Cleveland Beach** and **Queensland Beach.** With such sparkling sand, all are summer favorites.

Continuing on, the route passes the **Hooked Rug Museum of North America,** with both historic and contemporary exhibits on the fibre art.

In the pretty village of **Hubbards,** find the **Shore Club,** renowned for its lobster dinners and dances.

Just past the village, turn left on Fox Point Road which connects with Route 329 and traces the **Aspotogan Peninsula,** a rocky point separating St. Margarets and Mahone Bays. While this 40-kilometer (25-mile) coastal detour lacks definitive attractions, the docked boats and fishing nets drying alongside the road create an authentic scene. Watch for hand-painted signs advertising smoked mackerel or Solomon Gundy—a local specialty of pickled herring and onion—which might be available for sale at local homes.

Near the tip of the peninsula, you'll find **Bayswater Beach Provincial Park** at 4015 Rte. 329 to be emptier than most along the South Shore. But as the interment site of the Swissair disaster victims, the park also strikes a somber note.

From Bayswater, the road cuts along more sheltered territory for 4 kilometers (2.5 miles) to Blandford. You won't see it, but tucked in the core of the peninsula is the **Blandford Nature Reserve,** a protected area that was once a game sanctuary. The reserve was set aside by millionaire Cyrus Eaton to foster the birding area around Hollahan Lake.

Chester

At East River, the Lighthouse Route rejoins Highway 3 and passes the large family campground at **Graves Island Provincial Park.**

When you reach the village of **Chester,** make a left turn on Duke Street. Turn onto Water Street at the Front Harbour and drive into the heart of the New England–style village. The distinctly Cape Cod–feel comes from the Massachusetts settlers who arrived in this area during the 1750s.

Today, yacht races and seafood restaurants have turned the charming village into a refined destination. Bakeries and coffee shops complement the pretty

Chester Race Week fills the bay with spinnakers and sails.

waterfront scenery. The **Chester Playhouse** hosts a lively summer season of theater, and when **Chester Race Week** runs the third week of August, it fills the bay with spinnakers and sails.

For a day trip, take the ferry out to the year-round community of **Tancook Island;** the ferry runs two to four times daily. Summer savory crops and the herring fishery once provided a livelihood on the island, which as of 2018 still had an operating one-room school. Just off the coast of Tancook is Little Tancook and further out **East Ironbound,** the island that inspired the 1928 Frank Parker Day novel *Rockbound.*

Look out to the many islands as Highway 3 follows the coast of Mahone Bay through Chester Basin and Gold River. In the small fishing community of Western Shore, **Wild Rose Park** provides bathrooms and a convenient picnic area.

Just south of Western Shore, take Crandall Point Road down to the shoreline to give a look at **Oak Island,** where tales of treasure abound.

Since 1795, excavations to recover the **Oak Island treasure** have occupied many a mind and led to the death of six men. It began when three teenage boys discovered a depression in the ground beneath a tree. Curious, they dug into the earth and hit flagstones and layers of logs—but no treasure. A second excavation of the present "Money Pit" uncovered layers of coconut fibers as well as charcoal and putty. Digs have been hampered by the accidental deaths of six men, pit flooding, and dwindling funds. Franklin D. Roosevelt was even involved in a 1909 excavation.

Theories on the secret of the island's treasure range from the works of Shakespeare to the crown jewels of France, and of course pirate booty. Whatever it is—or isn't—Oak Island makes for a great tale.

Although the island is currently privately owned, the Friends of Oak Island Society have organized walking tours around the treasure island over the years. And like any location under the reality television spotlight, the destination has grown in popularity due to its profile on the History Channel show, *The Curse of Oak Island.*

Mahone Bay & Lunenburg

Follow Highway 3 into **Mahone Bay,** where views of the **Three Churches** greet you. Take photos from the large parking lot at the head of the bay, or venture

The famous three churches of Mahone Bay, Nova Scotia edge the town's waterfront.

Lunenburg has long had a working fishery, with dory-building shops, fishing boats, and a busy waterfront.

down Oakland Road for a water-framed view. For local information, stop in at the visitor center on the main road at 165 Edgewater St.

Come to a full stop at the three-way intersection that is a bit of a nightmare for unfamiliar drivers (tip: give way and go slowly; generally the alternating rule applies when crossing the other lane of traffic), and turn left toward Lunenburg.

Mahone Bay's Main Street is lined with vividly painted shops and galleries, the brightest of which is **Amos Pewter** at 589 Main St. The nearby **Mahone Bay Museum,** at 578 Main St., tells of the area's European settlement in 1754, although the Mi'kmaq fished and summered on the coast here long before.

Once known for its wooden boat festival (which is no longer running), it's now the autumn **Scarecrow Festival** that draws the crowds to see carved pumpkins and scarecrows decorating the town. Mahone Bay also hosts the winter **Father Christmas Festival.**

Highway 3 continues past typical Lunenburg Country waterfront homes. And at Maders Cove, the Lighthouse Route cuts inland toward UNESCO World Heritage Site Lunenburg. About 5 kilometers (3.1 miles) past Maders Cove, detour to the delightfully serene **Second Peninsula Provincial Park** along Second Peninsula Road. Trails and picnic tables trim a sheltered day-park.

Signs at the Highway 3 junction with Route 332 direct you left toward **Lunenburg.** Make the turn then take an immediate right onto Maple Avenue, which becomes Dufferin Street and heads directly into downtown.

Alternately, to see the best views of **Lunenburg Academy** at 97 Kaulback St., continue straight on Route 332 and then take Kissing Bridge Road. If choosing the latter route, you'll arrive in Lunenburg via the back harbor.

On a well-scheduled or lucky visit, Bluenose Drive will deliver its namesake, the **Bluenose II.** A replica of the famed fishing schooner sailed by Captain Angus Walters, the *Bluenose II* gives harbor tours when it is in its home berth. The original sailing schooner plied the waters from 1921 to 1946 and is now featured on the Canadian dime (10 cent coin).

Also on the waterfront, the **Fisheries Museum of the Atlantic** at 68 Bluenose Dr. engages visitors with a touch tank, moored vessels, and other activities.

Pass the bright red Adams & Knickle Building and dory-building shops to see men packing trucks with ice or a boat securing its mooring and then stroll the hilly Lunenburg streets. The colorful heritage buildings lie in theater-like rows up from the waterfront. Walk uphill to discover seafood restaurants as well as historic properties including the **Knaut-Rhuland House Museum** at 125 Pelham St. and **St. John's Church** at 64 Townsend St. The church is Canada's second oldest Anglican church and has been rebuilt following a destructive 2001 fire. Volunteers are often on hand in summer to give tours.

When in her homeport of Lunenburg, Nova Scotia the Bluenose II *takes visitors on tours of the harbor.*

The **Lunenburg Folk Harbour Festival** is a favorite for its musical entertainment and dozens of performers. Another delightful event with a strong following is the **Nova Scotia Folk Art Festival,** where vibrant folk art by local artists is on display and for sale. Both events take place in early August.

Extend the scenic drive with an overnight stay and more explorations—Drive 12 in particular makes a great pairing with the Lighthouse Route.

Check in to a heritage inn or comfortable bed-and-breakfast before sampling best-in-the-province fare at the buttercup-yellow **Fleur de Sel** at 53 Montague St. Or choose a lobster from one of the many live tanks at the local seafood restaurants.

14

Day Trip Beaches from Halifax

Dartmouth to Lawrencetown Beach to Martinique Beach

General Description: From views of downtown Halifax to a panorama of vast sandy beaches, this 88-kilometer (55-mile) scenic drive makes an outdoorsy day-trip escape from the Nova Scotia capital. Marshland boardwalks, surfable waves, and bike trails let you engage with the environment. Acadians, train conductors, Quakers, and fishermen all give a different perspective of the local history.

Special Features: Evergreen House and Quaker House, both run by Dartmouth Heritage Museum; McNabs and Lawlor Islands Provincial Park; Shearwater Aviation Museum; Fisherman's Cove; Rainbow Haven Beach Provincial Park; Shearwater Flyer, Salt Marsh, and Atlantic View trails; Cole Harbour Heritage Farm Museum; Cole Harbour Heritage Park; Lawrencetown Beach Provincial Park; Porters Lake Provincial Park; Acadian House Museum; Musquodoboit Harbour Railway Museum; Martinique Beach Provincial Park.

Location: East of Halifax, along the eastern shore.

Driving Route Numbers & Names: Macdonald Bridge, Wyse Road, Route 7, Alderney Drive, Octerloney Street, Pleasant Street, Route 322, Shore Road, Cow Bay Road, Bissett Road, Route 207, Lawrencetown Road, Highway 7, Marine Drive, East Petpeswick Road.

Travel Season: These beaches are sensational year-round. In winter, you'll have the place to yourself to beachcomb, but most museums will be closed. Easily enjoy the trails from May through October, but the best beach weather is in July and August. Fall and winter ocean swells bring surfers to these shores—you'll need a wetsuit to spend time in the saltwater.

Camping: Camp at Porters Lake Provincial Park, about 7 kilometers (4.3 miles) from Lawrencetown Beach along Crowell Road. The park has 80 campsites for tents and RVs, some lakeside. The picnic area and boat launches are also popular as a day trip.

Services: Halifax and Dartmouth, separate communities but both within the Halifax Regional Municipality, have a full complement of services. From shopping to gas stations to hospitals, the cities lack no comforts. Halifax and Dartmouth also offer dozens of accommodation options in heritage properties, motels, and full-service hotels. Heading along the drive, you'll find bed-and-breakfasts tucked in the sheltered harbors of fishing communities.

Nearby Points of Interest: Hope for Wildlife, Fisherman's Life Museum; in Halifax: Maritime Museum of the Atlantic, Canadian Museum of Immigration at Pier 21, Art Gallery of Nova Scotia, Halifax Public Gardens, Point Pleasant Park, Halifax Citadel National Historic Site, Alexander Keith's Brewery.

Time Zone: Atlantic time zone (GMT minus 4 hours).

The Drive

This 88-kilometer (55-mile) coastal scenic drive escapes the city to enjoy Nova Scotia's longest beach, surfing breaks, and salt-marsh trails. **Dartmouth**—for years overlooked by tourists—offers history and worthwhile vantages of the Halifax

Day Trip Beaches from Halifax

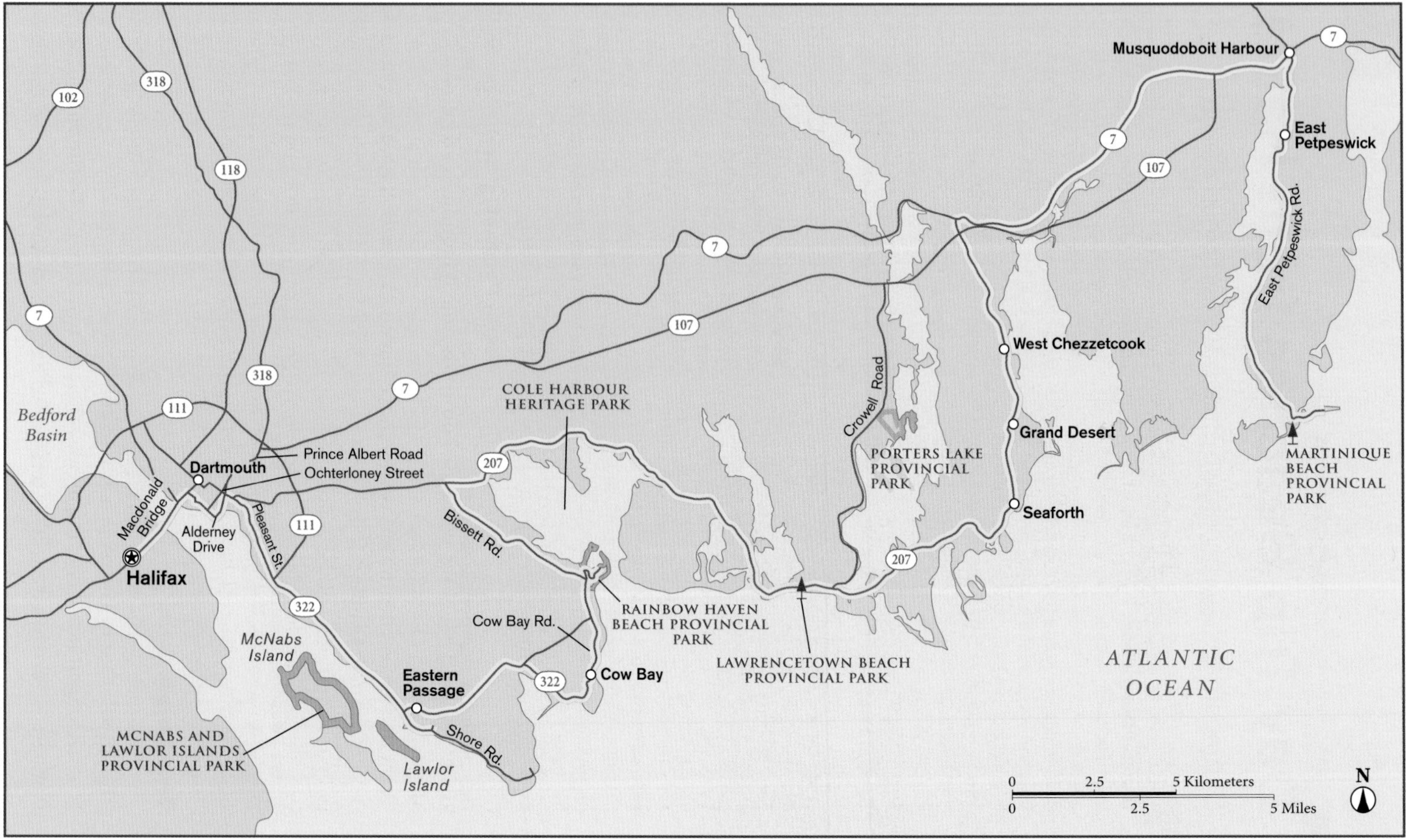

N

ATLANTIC OCEAN

0   2.5   5 Kilometers
0   2.5   5 Miles

East Petpeswick
Musquodoboit Harbour
East Petpeswick Rd.
MARTINIQUE BEACH PROVINCIAL PARK
West Chezzetcook
Grand Desert
Seaforth
PORTERS LAKE PROVINCIAL PARK
Crowell Road
LAWRENCETOWN BEACH PROVINCIAL PARK
RAINBOW HAVEN BEACH PROVINCIAL PARK
Cow Bay
COLE HARBOUR HERITAGE PARK
Cow Bay Rd.
Bissett Rd.
Shore Rd.
Eastern Passage
Lawlor Island
Prince Albert Road
Ochterloney Street
Pleasant St.
McNabs Island
MCNABS AND LAWLOR ISLANDS PROVINCIAL PARK
Dartmouth
Alderney Drive
Macdonald Bridge
Halifax
Bedford Basin

7
107
207
322
111
318
118
102

Start this drive in Halifax, where the Town Clock and Halifax Citadel National Historic Site watch over the city.

skyline as well as unusual island parks. Near the end of the route, three world-class beaches put a little sand in your driving shoes.

Cross from Halifax to Dartmouth on the Macdonald Bridge (toll $1 in 2018). Make an immediate right onto Wyse Road and drive to a T-junction with Windmill Road. Turn left at the lights. Just down the hill Windmill Road becomes Alderney Drive, or Highway 7.

In this across-the-harbor city, heritage homes sit in the sling of Alderney Drive. **Alderney Landing** is the waterfront hub of Dartmouth, with a boardwalk and panoramic view of the Halifax skyline. It's also where the Dartmouth–Halifax ferry docks. Branching inland, Ochterloney Street is the main route up from the waterfront, passing the **Quaker House Museum,** a 1785 home originally belonging to Quaker whalers from Nantucket. Farther northeast, Ochterloney joins Prince Albert Street and passes **Lake Banook,** ever busy in good weather with canoeists and kayakers.

Backtrack down to the intersection of Prince Albert Street (Highway 7) and Pleasant Street (Route 322) to drive east.

Just after the Portland Street intersection, turn right at Albert Street and venture a block closer to the waterfront to learn more about the city's history

In Eastern Passage, fishing boats and ocean-inspired galleries provide a prettified feel of the Atlantic.

at **Evergreen House Museum,** 26 Newcastle St. The blue house was home to Helen Creighton, the celebrated folklorist who recorded many of the province's traditional songs and tales, including the sad and rousing "Farewell to Nova Scotia."

Follow Pleasant Street, Route 322, as it heads southeast through the industrial side of town. At the junction with Highway 111 continue straight toward the community of **Eastern Passage**. The hospital, Canadian Forces Base Shearwater, and refinery towers have caused some folks to conjure unflattering impressions of this side of the harbor. **Shearwater Aviation Museum** at 34 Bonaventure St. displays aircraft and flight exhibits at its airbase location—established after World War I and the oldest military airfield on the east coast.

From Route 322 look right to **Georges Island National Historic Site,** best known for its lighthouse (visible from the Halifax side). On the small bare island, **Fort Charlotte** was a prison for expelled Acadians and a strategic World War II position. The national historic site is not open to the public.

Buskers are part of the lively entertainment in the Nova Scotia capital.

Other islands in the harbor include the **McNabs and Lawlor Islands Provincial Park.** The larger of the two, treed **McNabs Island** has Mi'kmaq shell middens, the stronghold of **Fort McNab National Historic Site,** long-abandoned summer homes, a lighthouse, and 22 kilometers (13.7 miles) of hiking trails. The smaller **Lawlor Island** sits closer to the shore. Both islands can be visited on a day trip from Halifax or Eastern Passage. Check in with Friends of McNabs Island (mcnabsisland.ca) for events and recommendations on local boat operators.

As you reach Eastern Passage, Route 322 bears inland to the left. Continue along the waterfront on Shore Road. **Fisherman's Cove,** 30 Government Wharf Rd., in Eastern Passage maintains its bustle as a working waterfront. Boats tied up to the government wharf and ocean-inspired galleries provide a prettified feel of the Atlantic. There's also a boardwalk for a stroll.

To continue the scenic drive, backtrack to Route 322 and turn right to continue east (the route is also labeled as Cow Bay Road).

Rainbow Haven Beach

The road leads through an unremarkable residential neighborhood for about 4 kilometers (2.5 miles). As Route 322 continues straight (to become Dyke Road), turn right onto Cow Bay Road. The road follows the coast out to Osborne Head and then curves around toward **Cole Harbour.**

Stop in at the drive's first beach—**Rainbow Haven Beach Provincial Park,** at 2248 Cow Bay Rd. The sheltered beach sits at the narrow mouth of a large protected area. Rainbow Haven has sandy shores, washrooms and showers, and family activities. Lifeguards supervise a swimming area during summer.

The park exit takes you across a causeway surrounded by saltwater marsh. Watch for herons fishing in the quiet waters on both sides of the causeway.

As you rejoin the pavement, turn right onto Bissett Road to continue on Route 322.

On the main route, about 2.5 kilometers (1.5 miles) from Rainbow Haven, you'll pass the trailhead for the **Shearwater Flyer Trail.** Cutting inland from the Canadian Forces Base Shearwater, the gravel pathway also connects here with the **Salt Marsh Trail** to cross the cragged bay of the **Cole Harbour Heritage Park** via islands and trails.

Many provincial railway lines were abandoned by the 1980s, and local groups throughout Nova Scotia began transforming the railbeds into recreational corridors available to walkers, runners, and cyclists. The Shearwater Flyer, Salt Marsh, and Atlantic View trails along this drive all form part of that network.

Lawrencetown Beach

Bissett Road ends at Route 207 in Cole Harbour. Here, turn right on Route 207 to drive along the head of the large marsh area toward **Lawrencetown.**

For a family-friendly detour, however, turn left on Route 207 to visit the farm animals and tearoom at **Cole Harbour Heritage Farm Museum.** The demonstration farm is located at 471 Poplar St., off Otago Drive.

Toward Lawrencetown, the road follows a network of coves and marshy islands where birds feed and take refuge.

Coming down the hill to **Lawrencetown Beach Provincial Park** you'll glimpse the full expanse of sand, although as you descend to sea level storm walls and dunes hide the views. Park and walk over the rock wall to the beach. Lawrencetown, like other beaches featured in this drive, has bathrooms and changing rooms.

In all seasons, surfers ride the waves along the Nova Scotia coast. Particularly as hurricane and winter swells reach the shores, surfers head out in their neoprene wetsuits, waiting for waves at Cow Bay, Lawrencetown, and Martinique.

The Salt Marsh Trail connects with the **Atlantic View Trail** near the beach. A turnoff on Crowell Road leads to **Porters Lake Provincial Park**—a lakeside park with picnic areas, a boat launch, and campsites.

To continue the scenic drive after tea or a surf lesson at Lawrencetown Beach, drive east on Route 207. Pass through Three Fathom Harbour and Seaforth before reaching the Acadian community of **Grand Desert,** named for the starkness of the landscape. You'll see Acadian flags posted on driveways and wharf poles, much like in other Acadian areas of the Maritimes.

Although Chezzetcook is a Mi'kmaq name meaning "water flowing rapidly in many channels," West Chezzetcook also has strong Acadian history. Visit the **Acadian House Museum** at 71 Hill Rd. to learn about the French-speaking history on the shore. The small, shingled house is a museum with hands-on exhibits (more like chores!). A garden, café, and barn fill the small grounds.

Before the Acadian deportation, starting in 1755, the area was sparsely settled. When the Acadians were released from imprisonment, they resettled this area in greater numbers and many locals spoke French here until the 1960s.

Martinique Beach

At the head of island-studded **Chezzetcook Inlet,** 17 kilometers (10.6 miles) from Lawrencetown Beach, Route 207 ends at Highway 7.

Martinique Beach is the longest sandy beach in the province.

Make a right turn on this busy route to Musquodoboit Harbour. Another 9 kilometers (5.6 miles) along Highway 7 and the route becomes Marine Drive.

The big rust-colored **Musquodoboit Harbour Railway Museum** stands out on Highway 7. The 1916 station is a well-preserved remnant on the now-decommissioned rail line. Historic cars, a visitor center, ice cream, and nearby trails all augment the stop.

From Musquodoboit Harbour, follow signs for Martinique Beach, making a right turn on East Petpeswick Road.

Over 12 kilometers (7.5 miles), the road along **Petpeswick Inlet** passes a yacht club and fishing wharves before arriving at the provincial park.

Known for its clean, near-white sands, **Martinique Beach Provincial Park** is often less crowded than more-accessible Lawrencetown. Measuring nearly 4 kilometers (2.5 miles) from end-to-end Martinique is the longest sandy beach in the province—a sure guarantee there'll be room for your beach blanket. Trails, a canteen, and pit toilets provide the necessities for a day trip. For camping, head

The Acadian House Museum in West Chezzetcook sees guides completing daily chores in the wooden house, barn, and small garden.

inland from Musquodoboit Harbour to off-the-main-trail **Dollar Lake Provincial Park.**

Side Trip: Halifax

Nova Scotia's capital city—and largest—makes a top destination for shopping, dining, theater, music, and galleries. Located at the start of this drive over the Macdonald and MacKay Bridges, **Halifax** has a dense downtown, making it easy to walk the historic streets on foot.

Along the waterfront, docked ships are open as historic and working exhibits. The **Maritime Museum of the Atlantic** on Lower Water Street gives perspectives on the *Titanic* sinking in 1912 and the catastrophic Halifax Explosion, which killed 2,000 and injured thousands more in 1917. Shipbuilding, fishing, and other local sea industries are explored.

The **Canadian Museum of Immigration at Pier 21** is located in the newer Halifax Seaport district, a hub for arts, tourism, and food—including the **Halifax Seaport Farmers' Market**. The museum's concrete architecture and historic Pier 21 location add a starkness to the poignant stories of immigrants arriving in Canada and young men going off to war.

The **Art Gallery of Nova Scotia** at 1723 Hollis St. features a permanent exhibit of work by Nova Scotia folk artist Maud Lewis, and even has her colorfully painted, garden-shed-size house on display.

The **Halifax Public Gardens** and **Point Pleasant Park** are two outstanding green spaces. The first is a manicured park of duck ponds and flower borders; the latter is a walking trail maze to gun batteries, historic towers, and ocean views.

Above the city, you'll often catch glimpses (and sounds) of the **Halifax Citadel National Historic Site,** with its protective stone walls, town clock, and cannons readying to fire a salute. Costumed interpretive guides tamp the gunpowder, play the bagpipes, and revive fort life.

Dining and accommodation options in Halifax are the most varied in the province. Dine on sushi and stay in a hostel, feast on seafood and bunk at a bed-and-breakfast, or pair local wine with a steak and stay in a waterfront hotel. On weekend evenings live music and locally brewed beers—including India Pale Ale from **Alexander Keith's Brewery**—flow freely.

15

Cape George—
The Little Cabot Trail

Antigonish to Cape George to Sutherlands River

General Description: The shoreline drive around Cape George is a 115-kilometer (71.5-mile) scenic route that's excellent in either direction. Take a rural detour when traveling to or from Cape Breton to visit lighthouses, geologically rich parks, and a tuna-fishing community. Hiking trails and quiet beaches are perfect for independent travelers.

Special Features: Antigonish Heritage Museum, Mahoneys Beach, Cape George Heritage School Museum, hiking trails, Ballantynes Cove Bluefin Tuna Interpretive Centre, Cape George Point Lighthouse, Arisaig Provincial Park, Merigomish Beach.

Location: Northern mainland Nova Scotia, on the Northumberland Strait.

Driving Route Numbers & Names: Highway 4, Main Street, Route 337, Mahoney Beach Road, Route 245, Big Island Road.

Travel Season: Clear weather will mean the best views out to Cape Breton and Prince Edward Island from along the coast and at Cape George Point. Most attractions—the parks, trails, and lighthouses—are outside, making a further case for fine weather. In the Maritimes, June through September offers the best chances of a sunny day. Museums on the route are open during the summer season.

Camping: Although no provincial camping parks lie directly on the scenic drive, Caribou-Munroes Island Provincial Park lies northwest of New Glasgow and close to the Prince Edward Island ferry. Private campgrounds in Antigonish provide options for tents and RVs.

Services: Two major centers—New Glasgow and Antigonish—bookend this drive. New Glasgow features more commercial options such as chain hotels, while Antigonish retains a little more heritage charm with downtown bed-and-breakfasts as well as budget accommodations on the St. Francis Xavier Campus (summer only).

Nearby Points of Interest: Nova Scotia Museum of Industry, Pictou County Sports Heritage Hall of Fame, Carmichael-Stewart House Museum in New Glasgow; Grohmann Knives Factory Tours, Hector Heritage Quay, McCulloch House Museum, Prince Edward Island ferry, Northumberland Fisheries Museum in Pictou.

Time Zone: Atlantic time zone (GMT minus 4 hours).

The Drive

Enjoy a relaxed pace and take the long, coastal route around Cape George Point between Antigonish and New Glasgow. This 115-kilometer (71.5-mile) scenic drive is perfect to tag onto a trip to or from Cape Breton, or as a summer day trip. Driven in either direction, the itinerary takes about an afternoon to a full day, dependent entirely on the length of your stops.

Cape George—The Little Cabot Trail

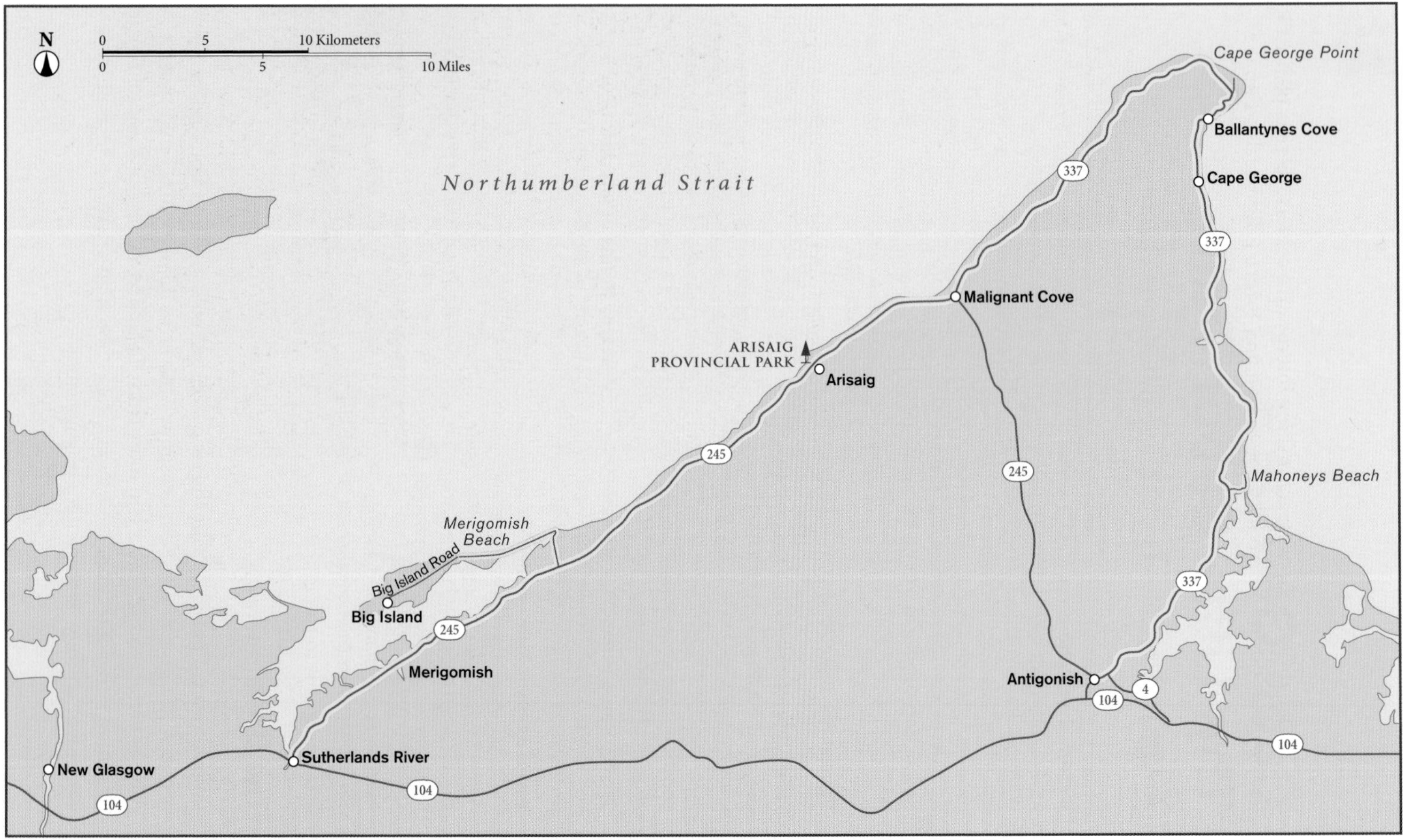

N

10 Miles
10 Kilometers

10
5

5

0
0

Cape George Point

Ballantynes Cove
Cape George

337

337

Mahoneys Beach

104

4

104

Antigonish

245

Malignant Cove

337

Northumberland Strait

Arisaig

ARISAIG
PROVINCIAL PARK

245

245

Merigomish Beach

Big Island Road

Big Island

Merigomish

Sutherlands River

104

New Glasgow

104

With lighthouses, parks, and fishing interpretive centers, there is plenty to explore with the views of both Cape Breton and Prince Edward Island on the horizons.

Antigonish

From exit 32 on Highway 104, take West Street (Highway 7 then Highway 4) into downtown **Antigonish.** To the east of the street, the campus of **St. Francis Xavier University** features multistory brick buildings on a compact campus. The route becomes Main Street, bearing east through the pretty downtown as part of Highway 4.

Cross the river, and at 20 East Main St. the **Antigonish Heritage Museum** displays local history exhibits in a preserved 1908 railway station. Following the drive east from the museum, the road becomes Route 337, which begins its coastal path out to Cape George Point.

Beyond Antigonish Route 337 passes through Lanark and Harbour Centre. Side roads lead down to residences on **Antigonish Harbour.** Farmlands of corn and hay show the region's arable land and agricultural history.

At Mahoney Beach Road turn right and follow the road to the shoreline at **Mahoneys Beach.** A broad beach with views of St. Georges Bay contrasts the sheltered Antigonish Harbour, which is nearly cut-off from the ocean by the beach. Look east to Cape Breton's Inverness County. This route out to Cape George is sometimes called the Little Cabot Trail for its coast-and-hills scenery that is similar to the Cabot Trail on Cape Breton Island. Geologically, the regions share the same beginnings.

Antigonish's Main Street is the feature of the historic community's pretty downtown.

Cape George Point

Cliffs, coves, farms, and secluded beaches down small side roads trim the 16 kilometers (10 miles) from Mahoneys Beach to the community of **Cape George.** The **Cape George Heritage School Museum** is a one-room school turned museum. The little white school opened in 1925, and one teacher taught as many as 50 local children here. The museum, with artifacts and information on the local heritage, opens in summer only. The rest of the year, use the school as a base to explore the **Cape George Hiking Trails.** Maps of the 37-kilometer (23-mile) trail network were available at the community notice board in the parking lot when I visited.

At Ballantynes Cove Wharf Road turn down to the docked fishing boats and stacked lobster traps. The waterfront **Ballantynes Cove Bluefin Tuna**

From the Cape George Point Lighthouse, Nova Scotia, look out to the shores of Cape Breton and Prince Edward Island.

Interpretive Centre gives a quick perspective on the local fishing industry. From the weathered tuna-fishing "fighting chair" to the dish-bucket retrieved from a tuna's stomach, the center provides an important and concerned perspective about these massive fish. Atlantic bluefin tuna can live to be 20 or more years old and weigh more than 450 kilograms (1,000 pounds). The largest bluefin tuna was caught in 1979 out of nearby Aulds Cove, on the Strait of Canso. The giant fish weighed in at 678.5 kilograms (1,496 pounds).

Eroding red cliffs hem in the marina, wharf, and seafood canteen. Above the cove a little roadside lookout savors views of sailboats in St. Georges Bay.

Ballantynes Cove, Nova Scotia is a port for fishing boats—and has a bluefin tuna interpretive center.

Driving up a hill that may remind you of the Cabot Trail inclines, watch for Lighthouse Road on the right. Make the turn and follow the half-kilometer road to **Cape George Point Lighthouse** at 152 Lighthouse Rd. A parking area and picnic tables are ideal for a lunch stop.

The present towering white lighthouse was built in 1968, the third on this point. The original lighthouse was established in 1861 but was destroyed by fire.

Arisaig Provincial Park

From the lighthouse, follow Route 337 as it rounds Cape George Point and follows the Northumberland Strait coast. At Malignant Cove, where there are an estuary and small beach, Route 337 ends and meets Route 245. One branch heads inland through Maryvale and returns to Antigonish, but continue west on the coastal Route 245.

Just before the provincial park, Arisaig Point Road leads off right to a wharf with a small lighthouse. The lighthouse is a replica of the original, which burned down in the 1930s, and is now the site of a visitor information center.

Arisaig Provincial Park sits on the Northumberland Strait, with faint views of Cape Bear at the southeastern end of Prince Edward Island. Interpretive signs provide clues to the ancient geology of the area. Search the shoreline for fossils, which can include snails, trilobites, and clams in the Silurian rock. While much of Cape George dates to the Precambrian (1,400 to 540 million years ago) and Devonian to Early Carboniferous periods (374 to 320 million years ago), a fault separates Arisaig. The park features the red sandstone, similar to that in Chéticamp on the Cabot Trail, which dates to the more recent Late Carboniferous period (320 to 286 million years ago).

Any fossils found are the property of the province, and it is illegal to remove fossils from the beach.

Crossing into Pictou County, land cleared for hay fields, grazing pastures, and summer homes allows great views out to the ocean. About 17 kilometers (10.6 miles) west from Arisaig, make a right on Big Island Road.

Starting at a sharp bend left, the rural road parallels perhaps one of Nova Scotia's most empty and gorgeous beaches. Drive over the causeway, and then park at the roadside stopping areas to walk through to enjoy the long sands at **Merigomish Beach.** On the other side of the road the sheltered, lagoon-like **Merigomish Harbour** is a rewarding spot for bird watching. Farms and summer homes lie farther down Big Island Road.

Return to the junction with Route 245 and continue southwest through the communities of Lower Barneys River and Merigomish. The scenic route ends at the Trans-Canada at Sutherlands River. Via both Highways 4 and 104 you can make a short 13-kilometer (8-mile) dash to **New Glasgow.** Plan to visit during the summer festivals, such as the early August **Riverfront Jubilee** or the mid-July **Festival of the Tartans,** featuring local Scottish heritage—ranging from kilted golf to caber tossing.

Antigonish, also easily accessible by the Trans-Canada, also celebrates its Celtic heritage in July with the **Antigonish Highland Games,** the oldest event of its kind outside Scotland.

Search the shoreline for fossils, which can include snails, trilobites, and clams, in Arisaig Provincial Park.

16

The Cabot Trail

Ingonish Beach to Meat Cove to Chéticamp

General Description: This 115-kilometer (71.5-mile) section of the Cabot Trail climbs and descends from Ingonish Beach to Chéticamp, passing through the truly dramatic Cape Breton Highlands National Park. Cliff-side roads, windswept plateaus, vibrant villages, and moose sightings form the main appeal of this well-traveled route. While many tour the Cabot Trail in a clockwise direction, owing to the larger visitor center in Chéticamp, and perhaps a nervousness about traveling beside the water, this version puts a counter spin on the trail. You'll see the same stunning views (saving the best for last) and likely enjoy less traffic. Add an additional 58-kilometer (36-mile) tangent out to isolated Meat Cove to see more incomparable coast.

Special Features: Giant MacAskill Museum, Cape Smokey Provincial Park, Cape Breton Highlands National Park, North Highlands Community Museum, Cabots Landing Provincial Park, Whale Interpretive Centre, Les Trois Pignons: Museum of Hooked Rug and Home Life, hiking, camping, wildlife watching, swimming, beaches.

Location: Northern Cape Breton Island in northern Nova Scotia.

Driving Route Numbers & Names: Cabot Trail, New Haven Road, Bay St. Lawrence Road, Meat Cove Road.

Travel Season: The fall colors of the old-growth sugar maples and other hardwoods make autumn in the Cape Breton Highlands vibrant and spectacular. In summer, camp at various locations throughout the park and enjoy the beaches, swimming, and hiking. The road is twisty, and winter weather can be treacherous. Sections of the Cabot Trail close in the worst weather, particularly the steep climbs at French and Mackenzie Mountains. But winter also brings an opportunity to ski at Cape Smokey and on cross-country trails.

Camping: Throughout Cape Breton Highlands National Park you'll find well-equipped and central campgrounds with hiking trails nearby. Six park campgrounds are spaced along the drive at Ingonish Beach, Broad Cove, Big Intervale, MacIntosh Brook, Corney Brook, and Chéticamp.

Services: As most of this roadway is inside the boundaries of Cape Breton Highlands National Park, take opportunities to fuel up and stock up when possible. Ingonish and Chéticamp have gas stations. For accommodations, you'll find the iconic Keltic Lodge in Ingonish Beach at the start of the drive. Motels, inns, and a hostel can be found in Pleasant Bay and Chéticamp.

Nearby Points of Interest: Great Hall of the Clans, Margaree Salmon Museum, Margaree Fish Hatchery, Alexander Graham Bell National Historic Site, Bras d'Or Lakes Interpretive Centre.

Time Zone: Atlantic time zone (GMT minus 4 hours).

The Drive

A coast and mountains scenic drive, the full **Cabot Trail** encircles the entire northwestern quadrant of Cape Breton. Along the way it touches provincial parks, Atlantic beaches, luxury hotels, and Acadian museums—not to mention the wild

The Cabot Trail

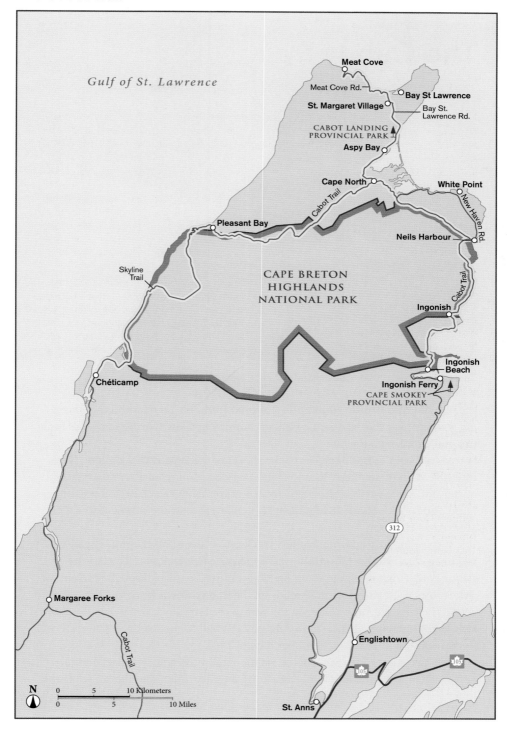

Gulf of St. Lawrence

Meat Cove

Meat Cove Rd.

Bay St Lawrence

St. Margaret Village

Bay St.
Lawrence Rd.

CABOT LANDING
PROVINCIAL PARK

Aspy Bay

Cape North

White Point

Cabot Trail

New Haven Rd.

Pleasant Bay

Neils Harbour

Skyline
Trail

CAPE BRETON
HIGHLANDS
NATIONAL PARK

Cabot Trail

Ingonish

Ingonish
Beach

Chéticamp

Ingonish Ferry

CAPE SMOKEY
PROVINCIAL PARK

312

Margaree Forks

Cabot Trail

Englishtown

105

105

N

| 0 | 5 | 10 Kilometers |

| 0 | 5 | 10 Miles |

St. Anns

There are dozens of roadside lookouts in the Cape Breton Highlands.

expanse of **Cape Breton Highlands National Park**. It's no question that this is the most iconic drive in Atlantic Canada, and if you allow two days or more for a trip you'll understand why.

Many begin in **Baddeck,** along the shores of the **Bras d'Or Lakes** on Highway 105. With its southerly location, good services, and regular *ceilidhs* (Gaelic music and dance parties), the pretty town features all the Cape Breton must-haves. From Baddeck it's about 18 kilometers (11 miles) to start the official Cabot Trail at St. Anns Harbour.

If traveling instead from Sydney, you'll cross Great Bras d'Or on Highway 105, then climb **Kellys Mountain** where there are two lookouts. To start the Cabot Trail, either continue south on Highway 105 to travel through St. Anns, or follow Route 312 and cross the harbor on the **Englishtown ferry** (info: 902-929-2404). If taking the latter route, on the way to the ferry dock you'll pass the **Giant MacAskill Museum,** dedicated to Angus MacAskill, who measured 2.36 meters (7 feet 9 inches) tall. The Cape Bretoner died in 1863.

The two routes—via St. Anns or via the Englishtown ferry—meet on the north side of Murray Mountain. Ahead, the mountains build to the left while the water is ever near on the right.

About 60 kilometers (37 miles) from St. Anns through forest and rural houses, the road approaches **Smokey Mountain.** Go slowly around the tight turns that elevate you to greater heights. A lookout to the right of the Cabot Trail and **Cape Smokey Provincial Park** thereafter are the first opportunities for real highland views—and they are already spectacular.

Although the roadside lookout is convenient, pull in to the provincial park and explore the short rocky trails that descend to fenced-off cliffs. Take your camera. A longer trail, 11 kilometers (6.8 miles) return, takes advantage of the elevated coastline and snakes out to Stanley Point.

Ingonish Beach to Cape North

The Cabot Trail cuts inland after the provincial park and descends to near sea level at Ingonish Ferry and **Ingonish Beach.** Fuel up here so you can explore side roads without being concerned about running out of gas.

Here you enter the eastern side of **Cape Breton Highlands National Park** and the official start of this scenic drive. A small visitor center off the main route sells park passes (mandatory for stopping at lookouts, beaches, or trails) and provides details on guided hikes, facilities, and safety. Accommodations are nearby, including a national park campground and (tipping the other end of the scale) the golf course, spa, and luxury accommodations at **Keltic Lodge.**

From Ingonish Beach, the Cabot Trail travels 115 kilometers (71.5 miles) to **Chéticamp** on the western side. The extra journey to Meat Cove adds an additional 58 kilometers (36 miles).

These sound like short distances, but consider this: Over those kilometers you'll round hairpin turns, climb and descend hills, picnic on beaches, hike to lookouts, and spot wildlife. Allow one full day at an absolute minimum; two, three, or more if you plan on activities such as hiking, whale watching, or swimming. The park boundaries end at residential areas, which they do here as you pass the community of Ingonish.

Reentering the park, the Cabot Trail quickly unveils more stunning views, especially as the road sits on the edge of the park, looking out over the Atlantic. **Broad Cove,** where there is a campground, is the first of many inlets, points, and beaches along the shore. Driving counterclockwise around the Cabot Trail makes it easier to pull over and enjoy the mountains-meet-ocean views. Bluffs and coves add beautiful curves to the coast and make for a fun drive.

The **Cape Breton Highlands** formed millions of years ago. The eastern Ingonish side is largely granite, an intrusive igneous rock. But faults through the center of the national park have also created a geological mix dating to the Precambrian, Ordovician to Devonian, and Devonian to Early Carboniferous periods.

Only Chéticamp shows the red sandstone of the late Carboniferous period, and is some of the youngest rock at 320 to 286 million years old. The late Carboniferous period also produced the major coal deposits in Cape Breton Island's Glace Bay, as well as elsewhere in the province in Stellarton and Springhill.

It's possible to stop almost every kilometer of this route to admire the scenery from a new vantage. But before spontaneously pulling over, watch for cyclists who are bravely pedaling up the hills.

Moose warning signs persist throughout the park. Although moose were wiped out in Cape Breton by 1924, Parks Canada reintroduced them with 18 animals from Alberta in the late 1940s. The moose refound their footing, and there are now about 2 animals per square kilometer (about 5 per square mile). Because the moose in Cape Breton descended from the Alberta animals, they are different subspecies from Nova Scotia's mainland moose, which is listed as endangered.

The pretty **Black Brook Beach** makes a good stop for a swim or hike. A coastal trail traces the shore from the beach to **Neils Harbour.** A branch trail circles **Jigging Cove Lake.**

The park boundaries break at **Neils Harbour,** where there are a hospital, gas station, and other services. The next stretch of driving cuts inland before an intense stretch of inclines and declines.

From Neils Harbour the Cabot Trail crosses fairly flat terrain for 13 kilometers (8 miles) toward South Mountain. To take a coastal detour, follow New Haven Road from Neils Harbour out to White Point. A hiking trail leads out to White Point. The driving detour is about 18 kilometers (11 miles), to where White Point Road reconnects with the Cabot Trail at South Harbour.

At Cape North, take a break at the **North Highlands Community Museum.** Displaying artifacts from the days of the early Highland settlers, the museum tells the story of an independent people. Watch the bellows blast in the forge and walk through the settlers' gardens. Next door the **North Highlands Cultural Centre** occasionally features music, ceilidhs, and lecture-style presentations.

Meat Cove

For those looking to explore the side roads, drive approximately 29 kilometers (18 miles) one way out on Bay St. Lawrence Road to **Meat Cove.** Along the route, sheltered North Harbour sits inside sandbars, islands dot the panorama, and North Mountain looms to the west, like a person sleeping under a sheet.

Along the coast at Aspy Bay, **Cabots Landing Provincial Park** features a quiet beach, picnic sites, and historical markers, including a **bust of John**

At Meat Cove, great slabs of rock seem suspended in a slide into (or out of) the ocean.

The Cabot Trail along the very edge of Cape Breton, Nova Scotia.

Cabot. A Venetian sailor, Cabot crossed the Atlantic in the *Matthew* and landed somewhere on the east coast of Canada on June 24, 1497. He was searching for a route to Asia but instead rooted Britain's claim on North America. The park also commemorates the **Atlantic Cable**—the line that connected Aspy Bay to Port-aux-Basques, Newfoundland, and was part of the first telegraph link with Europe.

At St. Margaret Village the road splits right to Bay St. Lawrence, a departure point for whale-watching tours, and left to Meat Cove. A 13-kilometer (8-mile) half-paved, half-dirt road winds up, down, and around to reach Meat Cove. There, great slabs of rock seem suspended in a slide into (or out of) the ocean. A canteen and campground at Meat Cove has the best location, and the most scenic spots along the cliff are part of the property.

Watch for kayakers below the cliffs or enquire about the hiking trail out around Cape St. Lawrence. Then backtrack on the dirt and paved roads to the main Cabot Trail at **Cape North.**

Pleasant Bay

West on the Cabot Trail from Cape North, the route traverses different scenery blending forest, valleys, and rivers together. **Big Intervale campground** is a home base for exploring the Cape Breton Highlands plateau. It's also a good halfway point for campers completing the route over two days.

Big turns and steep inclines cross branches of the North Aspy River. The tributaries sit in the valley between South and North Mountains, which are also divided by fault lines. North of the Cabot Trail lies the **Polletts Cove–Aspy Fault Wilderness Area**—an unmarred area that is popular for moose hunting and wilderness-only travel.

Lookouts on both sides of the river valley show the expanse of trees and vibrant life. The forests are a mix of deciduous and coniferous trees, making a lovely autumn scene when the leaves turn.

Atop North Mountain, which pans out at more than 400 meters (1,300 feet) elevation, the alpine plateau creates a stark contrast to the lush river valleys below. Windswept balsam fir and black spruce show signs of a harsh life: their stunted trunks and twisted branches battered by winter winds and snows.

Approaching the Gulf of St. Lawrence coast, watch for the hobbit-like cabin of Lone Shieling. In the Grande Anse Valley, the stone structure with a thatched roof pays tribute to the Scottish heritage in Pleasant Bay. It sits amid a forest of 350-year-old sugar maples.

The Cabot Trail exits the park boundary as it approaches **Pleasant Bay.** Drive down to the town wharf to visit the **Whale Interpretive Centre** on Harbour Road. Exhibits on 16 species provide an introduction to the largest ocean mammals. Apply the new-found knowledge with a whale-watching tour or use binoculars to look for pods of pilot whales off the coast. Like Ingonish and Chéticamp, Pleasant Bay is another good spot to secure accommodations or a meal with an ocean view.

From Pleasant Bay, the road slowly climbs up **MacKenzie Mountain** to cross another alpine plateau at 335 meters (1,100 feet). The plateau is part of the Appalachian Mountains chain that runs from Newfoundland down to Georgia.

Benjies Lake Trail provides access to the stark landscape, although the **Skyline Trail** with its headland coastal views is the national park's best-known hike. In the past there have been problems with coyotes (in 2009 a lone female hiker was attacked and killed by coyotes while hiking the trail) so venture out in groups—even if it means waiting at the trailhead for a hiking buddy, or joining one of the park's guided sunset hikes.

French Mountain, near the Skyline Trail, is one of the highest points in the park at 455 meters (1,493 feet). Descend from these heights via tight turns toward Chéticamp. This is the most-photographed section of the trail, where the road

snakes between deep green highlands, red cliffs, and blue ocean. You'll easily be able to pull off the road to look both up and down the route. Many of the park's dozens of lookouts also have interpretive signs.

At **Cap Rouge,** hike a trail to learn about the one-time Acadian community. Nearby, find **Corney Brook campground** and more options for walking. This is another great area to rest awhile and take in the monument-like surroundings.

Leaving the park is the red, wedge-shape sentinel **La Bloc,** the one-time site of a French fishing village and cannery.

Chéticamp

Past Pillar Rock you'll start to see **Chéticamp,** now just 12 kilometers (7.5 miles) off. The **spire of St. Peter's Church**—or St-Pierre in French—is unmistakable and was long a landmark for Chéticamp fishermen and sailors. For scenery, the mountains are still present to the left while the gulf lies to the right.

Before entering the town, stop in first at the larger national park visitor center. A campground provides longer-stay facilities. The relief map shows the valleys, slopes, and plateaus of the highlands, while interpretive exhibits detail park geology and wildlife.

In Chéticamp, the Stella Maris, or gold star, of the Acadian flag shines brightly. Museums and restaurants invite visitors into the culture—you'll eat, sleep, and even hook rugs with the locals. The first stop in town is **Les Trois Pignons**—a cultural center and hooked-rug museum at 15584 Cabot Trail. The museum centers on the work of **Elizabeth LeFort,** a legendary rug maker from the Chéticamp area. If you're rusty on your rug hooking know-how, take a look at the detail in LeFort's work. Biblical stories, fishing scenes, and portraits of politicians create a diverse body of work.

On the southwest end of Chéticamp Harbour, take a short scenic amble around **Chéticamp Island,** which has a soft-sand beach and is capped with **Enragee Point Lighthouse.**

Side Trip: Baddeck & the Bras d'Or Lakes

From Chéticamp the Cabot Trail heads south along the coast for 25 kilometers (15.5 miles) and then follows the Margaree River inland for 54 kilometers (33.6 miles) to the Bras d'Or Lakes.

The route passes through the **Margaree Valley,** where dramatic, towering views of the highlands will have tapered down to become a lush river valley. At

The Skyline Trail is the park's most popular hike and has a variety of scenic lookouts.

From the lovely town of Baddeck on the shores of the Bras d'Or Lakes, watch sailboats in front of Kidston Island Lighthouse.

Margaree Forks, and the confluence of the Southwest and Northeast Margaree Rivers, the Cabot Trail meets Highway 19 or the **Ceilidh Trail.**

The **Margaree Salmon Museum** at 60 East Big Intervale Rd. is worth a stop for its collection of fishing flies and tales of the "big one."

Continue southeast on the Cabot Trail to Highway 105. It's then just a short 10-kilometer (6.2-mile) hop to **Baddeck,** a central location where there's a ceilidh—Gaelic for "visit"—every night of the week in summer. From here, there is a lovely view of **Kidston Island Lighthouse.**

From the **Alexander Graham Bell National Historic Site** on Chebucto Street you can see the inventor's old home across the lake at **Beinn Bhreagh.** Exhibits at the historic site engage visitors with Bell's inventions—a short list of which includes the telephone, the metal detector, and the Silver Dart airplane.

Walk along the well-kept main street, and stop in at the stone **Bras d'Or Lakes Interpretive Centre.** There, learn more about the lakes that the French christened "arms of gold."

PRINCE EDWARD ISLAND

17

The Confederation Bridge

Cape Jourimain to Victoria to Rocky Point

General Description: When arriving on the island, most head straight for Charlottetown, Summerside, or Cavendish. Instead, drive this 75-kilometer (47-mile) scenic route over the Confederation Bridge and then along the south coast—it yields a string of interesting harbors, cultural sites, and farmland views. History is in full focus, from the iceboats that once transported the mail to the first European settlement on the island; this scenic drive makes a perfect summer detour.

Special Features: Cape Jourimain Nature Centre, Confederation Bridge, Gateway Village, Port Borden Back Range Light, Cape Traverse Ice Boat Memorial, Victoria Seaport Lighthouse Museum, Argyle Shore Provincial Park, Skmaqn–Port-la-Joye–Fort Amherst National Historic Site, Blockhouse Point Lighthouse, views of Charlottetown, beaches, swimming.

Location: Across the Confederation Bridge and along the Northumberland Strait, through southeastern Prince County and southwestern Queens County.

Driving Route Numbers & Names: Confederation Bridge, Highway 1, Route 10, Route 116, Route 19.

Travel Season: Waterfront towns are most fun to explore in the summer, when you can

walk along the beach at low tide in bare feet. The Canada Day fireworks in Charlottetown can be seen from the end of this drive, Rocky Point. In autumn, the red leaves add another hue to the red farm soil, red tractors, and red sands that give this drive its rosy reputation.

Camping: No provincial parks have campgrounds on this stretch of coast, but find private campgrounds in Borden-Carleton and Cumberland Cove, or head north to the hundreds of sites at Prince Edward Island National Park.

Services: Arriving on island, Gateway Village in Borden-Carleton covers the basics—from gas to wine to ice cream. Medical services are available in Summerside, about 25 kilometers (15.5 miles) from the bridge, as well as in Charlottetown, less than 25 kilometers (15.5 miles) from Rocky Point.

Nearby Points of Interest: Car Life Museum; in Charlottetown: Founders' Hall, Province House National Historic Site, Beaconsfield Historic House, Ardgowan National Historic Site, Confederation Centre of the Arts, St. Dunstan's Basilica, heritage walking tours, dining, live music.

Time Zone: Atlantic time zone (GMT minus 4 hours).

The Drive

A coastal drive, this 75-kilometer (47-mile) route includes the requisite lighthouse and beaches, but it also traverses the essential link to the island, the Confederation Bridge, and overlooked heritage sites. To cap the drive, you'll look out over the busy Charlottetown waterfront to see the skyline of the harbor city where Canada was born.

The Confederation Bridge

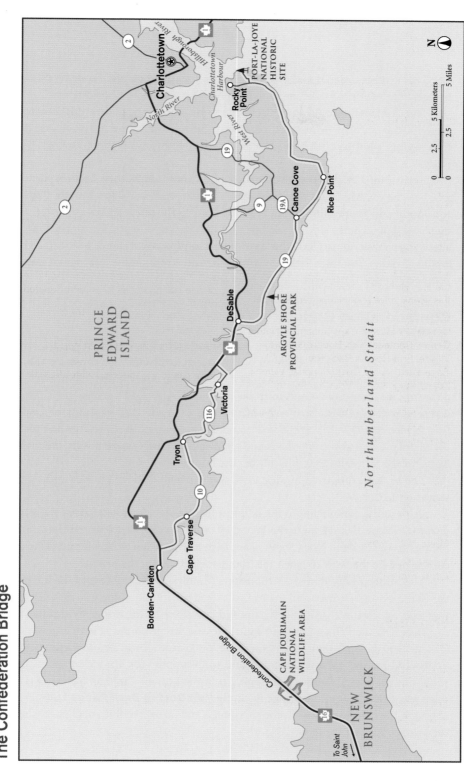

This drive is ordered for those arriving on the island via the Confederation Bridge, but it can easily be flipped to become a day trip from Charlottetown.

The Confederation Bridge links Borden-Carleton, Prince Edward Island, to Cape Jourimain, New Brunswick. Located just inside the New Brunswick side of the province's border with Nova Scotia, Highway 16 heads northeast toward the bridge.

Begin with a stop in **Bayfield** at the **Cape Jourimain Nature Centre,** part of a 662-hectare (1,636-acre) wildlife reserve that encompasses **Cape Marsh, Cape Jourimain** and **Jourimain Island.** Seabirds flock to the salt marshes as part of their migration routes, and ospreys fish off the coast. Hiking trails and beaches allow you to trek out to the **Cape Jourimain Lighthouse,** which is home to a cliff swallow colony. Facilities include washrooms and a restaurant, making it a well-planned stop for those who are mid road trip.

Confederation Bridge

After New Brunswick's Highway 16, the **Confederation Bridge** first gently climbs and then descends to the red shores of Prince Edward Island. The bridge is the final piece in fulfilling an 1873 promise by the federal government—to provide a continuous link to the island from the mainland. Although the idea of Canada was seeded at the Charlottetown Conference in 1864 and the Dominion of Canada was formed in 1867, Prince Edward Island did not join until 1873. This link to the mainland and absorbing the island's railway construction debt were the main gains for the farmland island in joining the dominion.

The bridge, completed in May 1997, was the final delivery on the Confederation promise.

Prior to the completion of the billion-dollar bridge, ferries provided transport to Prince Edward Island; the Wood Islands ferry still provides multiple daily sailings from Caribou, Nova Scotia from May to December. Many island visitors choose to take the ferry to reach the island and return via the bridge.

The bridge spans almost 13 kilometers (8 miles), and you'll avoid the toll on the island-bound journey and instead pay a roundtrip toll on the way off ($47 for two-axle vehicles in 2018). Pedestrians and cyclists cross the bridge by shuttle.

Reaching the Prince Edward Island side, the bridge connects with Highway 1 (Trans-Canada Highway)—the main route to Charlottetown. Before turning right on Route 10 to drive the Red Sands Shore, grab supplies (or just ice cream) at the shops and services at **Gateway Village.** From the Borden-Carleton waterfront, there are great views of the bridge from the **Port Borden Back Range Light,** although the lighthouse was decommissioned and moved to this small park when the bridge replaced the ferry.

The Confederation Bridge links Prince Edward Island to New Brunswick.

Throughout PEI, blue-and-white highway signs will direct you to restaurants, craft galleries, and accommodations. For travelers it's a refreshing helper that allows you to look at the scenery more than a GPS or iPhone screen.

About 2 kilometers (1.2 miles) past the tollbooths, turn right off Highway 1 to follow Route 10. The rural road passes **Amherst Cove** before reaching the **Cape Traverse Ice Boat Memorial,** where a roadside park displays an historic iceboat. Until a century ago, the iceboats scuttled mailbags and passengers across the ice-clogged Northumberland Strait to Cape Tormentine. The tin panels on the boat helped protect the hull from the ice, and runners allowed it to glide over the surface. The service started December 19, 1827—perhaps too late to post that year's Christmas cards—and ran until 1917 when an ice-breaker ferry began crossing.

Mountain ash hedges edge fields of baled hay, potato plants, and feed corn, and in each season the land will be in a different stage of preparing, planting, or harvesting. These are the initial scenes of the province's great tracts of farmland that make up the more than 1,350 farms. Note the red earth between the rows of potatoes—a soil that has made PEI and its spuds famous. But while potato is the island's best-known crop, the largest by land area is hay.

Cross the Tryon River at Tryon and, before reaching the Trans-Canada, turn right off Route 10 onto Route 116—the slow road (which includes a stretch of red dirt road) to the seaside town of Victoria.

Victoria

A picturesque setting, **Victoria** sits at the harbor edge where sand flats, a light-house, and fishing boats converge. A public wharf is the center of activity amid red cliffs and tidal flats. The **Victoria Seaport Lighthouse Museum** near the causeway maintains the local history along with the red-capped lighthouse, which is the island's second oldest. The narrow boat channel—look for it marked by red

Victoria sits at the harbor edge where sand flats, a lighthouse, and fishing boats converge.

and green navigation buoys—shows the limits of the harbor. Across the street there's a picnic area and welcome center.

The **Victoria Playhouse** produces theater shows and music performances during summer at the historic venue. The delectable treats at **Island Chocolates** on Main Street are also the centerpiece for chocolate-making workshops.

Causeway Road leads southeast from town.

Route 116 ends at Hampton, where you make a right turn on Highway 1, the main route, to DeSable.

About 4 kilometers (2.5 miles) along the Trans-Canada, turn right on Route 19 in **DeSable.** Less than 300 meters (0.2 mile) after the intersection, Monument Road leads to the **Franklin Knight Lane Monument.** Born in DeSable, Lane looms large south of the border. He excelled in US politics, serving as interstate commerce commissioner and secretary of the interior under Woodrow Wilson. A large grassy area and heritage sign commemorate his birthplace.

Through farm fields, Route 19 follows the coastline to **Argyle Shore Provincial Park,** a day-use park with a popular family beach, playground, washrooms, and picnic areas. The access road for the park runs parallel to a driveway for some private cabins. A small sign points the way, but mind to take the left road to reach the park.

The Argyle Shore refers to the area's Scottish heritage. While walking the beach you'll see the red cliffs that give this drive its official name: the Red Sands Shore.

Along this scenic drive or others on the island, note the distinct angles and straight lines of Prince Edward Island roads. In the 1760s Samuel Holland, a Dutch engineer and surveyor, was tasked with mapping the island—then called St. Johns Island. Holland divided the island into 67 lots and 3 royalties. Most lots had access to the waterfront and were fairly rectangular tracts given the variance of the coastline. Today, many roads follow these county lines or run parallel to the original land lot divisions.

As you drive up and down over rolling farmlands, try to identify the harvests. PEI is famous for its potatoes, but island farmers also grow corn, strawberries, oats, and Brussels sprouts, to name only a few crops. It's fascinating to watch the changes in the farming activities, as the workers and their giant machines seem to move in a great seasonal synchronization—be it ploughing the potato fields or bailing the hay.

At Canoe Cove, turn right to keep on Route 19 as it meets Route 19A.

Rounding Rice Point, crossing Nine Mile Creek, and then coming through Cumberland, follow the brown-and-white signs for the national historic site near Rocky Point.

Port-la-Joye

Skmaqn–Port-la-Joye–Fort Amherst National Historic Site tells a tumultuous tale—but there are some clues in its long, hyphenated name.

Prior to the arrival of the English settlers, the Mi'kmaq lived, fished, and hunted throughout the island. In 1720, 300 settlers arrived from France to establish a colony. Acadians from other parts of the Maritimes joined the settlement, which benefited from a good natural harbor and PEI's rich soil.

Skmaqn is a Mi'kmaq name, added to the national historic site in 2018, meaning "the waiting place" and referring to the cooperation of Mi'kmaq and French leaders—an alliance that was celebrated each year with feasting and gifts.

At Skmaqn–Port-la-Joye–Fort Amherst National Historic Site, find the Gallant memorial, and look out on the Charlottetown waterfront.

As French and British struggled over control of Atlantic Canadian regions, it led to much upheaval and the eventual expulsion of the Acadians from Nova Scotia and New Brunswick regions starting in 1755.

In August 1758 a British force came to seize possession of the region, which had been given up with the surrender of Louisbourg in July 1758. About two-thirds of the 4,600 colonists were deported that same year, mostly to France. About half died during the journey.

On the site of Port-la-Joye, the British built **Fort Amherst**—the grassy humps of which remain at the site today. Visitors can walk through these grassed-over fort walls, find the Gallant memorial, and look out on the Charlottetown waterfront.

A metal cross sits at the best viewpoint on the site. It commemorates the Great Upheaval of the Acadians, when 10,000 were deported from around the Maritimes to France, England, and the United States, including Louisiana where the Cajun culture took root.

Nearby at the end of Blockhouse Road lies **Blockhouse Point Lighthouse,** a square-set station that dates to 1876.

From this vantage, watch boats sailing in the harbor, which is the Fleur-de-lis–like confluence of three rivers: the Hillsborough, the North, and the West. Charlottetown's smokestacks and church spires, including those of the cathedral **St. Dunstan's Basilica,** rise above the city skyline. It's a concrete contrast to the meadows and trees sloping down from Port-la-Joye.

Rocky Point is a perfect location to admire the fireworks when displays take place above **Charlottetown Harbour.**

Side Trip: Charlottetown

The site is also less than 25 kilometers (15.5 miles) from the provincial capital city of **Charlottetown**, where varied dining options, heritage inns, live music venues, shops, and galleries line the historic streets.

Worthwhile city attractions include **Province House National Historic Site,** which although it was closed for extensive conservation and restoration in 2015 is still worth a look. **Beaconsfield House** is also lovely for its Victorian elegance, including furnishings and chinaware.

And for many, seeing an *Anne of Green Gables* performance at the **Confederation Centre of the Arts** will be an absolute must. Or, join costumed guides from the Confederation Players for walking tours around the city in French or English.

18

Acadians, First Nations & Oysters

Summerside to Malpeque Bay via the Acadian Coast and Lennox Island

General Description: This 150-kilometer (93-mile) scenic loop explores Celtic, Acadian, and Mi'kmaq heritage. The thrumming College of Piping in Summerside, a towering brick Catholic Church at Mont-Carmel, the serene water of Malpeque Bay, and the Mi'kmaq cultural center on Lennox Island each add a new curve to the route. Attractions include museums about Lucy Maud Montgomery, foxes, and shellfish, plus parks and trails.

Special Features: College of Piping, Eptek Art & Culture Centre, PEI Sports Hall of Fame, International Fox Museum, Wyatt House Museum, Linkletter Provincial Park, Acadian Museum, Union Corner Provincial Park and Schoolhouse Museum, the Bottle Houses, Lennox Island Mi'kmaq Cultural Centre, Indian Art & Crafts of North America, Malpeque Bay, Bideford Parsonage Museum, PEI Shellfish Museum, Green Park Provincial Park and Shipbuilding Museum, Yeo House.

Location: From Summerside in Prince County, along the coast of the Northumberland Strait to Lennox Island and Malpeque Bay.

Driving Route Numbers & Names: Route 11, Highway 2, Route 133, Route 12, Route 163, Bideford Road.

Travel Season: At its loveliest in summer, PEI is best visited between June and September. But the spring freshness and fall colors are also inviting, particularly in the bay-side Green Park Provincial Park. Book accommodations ahead if visiting in July and August, although campgrounds generally have availability outside of holiday weekends.

Camping: Both Linkletter Provincial Park (close to Summerside) and Green Park Provincial Park at the end of the drive have campgrounds. Showers and washrooms cover the basics, while playgrounds, kitchen shelters, and firewood make the stay more fun.

Services: Summerside, PEI's second largest city after Charlottetown, has all the needed services. Gas stations, medical care, and waterfront restaurants are all readily available in the Prince County center.

Nearby Points of Interest: L. M. Montgomery Lower Bedeque Schoolhouse Museum, Confederation Trail.

Time Zone: Atlantic time zone (GMT minus 4 hours).

The Drive

Begin this scenic 150-kilometer (93-mile) loop drive on Summerside's Water Street, part of Route 11. Located on the shore of Bedeque Bay, **Summerside** is a busy city with fishing wharves, shopping districts, and local colleges. The **College**

Acadians, First Nations & Oysters

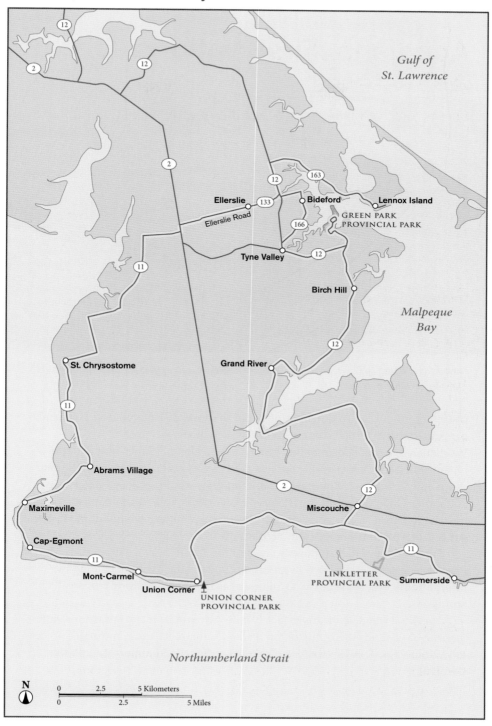

Gulf of St. Lawrence

Ellerslie ⟨133⟩ Bideford Lennox Island
Ellerslie Road
⟨166⟩ GREEN PARK PROVINCIAL PARK
Tyne Valley ⟨12⟩

Birch Hill

Malpeque Bay

⟨12⟩

St. Chrysostome Grand River

⟨11⟩

Abrams Village

Maximeville ⟨2⟩ Miscouche ⟨12⟩

Cap-Egmont

⟨11⟩ LINKLETTER PROVINCIAL PARK ⟨11⟩

Mont-Carmel Summerside

Union Corner UNION CORNER PROVINCIAL PARK

Northumberland Strait

N

| 0 | 2.5 | 5 Kilometers |
| 0 | 2.5 | 5 Miles |

Spinnaker's Landing in Summerside, Prince Edward Island, offers ice cream, souvenirs, and visitor information.

of Piping produces a summer performance to showcase bagpipes and Highland dancing. Inspired? Take a tour or a class at the school.

Follow the route down to the waterfront and along Heather Moyse Drive—renamed in 2014 after Olympic bobsled gold medalist, Heather Moyse. The cute shops and ice cream at **Spinnakers Landing** draw you in, as does a quick stop at the wharf-side visitor information center. Theaters, galleries, and music shows make Summerside a center for the arts. Regularly changing exhibits at the **Eptek Art & Culture Centre** range from needlecrafts to carvings.

For a historical look at the city, head to the Wyatt Heritage Properties. The historic properties encompass five locations open to the public, including the **International Fox Museum** at 33 Summer St. and **Wyatt Historic House** at 85 Spring St.

For those who fall for this Prince County city and its many attractions, Summerside boasts an inviting mix of top seafood restaurants and comfortable accommodations as well. In July, bibbed diners gather for the **Summerside Lobster Carnival.**

Back on Water Street, Route 11 continues west out of the urban center. And, after 5 kilometers (3.1 miles), a left-hand turn to **Linkletter Provincial Park** leads to a beachfront campground.

Acadian Shore

As the suburban-style properties become farms, you pass Lady Slipper Drive—an inland route to **Miscouche.** Either turn right to visit the **Acadian Museum** in Miscouche now, or include it at the end of the drive to discover PEI's Acadian heritage. It's about a 3-kilometer (2-mile) detour return.

To continue the scenic drive, follow the road (still Route 11) toward St-Nicholas and Union Corner. A half-dozen or so gravel roads branch off from the main road before the route emerges at Union Corner near the shoreline of the Northumberland Strait.

The **Union Corner Schoolhouse Museum** is situated at the top of Union Corner Road and above **Union Corner Provincial Park.** Drive down to the waterfront to look out from the red cliffs and see the Confederation Bridge to the southeast. Although the park has picnic tables, fire pits, washrooms, and change rooms, camping is not permitted.

Follow the shoreline for about 3.5 kilometers (2.2 miles) from Union Corner to **Mont-Carmel.** Above the tiny community—I strain to think how it supports such a large church—rise the twin spires of Our Lady of Mont-Carmel Church.

Route 11 traces the coastline to a tangent of attractions in the **Cap-Egmont** area. **The Bottle Houses,** at 6891 Rte. 11, present the work of a quirky island artist and builder. The original builder, Édouard Arsenault, constructed three, life-size buildings entirely from recycled bottles—about 25,000 empties in all. A house, chapel, and tavern welcome sunlight through the transparency of the glass. Nearby, drive along Phare du Cap Egmont Road to see the **Cap-Egmont Lighthouse,** which went into operation in 1884, and a nearby sea-carved arch, where birds roost.

Road names in the area show the blend of heritages: you'll see Scottish, French, and English surnames attached to roads, as well as those named for the ocean. A Labour Day weekend festival—the **Evangeline Area Agricultural Exhibition and Acadian Festival**—celebrates the region's farming history and Acadian roots.

Past Cap-Egmont Lighthouse, Route 11 hooks around and comes to the large **Egmont Bay** and crosses Haldimand River.

Fishing communities like **Abrams Village** (notable for the large Acadian Fishermen's Co-op building on the wharf) sit in the region known as the Evangeline coast. Abrams Village also hosts the July **Evangeline Bluegrass and**

Near Cap-Egmont Lighthouse is a sea-carved arch, popular with seabirds.

Traditional Music Festival, which features three days of music for a well-priced admission.

At the wetlands and forest of the **St.-Chrysostome Wildlife Management Area,** the road makes a series of sharp right-angle bends. Follow Route 11, keeping left at the intersections with Routes 128 and 130.

In **Mount Pleasant,** Route 11 ends at a T-junction with Highway 2. Turn left and follow the main highway north for a very short 500 meters (0.3 miles), before turning right onto Route 133 (Ellerslie Road).

After 6.5 kilometers (4 miles) on Route 133 through Ellerslie, turn left at the T-junction with Route 12. Drive 2 kilometers (1.2 miles) and then make a right on Route 163, or East Bideford Road, to Lennox Island.

Lennox Island

The one-way-in road follows a twisting arm of Malpeque Bay before connecting to the island causeway where the road becomes Sweetgrass Trail. **Lennox Island** is a First Nations community, its history stretching back thousands of years.

On Lennox Island, the small St. Anne's Church has the namesake of the Mi'kmaq patron saint.

At the **Lennox Island Mi'kmaq Cultural Centre** on Eagle Feather Trail, learn about the use of traditional plants in medicine, the songs in the Mi'kmaq culture, and the fine craft work. The cultural center offers guided tours in summer, and has info on walking trails in the western half of the island.

Across from the cultural center is the small white and pale yellow **St. Anne's Church.** When Grand Chief Membertou was baptized in Annapolis Royal, Nova Scotia in 1610 by French missionaries, Saint Anne was adopted as the Mi'kmaq patron saint.

On the village waterfront, an ecotourism complex provides clear views of the bay, including oyster aquaculture sites. Next door on Eagle Feather Trail, **Indian Art & Crafts of North America** displays finely crafted wares, from baskets to dream catchers to pottery.

Malpeque Bay

Return across the Lennox Island causeway and back to Route 12. Follow the main route south toward **Bideford** through the countryside scenery of goldenrod meadows and hay bales. After 2 kilometers (1.2 miles) turn left onto Bideford Road to visit the **Bideford Parsonage Museum** at 784 Bideford Rd.

As a 19 year old, *Anne of Green Gables* author Lucy Maud Montgomery boarded at this Methodist parsonage during her first teaching post at Bideford No. 6 School—a one-room schoolhouse. Built in 1878, the cute yellow home with white gingerbread trim is restored to that time, displaying a series of exhibits on the author as well as local shipbuilding—a strong industry on the island until the advent of steel-hulled liners. On Wednesday nights during summer, the parsonage museum hosts readings from Montgomery's works.

At the end of Bideford Road, on the Malpeque Bay shore, the wharf-side **PEI Shellfish Museum** explains the life cycle of spats, or baby oysters, as they grow into the world-famous table delicacy. Malpeque Bay's bivalve molluscs drew international recognition when they won accolades as the world's tastiest in the 1900 Paris Exhibition. The museum also covers info about lobsters, clams, and other tasty shellfish.

Either backtrack on Bideford Road or continue south to rejoin Route 12 in sweet **Tyne Valley.** The community hosts an oyster festival in early August.

Then it's on toward **Green Park Provincial Park** in Port Hill. An oasis of beautiful tree stands, camping, and history on Trout River, the provincial park is a lively spot during its mid-August blueberry social.

Penniless Englishman James Yeo arrived in Tyne Valley in 1819. He worked for a local businessman, opened a store, and then started building boats. More than 350 ships later, Yeo was considered the richest man on the island. The

At the Bideford Parsonage, Lucy Maud Montgomery boarded while she worked at her first teaching position.

impressive **Shipbuilding Museum** in the park tells more about Yeo and this significant island industry. The gorgeous Victorian gables invoke a time of hard-earned luxury. **Yeo House** is restored with historical furniture and open for visitors to peek into Yeo's life.

From Port Hill, Route 12 wends its way south toward Miscouche. Along the way you'll pass two pairs of facing churches in Birch Hill and a lovely wide estuary in Grand River. Aquaculture buoys bob, and bird life feeds along the shoreline.

As Route 12 meets Highway 2 in Miscouche, stop in now to the Acadian Museum or continue along the highway for dinner and a performance in Summerside.

19

Wind Turbines & Stompin' Tom

West Point to Skinners Pond to North Cape

General Description: A 95-kilometer (59-mile) coastal drive along PEI's windy northern shore, this route passes electricity-generating turbines and the home of "Bud the Spud" singer Stompin' Tom Connors. Unique rock formations, sandy beaches, fishing wharves, and shoreline trails provide lots to do. Nearby find museums that explore Acadian history and the island's favorite vegetable—potatoes.

Special Features: West Point Lighthouse Museum, Cedar Dunes Provincial Park, Giant's Armchair, Stompin' Tom Centre Homestead and Schoolhouse, Elephant Rock, Atlantic Wind Test Site, North Cape Interpretive Centre, North Point Lighthouse.

Location: Northwestern tip of the island, in Prince County.

Driving Route Numbers & Names: Route 14, Norway Road (Route 182), Route 12.

Travel Season: Boasting a long travel season, PEI has lovely temperatures from May through October. The wind turbines are fun to watch in any season, provided a breeze is blowing, but most museums keep seasonal hours, usually June through September.

Camping: Cedar Dunes Provincial Park, Mill River Provincial Park, and Jacques Cartier Provincial Park all offer camping facilities in close proximity to this drive. Expect washrooms, showers, kitchen shelters, and playgrounds at the provincial parks, which accommodate both tent and RV campers.

Services: O'Leary and Tignish provide the best options for services such as banks, gas stations, restaurants, and medical care. Ocean-side cottages are dotted along the drive, making it a fun beach getaway.

Nearby Points of Interest: Tignish Cultural Centre, Kildare Capes red sandstone cliffs, Jacques Cartier Provincial Park, Alberton Museum, Canadian Potato Museum, Mill River Provincial Park, Confederation Trail.

Time Zone: Atlantic time zone (GMT minus 4 hours).

The Drive

From the music of Stompin' Tom to sand between your toes, this 95-kilometer (59-mile) drive is a delight for the senses. Towering white wind turbines, quiet sandy beaches, and marshland trails give this more remote part of the island ample appeal. There are fantastic beaches along the entire length of this drive, including at West Point, Campbellton, Miminegash, and Skinners Pond.

From Summerside or Charlottetown, take Highway 2 northwest toward Tignish and the island's North Cape—the most northerly point in the province. Turn left onto Route 14 at Carleton, about 50 kilometers (31 miles) west of Summerside. (Here, don't confuse Carleton with Borden-Carleton—the community near the Confederation Bridge.)

Route 14 cuts west just south of O'Leary, through grain, clover, and potato fields.

Wind Turbines & Stompin' Tom

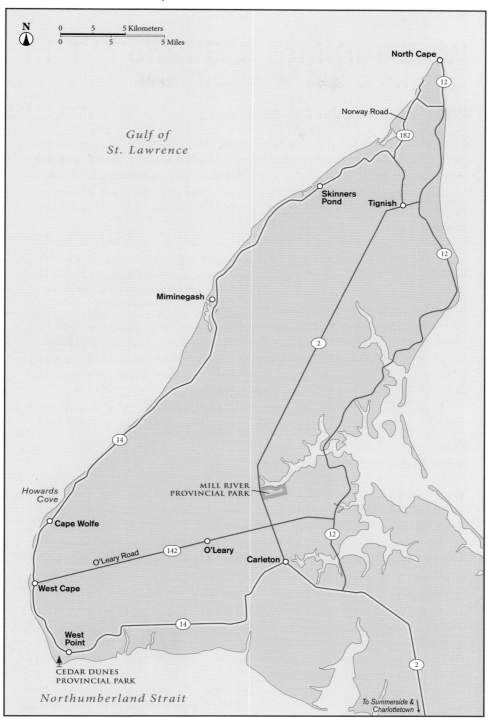

N

0 5 5 Kilometers
0 5 5 Miles

Gulf of
St. Lawrence

North Cape
12

Norway Road
182

Skinners
Pond

Tignish
12

Miminegash

12

2

Howards
Cove

MILL RIVER
PROVINCIAL PARK

Cape Wolfe

14

O'Leary Road
142
O'Leary

Carleton
12

West Cape

14

West
Point

2

CEDAR DUNES
PROVINCIAL PARK

Northumberland Strait

To Summerside &
Charlottetown

Following Route 14, make an unusual left at a yield sign and then bear right toward Milo. After traveling 21 kilometers (13 miles) in from Highway 2, make the first stop on the coast at West Point.

West Point & Cedar Dunes

The provincial park and lighthouse sit at West Point facing the Northumberland Strait. The picnic area, beach, and camping facilities at **Cedar Dunes Provincial Park** make an early stopping spot. Visit the **West Point Lighthouse Museum** to discover the history of the 1875 light station. Bold signature black-and-white bands define the island's tallest lighthouse. Boardwalks and comfortable accommodations add to the destination appeal.

Leaving the provincial park you'll spot the first of dozens of wind turbines on this scenic drive. **West Cape Wind Farm** is the island's largest and stretches from West Point to West Cape, farther along Route 14. Towering above the farmland hay fields, tractors, and cows, the churning wind turbines have the same shiny white sheen as *Star Wars* stormtroopers' armor.

Follow Route 14 along a smooth coastline around Carey Point and Cape Wolfe. In Howards Cove turn left on the Wharf Road to survey the large fishing wharf and sit in the **"Giant's Armchair"**—a seat-like stone that's only a good photo stop in clear weather because rainy days cause water to pool in the natural seat. Nearby is the squat **Howards Cove Lighthouse.**

From Howards Cove continue on Route 14, following signs for Roseville and Miminegash. The coast occasionally treats with sights of dramatic red cliffs.

Irish Moss & Skinners Pond

After Burton and a beach in Campbellton (which is a duplicate town name on the island, with another near New London), Route 14 curves slightly inland. As the ocean reappears, you arrive in **Miminegash.**

Once famed for large beach harvests and seaweed pie—sadly no longer available—the area is a producer of Irish moss. The seaweed is reported to be disappearing, but a little still grows on the ocean bed and coastal rocks, and then washes ashore to be harvested.

The seaweed is a source for carrageenan, an extract added as a thickener to ice cream and toothpaste. Seaweed pie was so named because it was made with carrageenan, but was neither green nor slimy.

West Point Lighthouse, near Cedar Dunes Provincial Park,
offers accommodation in its distinct tower.

It's a melancholy turn of a community, but there is still a local passion for seaweed, and the **Irish Moss Festival** is an annual, early summer event in nearby **Tignish** that coincides with the traditional beach harvest.

As Route 14 follows the coast, PEI farmlands become less prevalent and the fleets of lobster fishing boats grow larger. Acadian flags and five-point stars on houses show the region's French-speaking heritage.

About 14 kilometers (8.7 miles) past Miminegash, you'll arrive in the unexpectedly famous **Skinners Pond**, the home of **Stompin' Tom Connors.** A folk singer and songwriter, Stompin' Tom is best known for "The Hockey Song" and "Bud the Spud"—true Canadian anthems.

Born in Saint John, New Brunswick, Stompin' Tom was adopted by a family in Skinners Pond; at the age of just 13, he hitchhiked around the country working odd jobs. His ensuing music career spanned six decades.

At the intersection of Route 14 and Knox Lane sits a historic schoolhouse. Originally built in the early 1800s and thought to be the oldest on the island, Skinners Pond School was preserved at the behest of Stompin' Tom, who attended the one-room schoolhouse. Added in 2017, the **Stompin' Tom Centre Homestead and Schoolhouse** is a complex with dining, regular entertainment, and exhibits about the musician. There's a Canada Day weekend festival too.

Skinners Pond is also a fishing community, and is the location of a lovely, smooth-sand beach. Across from the schoolhouse, Stompin Tom Road heads down to the harbor, wharf, and beach. From here you can spy the wind farm at North Cape.

Continue northeast along the coast and after Nail Pond, turn onto Norway Road (Route 182).

As it makes a doglegged turn east, keep straight on the dirt-surfaced road to see the eroding coastline and more views of the wind turbine farm. **Elephant Rock** was a sea stack off this coast. And while it once looked like its namesake mammal, it has since largely eroded away.

Still, the green meadows, sharp drop offs, ochre-red cliffs, and white wind turbines create a vibrant contrast. From this point the **Black Marsh Trail** also connects to North Cape over a 2.5-kilometer (1.5-mile), one-way route of boardwalk and trails.

North Cape

Follow the dirt road back to Route 182 and make a left, taking the paved Nelligan Road to the T-junction with Route 12. Make another left toward Seacow Pond and North Cape. After a short distance, Route 12 ends at the parking lot of the **Atlantic Wind Test Site** and **North Cape Interpretive Centre.**

You'll see two types of towering wind turbines: the V47s that stand 73 meters (240 feet) and the V90s that stand 125 meters (410 feet) in total height. Three slim blades per turbine churn with the power of the wind. Only until you walk through the exhibits (inside and out) and see the blades up close does their size—similar to that of an airplane wing—make an impact.

Walk out to **North Cape Lighthouse** to see the northernmost tip of Prince Edward Island. Local residents placed an impromptu light here before the lighthouse was completed in 1867. The light marks the longest natural rock reef in North America, a 2-kilometer (1.2-mile) stretch that's exposed at low tide. This is the boundary between the Gulf of St. Lawrence and the Northumberland Strait and visitors can walk on this special slice of the ocean floor.

Windmills, grasslands, and hay fields surround North Cape, Prince Edward Island.

20

Green Gables & Red Sands

New London to Cavendish to Dalvay-by-the-Sea

General Description: This 84-kilometer (52-mile) scenic drive encompasses PEI's most famous icons: *Anne of Green Gables* and Cavendish Beach. The route journeys over farmlands and rivers to the shoreline where lighthouses, fishing boats, and red sandstone cliffs await in the island's only national park. Offbeat attractions include a farmer-started bank, a display of mounted birds, and a mansion-sized summerhouse. Of course, the drive couldn't miss a stop at Cavendish, Brackley Beach, or the near-countless Green Gables attractions.

Special Features: Lucy Maud Montgomery Birthplace, Stanley Bridge Marine Aquarium, Prince Edward Island National Park, Cavendish Beach, Green Gables Heritage Place, Site of Lucy Maud Montgomery's Cavendish Home, North Rustico Harbour Lighthouse, Farmers' Bank Museum, Doucet House, Brackley Beach, the Dunes Studio Gallery and Café, Covehead Lighthouse, Dalvay-by-the-Sea National Historic Site, boat tours, hiking, cycling, beaches, bird watching.

Location: Central PEI, on the northern shore of Queens County.

Driving Route Numbers & Names: Route 6, Grahams Lane, Cawnpore Lane (Route 13), Gulf Shore Parkway West, Harbourview Drive, Church Road, Route 15, Gulf Shore Parkway East.

Travel Season: In summer the national park swells with beachgoers. But with about 40 kilometers (25 miles) of shoreline, it's still possible to find a quieter spot in the park, even in the height of the season. Attractions, in general, are open from June through September.

Camping: Stay in Prince Edward Island National Park, with campgrounds at Cavendish, Brackley, and Stanhope. Campgrounds are equipped with the basic facilities such as water, washrooms, showers, and play areas. There are also a number of private campgrounds in the area.

Services: This drive starts near Kensington and ends about 10 kilometers (6.2 miles) from Charlottetown. Gas stations, groceries, and supplies are available in both. For medical services, head to Charlottetown or Summerside. Along the entire stretch of the drive, cabins, cottages, bed-and-breakfasts, and motels will mark the meters. But book ahead in summer as even with the density of accommodations, favorite spots do put up No Vacancy signs.

Nearby Points of Interest: Kensington Railway Station, Kensington Haunted Mansion, Old Millman Heritage Road, Anne of Green Gables Museum at Silver Bush.

Time Zone: Atlantic time zone (GMT minus 4 hours).

The Drive

With a little of everything that makes the gentle island such a summer vacation favorite, this coastal 84-kilometer (52-mile) scenic drive features the most famous icons of the island—from *Anne of Green Gables* attractions to perfect beaches and lobster suppers. Its winding curves are buzzing with tourists in July and August,

Green Gables & Red Sands

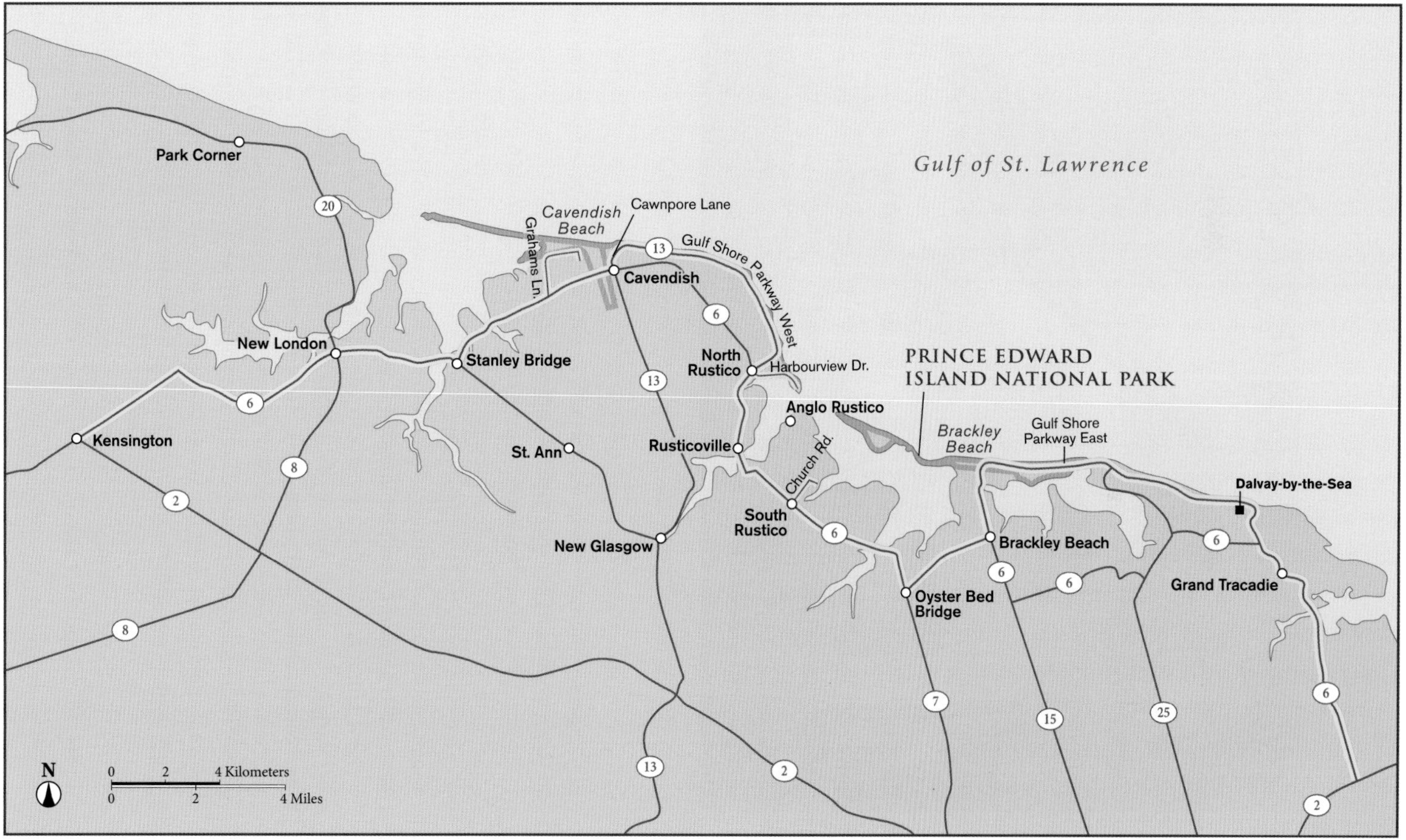

Gulf of St. Lawrence

PRINCE EDWARD
ISLAND NATIONAL PARK

Dalvay-by-the-Sea

Grand Tracadie

Gulf Shore
Parkway East

Brackley Beach

*Brackley
Beach*

Oyster Bed
Bridge

Anglo Rustico

Church Rd.

South
Rustico

New Glasgow

Rusticoville

North
Rustico

Harbourview Dr.

Gulf Shore Parkway West

Cawnpore Lane

Cavendish

*Cavendish
Beach*

Grahams Ln.

Stanley Bridge

St. Ann

New London

Park Corner

Kensington

N

0   2   4 Kilometers
0   2   4 Miles

Green Gables Heritage Place is a favorite for Lucy Maud Montgomery fans from around the world.

so the quieter shoulder-season months will reward with oysters, emptier roads, and more availability for overnight accommodations.

To reach New London, travel from Kensington along Route 6 or from Summerfield along Route 8 (both communities are on Highway 2). Route 6 is the prettier drive, and between Kensington and New London the rolling hills of farmland undulate down to the Southwest River. Smaller waterways join the larger, and the road crosses Durant Creek and Harding Creek.

New London sits at the busy crossroads of Routes 6, 8, and 20. A tour-bus-sized parking lot signals the site of an *Anne of Green Gables* attraction: the **Lucy Maud Montgomery Birthplace.** Here, on November 30, 1874, Lucy Maud Montgomery was born. The town was then called Clifton, and Montgomery's parents lived in this small wooden home. But before Montgomery was two, her mother died from tuberculosis, and her father turned custody over to her maternal grandparents. Exhibits of clothes, writings, and photos fill the two floors.

For more Anne Shirley than one scenic drive can perhaps hold, make a side trip northwest on Route 20 from New London to Park Corner. Here, along Cousin's Shore and the Lake of Shining Waters, is the **Anne of Green Gables**

Museum at Silver Bush—Montgomery's aunt and uncle's home and where the author married Ewan Macdonald.

For beaches, walking trails, and fishing villages, however, continue on the main scenic drive and travel east from New London on Route 6 through Stanley Bridge and Cavendish—toward the national park.

Stanley Bridge & Cavendish

About 4 kilometers (2.5 miles) from New London, **Stanley Bridge** bestrides its namesake river. Descend the gentle hills to the pretty riverside location. On river left, you first pass **Carr's Oyster Bar and Restaurant,** which serves the locally grown delicacies, Malpeque Bay oysters. Next door to the restaurant, the **Stanley Bridge Marine Aquarium** at 32 Campbellton Rd. features touch tanks, fish aquariums, and a collection of mounted birds and butterflies.

But the Stanley Bridge fishing wharf—where boat tours and working fishing vessels come and go—is the most fascinating part of the community, and there's also an excellent seafood market. Venture from the wharf with a deep-sea fishing tour or just admire the views of seabirds perched on aquaculture buoys. Boats slip out through a narrow, silted-in harbor mouth. Here you can also see the long stretch of dunes that form the western end of **Prince Edward Island National Park** and shelter the harbor.

The **River Days Festival** celebrates the Stanley Bridge area with events and entertainment in late August.

Driving east from Stanley Bridge there's a roundabout at the junction with Routes 254 and 224. Take the third exit for Route 6. "Roundabouts are cheaper than traffic lights," a local told me.

Crossing an inlet you'll see more aquaculture sites and sand dunes, along with farmland hedgerows and fields. As the road approaches Cavendish, signs for accommodations increase and vacation cabins sit between hayfields and perhaps, depending on the season, flowering potato plants.

At a stoplight, Grahams Lane leads left to **Cavendish Beach** and the western end of **Prince Edward Island National Park.** The one-way-in road accesses the campground and the sandy shores of Cavendish. At the shoreline you can follow interpretive trails, relax at the beach, and look out over the dunes.

When near the dunes it's essential to keep on marked paths, as walking on dune or marram grass kills the plant. These grass roots help stabilize the dunes, but once they die the dunes simply drift away. A surprising note from a park brochure says that as few as 10 steps can kill marram grass. Also fragile in the park are the coastal piping plovers. The endangered black-collared, white-bodied birds

Sand dunes and red cliffs mark the shoreline of Prince Edward Island National Park.

nest on the beaches from May through to mid-August. But the quiet of the park and the tourist center of Cavendish have few similarities.

Early on a summer morning **Cavendish** is an empty spot. But as the heat of a summer's day increases, so does the traffic. Allow for "tourist driving" (i.e., drivers slowing down looking for attractions or accommodations, or turning without using a signal light) as folks navigate a new place.

The attractions they seek are plenty: You'll pass **Ripley's Believe It or Not Odditorium, Avonlea Village, Grandpa's Antique Photo Studio,** plus dozens more along Route 6, also called Cavendish Road. Enjoy the tackiness: There are few places in Canada that can match the attention-grabbing appeal you'll see along this stretch.

For many, however, the main draw in Cavendish is **Green Gables Heritage Place.** Amid gardens, barns, and woodland trails sits **Green Gables House,** its white shingles edged with forest green trim. The house, which belonged to cousins of Lucy Maud Montgomery's grandfather, is now refurbished as the fictional house where orphan Anne Shirley came to live with Matthew and Marilla Cuthbert—a tale that has made Green Gables and PEI famous internationally. Trails lead to **Lovers' Lane,** the **Haunted Woods** and the **Green Gables Golf Course.**

For those more intrigued by the story of Montgomery herself, visit the **Site of Lucy Maud Montgomery's Cavendish Home,** where grandparents Alexander and Lucy Macneill raised Montgomery after her mother died. The home at 8521 Cavendish Rd. is now only a foundation, but it is still the "hallowed ground" where Montgomery penned the most legendary of her books, *Anne of Green Gables.*

Continue on the main vein through Cavendish, following Route 6. Turn left at the traffic lights onto Cawnpore Lane or Route 13.

There's a large visitor information center on the way back into the national park. You'll need a park pass to stop at lookouts and beaches in this section. Trees screen the right side of the road, and to the left stand fragile red sandstone cliffs. Boats and birdlife provide lots to watch along the shoreline.

After a 9-kilometer (5.6-mile) scenic drive, Gulfshore Parkway West arrives at Beach Lane.

The Rusticos

Although Beach Lane leads along **North Rustico Beach**, continue on Church Hill Avenue into **North Rustico** and then turn immediately left on Harbourview Drive to reach **North Rustico Harbour.**

From the heavily silted harbor mouth, the **North Rustico Harbour Lighthouse** beams its navigational signal. Views of distinct red bluffs and the Gulf of St. Lawrence provide a stunning panorama. Amid the restaurants, fishing charters, kayak tours, and other visitor comforts, a trail leads out to the beach.

From the center of town, Route 6 heads southeast, passing through **Rusticoville.**

At **South Rustico,** Church Road travels a short distance to a series of historic Acadian attractions. A stone stronghold, the **Farmers' Bank Museum National Historic Site** at 2188 Church Rd. was one of the first people's banks in the country. In operation for 30 years, the bank supplied inexpensive credit to the local Acadian population. Tour the solid sandstone bank and learn about the Catholic priest who organized the project, Rev. Georges-Antoine Belcourt.

Neighboring **Doucet House** displays daily life for Acadians during the 1800s through a garden, small wooden house, and guides. Also in South Rustico, **St. Augustine's Catholic Church** is the one of the oldest Catholic churches on Prince Edward Island, having been built in 1838.

Wharf Road ventures out to the coast, where the harbor is almost sealed off by dunes, like many areas along this northern coast. In some places, dunes can close off a saltwater bay creating a *barachois*—a term particular to Atlantic Canada that refers to a coastal lagoon largely cut off from the ocean. A barachois may be tidal, but generally fills with freshwater over time.

North Rustico has a busy fishery—as well as popular lobster suppers.

Return to Route 6 and follow it east across the Wheatley River. At Cymbria—just before **Oyster Bed Bridge**—see more aquaculture sites in the sheltered bay, where oysters and mussels are cultivated and harvested.

At a roundabout, make the third turn to continue following Route 6 as it intersects with Route 7.

Brackley to Dalvay

On the drive to the community of Brackley Beach, stop to indulge in the soft scents and suds at the **Great Canadian Soap Company.** Then, at a true farm-country intersection, turn left on Route 15. (Route 6 continues to the right, and passes the local community center where ceilidhs are a regular summer event.)

On roughly the 3-kilometer (2-mile) stretch out to the shore, you'll pass the **Dunes Studio Gallery and Café,** noted for its restaurant and gallery as well as a lush summer garden. Through this marshy stretch, the road almost seems to dip below the water level before reaching a huge beach-goers parking lot near the shoreline. Here we pick up another stretch of Gulf Shore Parkway to explore the final kilometers of this coastal national park drive.

There are viewpoints and trails down the road to Robinsons Island, as well as **Brackley Beach,** where the day-use area includes a beach, picnic tables, and a canteen. The campground provides tent sites only.

But I prefer the lookouts to the east, where the paved scenic road parallels a cycling and walking path—watch for pedestrians who may be crossing to admire the views.

First along Gulf Shore Parkway a bridge spans the mouth of **Covehead Bay** where the square **Covehead Lighthouse** serves as a beacon for the fishing boats that return here to dock. At the lighthouse, walk along the beach and visit the fishing shacks.

First along Gulf Shore Parkway, the square Covehead Lighthouse marks the mouth of Covehead Bay.

Erosion problems are apparent throughout the park as wind and water shave away the soft red shoreline. Even the Tarmac parking lots have crumbled into the ocean in some places. The PEI coastline erodes about on average about half a meter (1.5 feet) every year, although this varies greatly from one region to the next.

Gulfshore Parkway measures 10 kilometers (6.2 miles) from Brackley Beach to Dalvay-by-the-Sea. Stop frequently along this stretch to enjoy hikes, lookouts, and picnic areas. Although the sand and cliffs are lovely, head inland to hike over marshland boardwalks and through quiet forests. Just be sure to bring bug repellant and long sleeves.

While mosquitoes might be your only *guaranteed* wildlife sighting, beaver and birdlife also frequent the marshes.

Choose **Stanhope campground** if you're keen to have a campfire. The campground also has serviced sites for RVs.

The last stopping place along this coastal stretch is the impressive summer home turned inn, **Dalvay-by-the-Sea National Historic Site** at 16 Cottage Crescent. The Victorian mansion provides antique-furnished guest rooms with no telephones, televisions, or alarm clocks. The Adirondack chairs under the garden pine trees make the perfect resting spot after a long drive.

The gardens at Dalvay-by-the-Sea have views of Long Pond, also known as "Dalvay Lake."

Dalvay-by-the-Sea, started in 1895, was once the summer home of Alexander MacDonald. The Scottish-born businessman made his fortune serving as president of Standard Oil Company and a director in the mining, railway, and banking industries.

When MacDonald died, his fortune fell to his two granddaughters, the children of his only child Laura. But under the management of their father, the granddaughters' million-dollar fortune disappeared with bad investments. Unable to afford the house that had cost $50,000 to build, MacDonald's granddaughters sold the house to the caretaker, William Hughes, for their debt in back taxes: $486.57.

In 1938 the house and land was sold to the government so it could be included in the national park. For the best views, drive past the house to admire the mansion across **Long Pond** (also known as Dalvay Lake) just as Alexander MacDonald did on his last visit to the house in 1909.

Gulf Shore Parkway makes its final connection with Route 6, about 2 kilometers (1.2 miles) past Dalvay.

After 10 kilometers (6.2 miles) through Grand-Tracadie and past Winter Bay, Route 6 ends at Highway 2.

Side Trip: Lobster Suppers

Prince Edward Island **lobster suppers** are an enduring local tradition, owing to good fishing grounds around the island and the lobster boats that dock in local harbors. Days of an abundant fishery are declining, but it's still possible to get a fresh, PEI lobster dinner.

PEI lobster suppers offer an authentic, down-home feel. Full meals usually include the main attraction of a 1-pound crustacean plus steamed mussels or seafood chowder, homemade rolls, and local vegetables—all capped with berry shortcake or pie and a cup of tea.

In June 1958, **New Glasgow Lobster Suppers** served their first lobster dinner as a fundraiser. The cost? $1.50 each. It has since become a private restaurant.

Owing to its popularity as a dining option—some dining rooms can seat hundreds—you can find PEI lobster dinners in many restaurants as well as full suppers in Cardigan and (my uncle Tom's favorite) at the **Fisherman's Wharf** in **North Rustico.**

21

Ferries & the *Titanic*

Wood Islands to Panmure Island Provincial Park

General Description: Ending at a serene beach, this 70-kilometer (43.5-mile) scenic drive skirts the southeastern coast of Prince Edward Island. It begins at the Wood Islands ferry terminal—the dock for a May to Dec service between Nova Scotia and the island. En route you'll discover a winery, parks, and lighthouses—one of which was the first land station in Canada to receive the *Titanic*'s SOS call. Take side trips to see a buffalo herd, dine on local mussels, and take a boat tour.

Special Features: Wood Islands Ferry, Wood Islands Lighthouse, Northumberland Provincial Park, Rossignol Estate Winery, Cape Bear Lighthouse, Kings Castle Provincial Park, Panmure Island Provincial Park, Panmure Island Lighthouse.

Location: Located in southeastern Kings County, Prince Edward Island.

Driving Route Numbers & Names: Trans-Canada Highway (Highway 1), Route 4 (Shore Road), Route 18, Cape Bear Road, Black Brook Road, Fox River Road, Route 348 (Gladstone Road), Route 17, Route 347 (Panmure Island Road).

Travel Season: This is another lovely summer drive, although on a clear fall day,

walking on the beaches is perfectly enjoyable too. Museums and attractions tend to maintain regular hours from June to September only.

Camping: Camp at Northumberland Provincial Park near the start of the drive, where services include washrooms, showers, and laundry. At the drive's end, Panmure Island Provincial Park provides a lovely vantage near sandy beaches and accepts reservations. Private campsites can be found along the way in Murray Harbour and Murray River—while Seal Cove Campground is known for its sea-life sightings.

Services: Although gas and basic groceries can be found in Murray River, the closest hospital is in Montague. Most of the accommodations on this stretch are vacation cabins or cottages, requiring greater self-sufficiency than in better-serviced areas such as Charlottetown, Cavendish, and Summerside.

Nearby Points of Interest: Buffalo-land Provincial Park, Garden of the Gulf Museum, Orwell Corner Historic Village, Sir Andrew MacPhail Homestead.

Time Zone: Atlantic time zone (GMT minus 4 hours).

The Drive

If your schedule allows, arrive on PEI via the ferry. When heading to the eastern end of the island from Nova Scotia, it will cut down on driving time without adding to the overall travel time. Getting to the island is no charge; instead ferry and bridge tolls are collected when you leave.

Northumberland Ferries Limited operates the route from Caribou, Nova Scotia, to Wood Islands, Prince Edward Island. Since 1941 ferries have made the

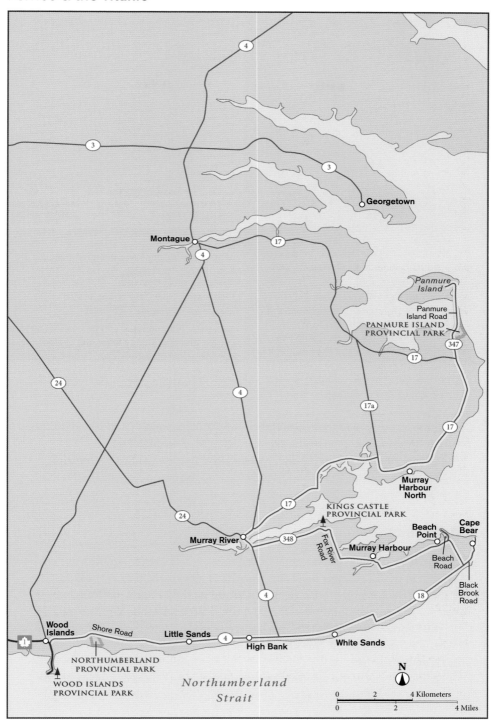

Georgetown

Montague

Panmure Island

Panmure Island Road

PANMURE ISLAND PROVINCIAL PARK

Murray Harbour North

KINGS CASTLE PROVINCIAL PARK

Beach Point

Cape Bear

Murray River

Murray Harbour

Beach Road

Black Brook Road

Wood Islands

Shore Road

Little Sands

High Bank

White Sands

NORTHUMBERLAND PROVINCIAL PARK

WOOD ISLANDS PROVINCIAL PARK

Northumberland Strait

Fox River Road

N

0   2   4 Kilometers

0   2   4 Miles

Northumberland Ferries Limited operates the ferry route from Caribou, Nova Scotia, to Wood Islands, Prince Edward Island.

75-minute crossing over the Northumberland Strait, passing Pictou Island on the way. The ferry operates 8 months per year, from May through Dec.

But this 70-kilometer (43.5-mile) scenic drive doesn't require a ferry trip: Simply follow signs for the Wood Islands ferry on the island, or take the Trans-Canada Highway from Charlottetown.

Wood Islands

After the ferry docks at the terminal in Wood Islands Harbour—in the southernmost region of PEI—follow the Trans-Canada Highway that begins at the wharf for 500 meters (0.3 mile). Turn right into **Wood Islands Provincial Park,** which features a museum and interpretive center at the **Wood Islands Lighthouse.**

The lighthouse, built in 1876, has ushered the ferry into the harbor since the MV *Prince Nova* made the first crossing in 1941, and the light guided iceboats and ships long before that.

Learn the tales of the sea: from rumrunning during Canada's longest prohibition (1901–1948) to sightings of a phantom ship off the coast. Climb the light station and see the lighthouse-keeper's quarters. Long before the regular ferry run, iceboats crossed to Nova Scotia with mail and also provided passenger service.

The provincial park offers a beach, washrooms, picnic tables, play area, and a boat ramp.

The Trans-Canada branches west to Charlottetown at the junction with Route 4. Turn right, or east, passing the **Wood Islands Welcome Centre**—where a collection of services includes an information center, ice cream shop, liquor store, cafe, and gift store. Ask at the visitor center about the annual **70-Mile Yard Sale,** held in mid-September.

A branch of the **Confederation Trail** also starts nearby. Built on the old railway beds after the train service was decommissioned in 1989, an 80-kilometer (49.7-mile) branch of the trail runs from Charlottetown to Murray Harbour. Traversing the island from tip to tip covers 273 kilometers (170 miles) of walking and biking trails, while all branches of the Confederation Trail cover 435 kilometers (270 miles) total distance.

This scenic drive is a portion of the **Points East Coastal Drive**, so watch for the blue-and-orange starfish marking the route.

As the road follows the coast, you'll pass **Northumberland Provincial Park,** about 3 kilometers (2 miles) from Wood Islands. Bluffs look out over the shoreline, where there is a beach and supervised swimming during summer. The campground has good basic facilities.

The straight road sits on an eroding coastline. Farmlands and vacation properties stretch down to the waterfront. Pass through Little Sands where a roadside Winery sign marks **Rossignol Estate Winery.** Widely spaced vine rows slope down to the strait. Although fruit wines are the winery's signatures, it is producing increasing varieties of specialty products, whites, and reds—including Atlantic Canada favorite vines like Marechal Foch and L'Acadie Blanc.

After High Bank, Route 4 turns to cut north (becoming Normans Road) in a direct line to Murray River. Instead, continue east and follow Route 18 out to Cape Bear.

Cape Bear

The trees thicken to a forest as the road enters **Cape Bear.** Black Brook Road leads to the 1881 **Cape Bear Lighthouse.** Having been moved multiple times away from the quickly eroding cliffs, the lighthouse was repositioned in 2015. The site has views of the crumbling red shoreline and long sand beaches, as well as a picnic area.

The now-demolished **Marconi station** at Cape Bear was the first land station in Canada to receive the *Titanic* SOS call. (Although Cape Race in Newfoundland

The Marconi station, near the Cape Bear Lighthouse, was the first in Canada to receive the Titanic *distress call.*

received the message first, the rocky province did not join Canada until 1949.) It's worth the small fee to climb the lighthouse and view the exhibits on past lighthouse keepers and see the light.

From Cape Bear, return via Black Brook Road to Route 18 and continue on toward Murray River. Beach Point lives up to its name with a local-favorite beach and guiding lights at the mouth of Murray Harbour.

Follow the starfish scenic-drive signs along Route 18 as it bears right and cuts through the small fishing community of **Murray Harbour.** There's a busy town wharf.

About 2 kilometers (1.2 miles) past the town, turn right onto Fox River Road and then left to travel on Route 348 toward Gladstone. Along the way a small day-use park, **Kings Castle Provincial Park** at 1887 Gladstone Rd., offers a unique cast of guides: Storybook statues ranging from the Three Bears to Mother Goose decorate the park. Washrooms, a picnic area, a themed playground, and a beach make the park a wonderful budget day trip for families. Check for details of planned summer activities.

Both Route 348 (Gladstone Road) and Route 18 come to T-intersections with Route 4. Turn right and drive through the small town of Murray River.

Cross the Murray River waterway, and then turn right on Route 4 (to Montague) and then on Route 17 toward Point Pleasant and Murray Harbour North. The largest seal colony on the island is in the area. Often regarded as pests by fishermen, harbor seals and gray seals feed on fish and love to bask on rocks, making for easy viewing from beaches such as the sands at Seal Cove Campground.

Panmure Island

Cranberry bogs, farms, and marshes lie on either side of Route 17 as it twists along the coast. When sightlines allow, catch glimpses of a small island chain, the Murray Islands, in the sand-spit-protected harbour. At Murray Harbour North, keep left on Route 17.

Climb the historic lighthouse above Panmure Island beach.

About 18 kilometers (11 miles) from Murray River, leave Route 17 and turn right onto Route 347: the no-exit road out to **Panmure Island.** The road soon enters **Panmure Island Provincial Park** at 350 Panmure Island Rd. A campground with washrooms, laundry, water, and a play area are located on the mainland side of the park.

A sandbar connects Panmure Island to the mainland. To the ocean side, enjoy the walks and views from a golden-sand beach. Lifeguards supervise the swimming area in summer. On the west side of the road is sheltered **St. Marys Bay,** where a red shoreline faces mussel aquaculture sites. Enjoy the sand to its fullest with the **Panmure Island Sandcastle Competition**—a fun amateur event held in August.

St Marys Bay leads into a larger bay known as Three Rivers for the freshwater tributaries that meet here. The Montague, Brudenell, and Cardigan Rivers flow into the bay.

Atop the northern hill, the **Panmure Island Lighthouse** overlooks the area. It's the province's oldest wooden lighthouse, built in 1853, and in summer you can view exhibits and climb the tower to see the lantern.

The Mi'kmaq were Panmure Island's first inhabitants, drawn to the rich shellfish grounds to harvest clams and mussels. Each summer First Nations gather for the **Abegweit Pow Wow.** Learn ancient teachings, buy crafts, and watch traditional dance during the August cultural weekend event, which ends with a feast.

Panmure Island Road cuts through farm fields to cross to the west side of the island. Scottish settlers came to the area in the early 1800s and the original one-room schoolhouse, built in 1897 and now used as a community hall, still stands.

From Panmure Island, retrace the road along the sandy causeway. Route 17 continues west 20 kilometers (12.4 miles) to Montague and 37 kilometers (23 miles) to Georgetown—offering the best options for dining and accommodations.

Side Trip: Montague and Georgetown

Continuing west of Panmure Island, Route 17 skirts coves and riverbanks to **Montague.** From there, Routes 4 and 3 head out to **Georgetown.** Both are small but busy communities, and their charm comes from historic architecture plus their riverside and coastal locations.

On the Montague Main Street and housed in a historic sandstone building, the **Garden of the Gulf Museum** delves into pioneer life with exhibits and local photos.

Georgetown is the seat of Kings County. The peninsula on Cardigan Bay was set aside for this purpose when Samuel Holland surveyed the island and divided it into 67 lots and 3 royalties. Theater, storied churches, and golf courses draw visitors to the area.

22

Singing Sands

Souris to East Point to New Harmony Heritage Road

General Description: Round the eastern tip of Prince Edward Island on this 70-kilometer (43.5-mile) scenic loop to discover the famed Singing Sands, lighthouses, and red-dirt heritage roads. Watch for whales and gannets, amble over coastal trails, bike the Confederation Trail, or take a train ride. This drive requires a slower pace: one that includes stopping at beaches, walking out at low tide, and scanning the water of the Gulf of St. Lawrence with binoculars.

Special Features: Souris Beach Gateway Park, Souris East Lighthouse, Magdalen Islands ferry, St. Mary's Roman Catholic Church, Black Pond Bird Sanctuary, Red Point Provincial Park, Basin Head Provincial Park, Singing Sands, Basin Head Fisheries Museum, East Point Lighthouse, Elmira Railway Museum, Confederation Trail, New Harmony Demonstration Woodlot, New Harmony Heritage Road.

Location: Eastern tip of Prince Edward Island, Kings County.

Driving Route Numbers & Names: Main Street, Route 16, Lighthouse Road, Elmira Road (Route 16A), Northside Road, Route 302 (Baltic Road), Route 303 (Glen Road/New Harmony Road), Route 335.

Travel Season: A perfect summer drive, this route journeys to PEI's eastern beaches. Attractions on this route tend to be open only in the summer months—June to September. The dirt heritage road is best avoided in wet weather.

Camping: Red Point Provincial Park lies about halfway through this drive and has hot showers, washrooms, and RV sites. The campground takes reservations, and is also adjacent to the family-friendly Basin Head Provincial Park, where there is no camping.

Services: Souris is the best bet for restaurants, supplies, and gasoline. For medical care, there is a hospital. For extensive shopping, journey the 80 kilometers (50 miles) to Charlottetown—a trip that takes about 1¼ hours. Vacation chalets and cottages are extremely prevalent in this area. Book a stay in St. Peters Bay for a pretty, central location, or in Red Point, which is convenient to parks and beaches. There are also a few large golf resorts on this coast.

Nearby Points of Interest: Myriad View Artisan Distillery, PEI National Park (Greenwich).

Time Zone: Atlantic time zone (GMT minus 4 hours).

The Drive

The Singing Sands, great wildlife watching, and the province's easternmost point all delight on this 70-kilometer (43.5-mile) drive. Arrive in the east via the main roads: Highways 2 and 4. Rural Kings County is filled with farm roads that run parallel to the original land lots—from the northwest to the southeast in this area. With a well-marked road map you can find quick—if not exactly direct—routes throughout the island. PEI tourism provides above-average highway maps for no charge.

Singing Sands

Highway 2 strikes in from the west. The Souris River lets out into Colville Bay with the Northumberland Strait beyond. Between Souris West and Souris, find the sandy shores of **Souris Beach Gateway Park** at 8 Main St. The narrow sand spit protrudes into the harbor mouth, anchored by the pavement. Showers, washrooms, a play area, and beachside businesses provide more than the basic day-park services. The area is also popular with boaters—from canoeists and kayakers to windsurfers.

In **Souris,** services cluster (conveniently, if a little unattractively) along the main road. The **Matthew and McLean Building** at 95 Main St. houses the visitor information center as well as some historical exhibits about the Acadian community. In 1727 Acadians established fisheries and farms here. It's said the town's name—meaning "mice" in French—comes from three plagues of rodents that swept through the fields during the 1720s and 1730s.

The town is the hub of the east, and a ferry runs from Souris to the **Magdalen Islands (Îles de la Madeleine).** The picturesque islands are an isolated network of about 12 sandy islands, about 5 hours offshore by ferry. Part of Quebec, the islands share a similar French-speaking heritage. Most are linked by sand dunes, making the archipelago easy to explore. The islands' history spans shipwrecks and a feudal landlord, but the people—the Madelinots—are perhaps the best reason to visit.

Above the town, the round tower of **St. Mary's Roman Catholic Church** silhouettes a stern profile. The church, first built in 1838, is a testament to the strong Acadian heritage in the area. The church was rebuilt three times: in 1849 due to fire, 1901–1902 to use the island sandstone, and 1929 again due to fire.

To the east of the ferry dock, look for the **Souris East Lighthouse.** Dating to 1880, the lighthouse houses a small gift shop. Perhaps most unique, however, is that as recently as 1991 Frank McIntosh was a lighthouse keeper here. When he retired, McIntosh became the last lighthouse keeper of Prince Edward Island. In late July, visit Knight Point for entertainment and beach glass treasures at the **Mermaid Tears Sea Glass Festival.**

Singing Sands

Follow Route 16 east through Souris, past Chepstow, and toward Little Harbour. The road bridges the **Black Pond Migratory Bird Sanctuary,** first established in 1936. A total of 368 bird species have been spotted in the province, but Canada geese and nesting waterfowl in the thousands are most common in this migratory sanctuary. Great blue herons nest in eastern PEI, as do ospreys, kestrels, hummingbirds, and sandpipers. The province publishes its Field Checklist of Birds online as a downloadable guide.

Swimmers thrill at bridge jumping in Basin Head Provincial Park.

Although Route 16 sits inland from the coast, you'll find the best views at the provincial parks along the way. The first, **Red Point Provincial Park** at 249 Red Point Park Rd., features more than 100 campsites plus washrooms, showers, fire pits, and a playground. A dump station and serviced sites accommodate RVs. The park is situated on the beach—a great spot for swimming in the supervised area.

For a better day trip option, continue 2 kilometers (1.2 miles) past the Red Point turnoff and then make a right to **Basin Head Provincial Park.** It's known for its **"Singing Sands,"** because scuffing your feet along the beach produces a so-called singing sound—a noise that hits a pitch somewhere between a squeak and the zip of a tent fly closing. Scientists haven't determined what causes the sand's sound, although speculations identify the high amount of silica or perhaps the amount of quartz in the sand. The beach is a summer frenzy of activity as kids jump from the pier into the basin's small mouth, also known as the run. Families picnic on the busy beach and make use of the generally good facilities.

At the park visit the **Basin Head Fisheries Museum,** which sits above the beach on a bluff. It tells the history of the inshore fishery: the boats, workers, and the cannery. A harbor to Basin Head was dredged in the late 1930s and a wharf built to maintain access to the basins.

Basin Head is known for its "Singing Sands," because scuffing your feet along the beach produces a so-called singing sound.

You won't likely see it, but the lagoons at Basin Head are the only place where **giant Irish moss** grows. The moss contains high amounts of carrageenan, a thickening agent used in ice cream and toothpaste. Unlike other types of Irish moss, the strain that lives in Basin Head never roots to the ocean floor and has an even higher concentration of carrageenan—but unfortunately similar to the decline of Irish moss on the west side of the island, the seaweed harvests are greatly reduced in recent years.

From Basin Head, follow PEI's coastline of sand dunes for 12 kilometers (7.5 miles) to reach the island's eastern tip.

East Point

In **East Point** turn right on Lighthouse Road to reach the **East Point Lighthouse.** Built in 1867, the octagonal light station is one of the oldest on the island. (Newer beacons are four sided.) Three tidal forces—from the Atlantic Ocean, Gulf of St. Lawrence, and Northumberland Strait—meet off this point. Add in reefs and a foggy day, and shipwrecks were once common here.

Tidal forces of the Atlantic, Gulf of St. Lawrence, and Northumberland Strait converge off East Point.

Looking across the Gulf of St. Lawrence, when the day is clear, you'll see the Cape Breton Highlands rise up from the lowlands of the Margaree Valley. Watch the horizon for whales or nose-diving gannets. Across from the lighthouse a gift shop is well stocked with local, handmade goods.

Walk along the bluffs and down to the shore: A large, empty, red-sand beach stretches to the horizon.

From East Point, Route 16 continues around the coast as Northside Road. You'll spot a string of white wind turbines that form **East Point Wind Farm.** The power-generating complex has ten V-90 turbines, each with a diameter of 90 meters (295 feet).

At North Lake, Elmira Road is a shortcut across the eastern tip through to Elmira. As the terminus of the Confederation Trail—which was reclaimed from railway lines abandoned in 1989—Elmira focuses on its locomotive history. The **Elmira Railway Museum** revives the glory days of train travel with photos and artifacts. Take a miniature train ride, size up the model train collection, and enter the stationmaster's office.

The Confederation Trail ends (or begins) in Elmira, connecting to Tignish in the west via 273 kilometers (170 miles) of gravel paths. The trail is a particular favorite with cyclists as the hills are well graded.

From Elmira, return north to Route 16 (Northside Road) and follow the shore to my favorite section of the drive: a scenic heritage road.

New Harmony Heritage Road

At Priest Pond turn left on Route 302, or Baltic Road. After about 4 kilometers (2.5 miles) make a right turn for the packed-dirt New Harmony Road, or Route 303. Including one of a dozen or so sections of **scenic heritage roads** on the island, the route follows old farm lanes and takes visitors back to a long-lost Prince Edward Island. This stretch is also called "The Glen" for the old farming community of Glencorradale.

In hot, dry weather the dust can be bad if traveling behind another vehicle, plus it reduces visibility. Conversely, after the spring thaw the roads are muddy, and wheels easily rut the soft, soggy clay. Stick to clear, dry summer days for this section of the drive. Bicycles, tractors, and other vehicles also use these roads, as do animals. Enjoy the quiet of the heritage road by driving slowly—hedgerows often grow close to the road edges, so scan them for wildlife and farm animals.

The first stretch of the full 12.5-kilometer (7.8-mile) scenic route through to St. Catherines passes farm fields of grains and potatoes. Note how the scene is void of power lines and houses. During PEI's long prohibition, which stretched from 1901 to 1948, rumrunners used this route as they unloaded boats off the shore.

After 5.5 kilometers (3.4 miles) on New Harmony Road, Kelly Road meets it from the right. Hang left here to continue following Route 303. As the red clay road crosses the **Confederation Trail,** it enters a lush tunnel of tree canopies. The mixture of foliage makes this drive a lovely trip on a clear fall day.

Glen Road, Route 304, intersects the heritage road about 3 kilometers (2 miles) after the last left.

This section from Route 304 (Glen Road and Tarantum Road) through to Greenvale Road is officially designated as **The New Harmony Road.** The diverse, mature hardwood stands at the **New Harmony Demonstration Woodlot** add to the appeal, with a canopy of yellow birch arching over the road. There's a short trail through the woodlot.

At the junction with Route 335 in St. Catherines, turn right to head back into Souris. Alternately, follow the heritage road as it bends left as a mix of paved and dirt roads back to Route 16 at Little Harbour.

Side Trip: St. Peters and Greenwich

The rural, low-trafficked roads of eastern Prince Edward Island make exploring farther a welcome option. **St. Peters,** noted as one of the prettiest destinations to enjoy the Confederation Trail, is also the access point for the Greenwich section of **Prince Edward Island National Park.**

Separated from the family beaches and red dunes of the western and largest section of the national park—and a world away from the tourist-vibe of Cavendish—**Greenwich** features marshlands, bird-watching opportunities, and boardwalks. The park interpretive center enlightens visitors about the protected habitat, while the supervised beach lets visitors escape the usual national park crowds.

NEWFOUNDLAND & LABRADOR

23

The Tablelands

Wiltondale to Woody Point to Trout River

General Description: Through winding forested roads to the vast mountain plateau of the Tablelands, this 50-kilometer (31-mile) scenic drive along Route 431 enters a lesser-visited side of Gros Morne National Park. Fishing villages on Bonne Bay, a national park discovery center, and short hikes provide a day or two of explorations. Nearby lies the northern shore of Gros Morne National Park with its looming inland fjords and dramatic slopes of the Long Range Mountains.

Special Features: Lomond River, St. Patrick's Church, Woody Point Heritage Theatre, summer passenger ferry, Gros Morne Discovery Centre, Green Gardens, Tablelands, Jacob A. Crocker House, Trout River Pond, hiking, geology.

Location: On the Gulf of St. Lawrence coast, northwest of Deer Lake.

Driving Route Numbers & Names: Route 431, Water Street, Main Street.

Travel Season: Boat tours to Western Brook Pond run up to six times daily in July and August, which is also the most pleasant season for hiking and camping. June and September are shoulder seasons along this coast of changeable weather. But perhaps more than the weather, you'll want to check in on a bug forecast—late August often fares the best in this respect. Summer also offers an array of arts festivals.

Camping: Throughout the national park find well-equipped campgrounds for tents and RVs. Closest to Route 431, Lomond campground includes sites on the shore of Bonne Bay and has a wharf and boat ramp. At the end of this scenic drive, Trout River campground offers the benefit of services in the nearby community, including excellent restaurants. In the larger section of the park, you can camp at the wooded Berry Hill or along the coast at Shallow Bay or Green Point. Some campgrounds even offer wireless Internet—ask when you buy your park pass for an updated list.

Services: Fuel up in Rocky Harbour across Bonne Bay or grab supplies and seek medical attention in Norris Point. National park staff members are best equipped to direct you to the closest services. Wiltondale, Lomond, and Trout River offer a greater selection of cabins, while heritage homes in Woody Point have been converted to comfortable bed-and-breakfasts.

Nearby Points of Interest: Bonne Bay Marine Station, Jenniex House, Dr. Henry N. Payne Community Museum, Lobster Cove Head Lighthouse, Western Brook Pond, hiking, camping, wildlife watching.

Time Zone: Newfoundland time (GMT minus 3.5 hours).

The Drive

A one-way-in scenic road travels 50 kilometers (31 miles) along the shore of Bonne Bay, through the Tablelands, and out to the clustered community of Trout River. Hikes branch off the main route and lead to a stark but geologically rich

The Tablelands

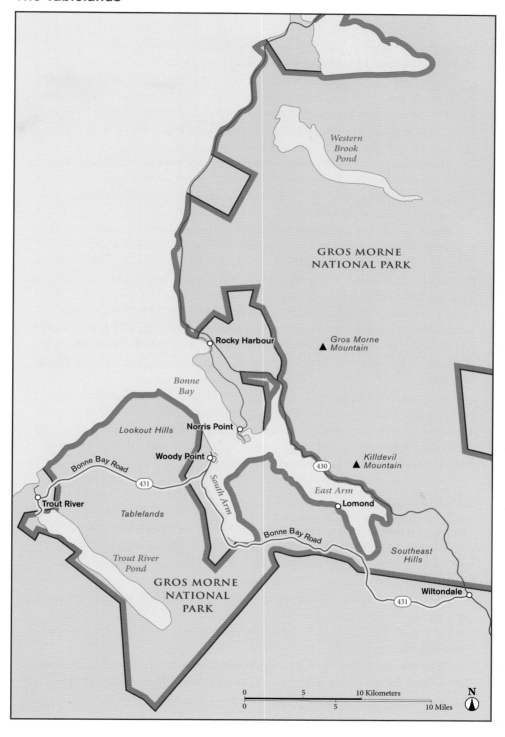

Western Brook Pond

GROS MORNE NATIONAL PARK

Gros Morne Mountain ▲

Rocky Harbour ○

Bonne Bay

Lookout Hills

Norris Point ○

Bonne Bay Road

Woody Point ○

Killdevil Mountain ▲

430

East Arm

431

Trout River ○

South Arm

Lomond ○

Tablelands

Bonne Bay Road

Southeast Hills

Trout River Pond

GROS MORNE NATIONAL PARK

431

Wiltondale ○

| 0 | 5 | 10 Kilometers |
| 0 | 5 | 10 Miles |

N

landscape and rugged coastline. Visit a heritage church, fisheries museum, or impressive exhibits at the Discovery Centre in Gros Morne National Park.

From Deer Lake on the Trans-Canada Highway, drive north on Highway 430 for 30 kilometers (18.6 miles) toward **Wiltondale.** Visit the park gate to purchase a visitor pass and pick up a guide to the national park. From the Southeast Hills, Route 431 (also called Bonne Bay Road) cuts west, leading out to Woody Point and then through the Tablelands to Trout River.

Thick coniferous forests smother bulging rock mountains, which bear down on the road like guards. A 5-kilometer (3.1-mile) stretch of road edges the narrow but long Bonne Bay Little Pond. The skyline of knobby mountains continues to change as the road twists west.

About 13.5 kilometers (8.4 miles) from Wiltondale, Lomond Road leads down to a national park campground on the right. With a mix of drive-in and walk-in sites, the campground accommodates all. The usual amenities—showers, washrooms, a kitchen shelter, and playgrounds—make for a comfortable stay, while the wharf and boat ramp provide access to the water.

Hikes follow old logging roads. A 4-kilometer (2.5-mile) hike leads through forest to the abandoned community of **Stanleyville.** The loggers have moved on, and it's now just the garden plants that live here on the **East Arm of Bonne Bay.**

Other hikes follow the **Lomond River** or circumnavigate heart-shaped **Stuckless Pond.**

The main drive along Route 431 begins to climb at Tappers Mountain, just past Lomond Road. The scenery closes in with larger multipeaked hills. It's about a 9-kilometer (5.6-mile) stretch through to **MacKenzie Brook,** where a picnic site marks the head of Bonne Bay's South Arm. Treed slopes and ponds giveaway to residential houses as the park boundary ends.

Woody Point

The park boundaries end just before the coast to accommodate the communities of Glenburnie, Birchy Head, and Shoal Brook. The houses of one abut the next, and the road twists severely along the coast. Take it slow, and pull over for the locals to pass if you're being followed closely.

At the turnoff to the Tablelands and the continuation of Route 431, either turn left now and head west to explore the Tablelands and Trout River first, or head to Woody Point for lunch and return shortly. Here, I describe the Woody Point tangent first.

After following the main route into **Woody Point,** 20 kilometers (12.4 miles) from Lomond Road, turn right on Cox's Lane down to Water Street. Heritage buildings and homes line the waterfront, looking out across Bonne Bay to Norris Point. There's a summer passenger ferry that'll take you over to the far shore.

This region was originally home to First Nations people, then ceded to the French as part of a treaty with the British. Used as a seasonal fishing base for the British in the 1800s, Woody Point wasn't considered permanently settled until seasonal fishermen started to overwinter in Bonne Bay. As the herring fishery boomed so did the community, growing to include a telegraph station, customs office, tinsmith, and bank, among other services. But a raking fire in 1922 burned much of the town, and Woody Point never totally recovered its former prosperity.

Heritage fishing sheds, some still with lobster traps outside, recall the days when Woody Point was a commercial fishing center, harvesting the wealth of the offshore waters. Today, seafood restaurants, heritage bed-and-breakfasts, and small town essentials such as a library and post office stand in strong force along this short waterfront street.

Particularly notable is the **Old Loft Restaurant.** In a gleaming refinished fishing loft complete with barrel chairs and historic photos, the restaurant serves fresh and local seafood. Downstairs a craft gallery presents some handmade souvenirs as well as dessert—an ice cream shop. The building dates postfire to 1936.

On the main upper street, find St. Patrick's Church. The tiny white structure was built in 1875 and is one of the oldest in the diocese. Nearby, **Woody Point Heritage Theatre** may be hosting a music performance or a show. The theater is the former Lord Nelson Orange Lodge No. 149, originally a meeting place for a Protestant fraternal order, but the hall has long been used for local weddings and dances as well.

In August, wordsmiths gather for **Writers at Woody Point**—a literary festival showcasing writers and musicians. The Gros Morne area, in fact, is a center for arts festivals and also hosts summer theater and music events.

Tablelands

From Woody Point, backtrack to Route 431 and turn uphill toward the Discovery Centre, the Tablelands, and Trout River.

Due to its rich geology, inaccessible wilderness, and rugged coastline, **Gros Morne National Park** became a UNESCO World Heritage Site in 1987. The national park **Discovery Centre** sits overlooking Bonne Bay. Stop at the yellow building, the biggest visitor center in the park, to view exhibits on the importance of the environment, wildlife, and human history. A 5-kilometer (3-mile) lollipop-loop hike climbs to a lookout over the bay.

Continue driving west as the route climbs from near sea level to more than 200 meters (656 feet) elevation. There's a roadside lookout for a quick stop. The

This Gros Morne National Park drive heads through the Tablelands and out to a rugged coastline near Trout River.

route then cuts a fairly straight but dramatic path between the Lookout Hills to the right and the Tablelands to the left.

In some ways it's not hard to imagine the forceful collisions that created this scenery. The **Lookout Hills** share the rocky gray and deep forest green of other Gros Morne landscapes. But to the south, the stark dryness of the orange Tablelands overpowers.

A half billion years ago, the **Tablelands** lay below sea level, part of an ocean bed. Moving plates forced Africa and North America together, thrusting up the ocean floor to create the Appalachian Mountains. Rising to 719 meters (2,359 feet), the Tablelands have steep edging slopes and a far-reaching plateau at the top. The orangey rock is peridotite, part of the earth's mantle. The Tablelands are a rare opportunity to see this mantle, and have provided evidence to help develop the theories of plate tectonics.

If available, take a guided hike on the 4-kilometer (2.5-mile) return trail in this area of the park. A rocky landscape leads to the entrance of **Winterhouse**

Boat tours explore the inland fjord of Western Brook Pond in Gros Morne National Park.

The Arches Provincial Park makes a quick and scenic stop close to Route 430, north of Gros Morne.

Brook Canyon. Fragile flowering plants and engaging geology define the explorations.

Continuing the drive along Route 431, a large trailhead provides a hike to the shoreline at **Green Gardens.** Sea stacks, an ocean cave, and primitive camping provide destinations for a longer hike over steep terrain.

Trout River

Follow Route 431 through the barren landscape to its terminus at **Trout River,** about 18 kilometers (11 miles) from Woody Point and 50 kilometers (31 miles) from Wiltondale. This is the western edge of the national park, where the land meets the Gulf of St. Lawrence.

The road exits the boundaries of the park as it reaches the community. Follow Route 431 to a junction with Main Street.

A left turn away from the town leads inland to **Trout River Pond,** also called Big Pond. The lake is deceptive in its size—measuring about 15 kilometers (9 miles) long but rarely more than a kilometer wide. The glacier-carved fjord features a boat ramp and is popular with anglers. A campground provides excellent services for walk-in and drive-in campers; however, there is no dump station.

Return on Main Street to the commercial center of Trout River along the waterfront. The town wharf juts out like a hitchhiking thumb into the river mouth. Near the wharf, a boardwalk trims the edge of Trout River Bay to pass the beach where caplin (a small saltwater fish) wriggle onto the sand to spawn.

From 1815 to 1880, Crocker families were the only residents in Trout River. Since its days as a one-family community, Trout River has grown to include restaurants and cabins that accommodate the visitors drawn to the outstanding national park.

But to get to know the locals, visit the **Jacob A. Crocker House** at 221 Main St., which shows a traditional area home dating to 1898.

Side Trip: Route 430

Returning back to Wiltondale, **Route 430,** also called the **Viking Trail,** leads through the most-visited portion of Gros Morne National Park. It is also the route to the Northern Peninsula and southern Labrador, featured in Drives 25 and 24 respectively. The **Long Range Mountains** create an intimidating scene as they meet the boggy coastal plateau.

Traveling northwest, **Killdevil Mountain** is the first great height along East Arm. The road then journeys inland past the bare mound of Gros Morne. The mountain's name translates literally from French as "big gloomy," but *morne* is also a Creole word meaning "rounded hill."

There's another visitor center and then offshoot roads lead to the communities of **Norris Point** and **Rocky Harbour,** where you'll find supplies and accommodations. **Bonne Bay Marine Station** sits on the waterfront in Norris Point and is where the summer passenger ferry arrives from Woody Point.

Follow side roads through Rocky Harbour and out to **Lobster Cove Head Lighthouse**, a light station at the entrance to Bonne Bay. Walk along trails edged with weather-twisted branches of tuckamore—the name given to conifers stunted by coastal winds.

In the northern section of the park, daily summer boat tours to **Western Brook Pond** are the most dramatic way to experience the high cliffs and waterfalls around. (Well, the most dramatic unless you're prepared for a multiday wilderness trek using only a compass and map to find the route!) The stunning inland fjord is the park's most famous feature.

Various museums in park communities recall the commercial-fishing lifestyle that first saw European settlement take root along this coast. The **Jenniex House**

Lobster Cove Head Lighthouse is at the entrance to Bonne Bay.

in Norris Point caters to photographers with tea and muffins, while the **Dr. Henry N. Payne Community Museum** in Cow Head explores various aspects of outport history.

Explore the coast at a slower pace by hiking the trails at Green Point, Broom Point, and Shallow Bay. But throughout these adventures, you'll not escape the panoramic presence of the grand Long Range Mountains—the northern end of the Appalachian chain.

24

Labrador Coast & Basque Whalers

St. Barbe to Point Amour to Red Bay

General Description: With a rare and compelling taste of Labrador, this 140-kilometer (87-mile) scenic drive explores the coast along the Strait of Belle Isle. It's an isolated shoreline of icebergs and whales. Cross from Newfoundland to Labrador by ferry and follow the barren highway through small communities. Lighthouses, rivers, and dramatic bluffs mark the coastline. With few trees, your gaze travels farther to the horizon. In the 1500s Basque sailors made the long journey across the Atlantic to hunt whales in Red Bay. These Basque seafarers set up seasonal communities where they rendered blubber into whale oil. The national historic site at the end of the paved road lets you explore what they left behind.

Special Features: St. Barbe–Blanc-Sablon ferry, Gateway to Labrador visitor center and museum, Point Amour (Canada's second tallest lighthouse), Maritime Archaic Burial Mound Historic Site, Pinware River Provincial Park, Tracey Hill Trail, Boney Shore Trail, Right Whale Exhibit, Red Bay National Historic Site, hiking, iceberg watching.

Location: Southern Labrador coast.

Driving Route Numbers & Names: St. Barbe–Blanc-Sablon ferry, Route 138, Route 510 (Trans-Labrador Highway), L'Anse-Amour Road.

Travel Season: In spring and early summer, icebergs often float through the Strait of Belle Isle, grounding themselves on the bays and becoming visible from shore. The provincial ferry runs year-round, although it is susceptible to winter ice conditions (and sometimes re-routes to Cornerbrook). In fall and winter the northern lights are visible along this coast, making it a special but cold and unpredictable season to visit. The handful of attractions—Red Bay and Pinware Provincial Park—have the longest hours during the height of the season, usually June through September.

Camping: Pinware Provincial Park has camping facilities along with a day-use area and a lovely beach. Campers have access to flush and pit toilets, showers, drinking water, fire pits, and garbage disposal while staying at one of 22 campsites.

Services: Find medical services at the regional hospital in Lourdes-de-Blanc-Sablon, Quebec, west of the ferry terminal as well as in Forteau. Fuel up or stay in Forteau. L'Anse-au-Loup is a good bet for supplies, while there's also accommodation in L'Anse-au-Clair and West St. Modeste.

Nearby Points of Interest: Thrombolites at Flower's Cove, Deep Cove Winter Housing Site, Musée Scheffer, Battle Harbour National Historic Site, highway to Happy Valley–Goose Bay.

Time Zone: Newfoundland time zone (GMT minus 3.5 hours) in Labrador and Atlantic time zone (GMT minus 4 hours; does not observe DST) in Quebec.

Labrador Coast & Basque Whalers

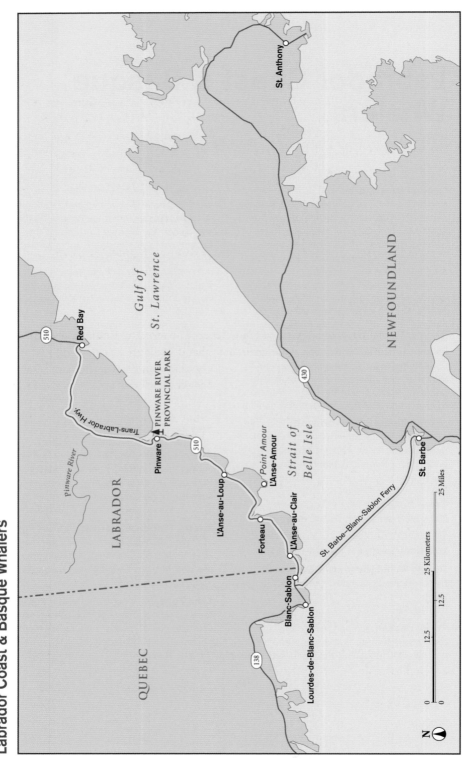

The Drive

Cross the Strait of Belle Isle on the provincial ferry to travel 140 kilometers (87 miles) along the vast Labrador coast. The bare coast of bluffs, coves, and tiny communities (some just a few houses large) create an empty yet engaging landscape. The final portion of the drive follows the Pinware River before reaching Red Bay.

Begin by catching the ferry in **St. Barbe,** Newfoundland—about 175 kilometers (109 miles) from the northern end of Gros Morne National Park and 120 kilometers (75 miles) southwest from St. Anthony. It's best to make reservations for the Labrador Marine ferry, which runs up to two or three times daily in summer. Those with reservations must arrive at the terminal and check in a full hour in advance. The 1.5-to-2-hour trip crosses the **Strait of Belle Isle,** providing great views of both coasts.

Quebec to Labrador

The provincial ferry actually arrives in Quebec. The terminal in **Blanc-Sablon** is located in the Atlantic time zone, in an area that doesn't observe daylight savings time. In summer, that puts Blanc-Sablon 1.5 hours behind Newfoundland. Thankfully, despite docking in Quebec, the ferry runs on Newfoundland time—making the schedule far less befuddling.

After exiting the ferry, follow Jacques Cartier Avenue to a T-junction with Route 138 or Dr. Camille Marcoux Boulevard. Head east, crossing the Blanc-Sablon River and passing through the small Quebec community.

Route 138 leads to the Quebec-Labrador border, where a sign welcomes visitors to the "Big Land." Begin the eastward trek over the Labrador landscape. It's a challenge to spot a tree on this panorama of rocky hills and coastal bluffs. Just imagine trying to build a house or collect firewood!

Climb and descend the bluff above **Charles Point** on what is now **Route 510,** or the **Trans-Labrador Highway.**

The village of **L'Anse-au-Clair** centers on a wide beach tucked in a narrow cove. The **Gateway to Labrador Visitor Centre** and museum is located on the right when arriving in town. Housed in a 1909 church that was constructed with volunteer labor, the visitor center serves equal parts historical tales and local information.

Over the 10-kilometer (6.2-mile) stretch from L'Anse-au-Clair to **Forteau,** the slightly inland road still affords excellent views of the coast. The highway rounds Forteau Bay, where houses cling to the road. Forteau celebrates the hardy orange **bakeapple berry**—elsewhere known as a cloudberry—with an August festival.

A bare coast of bluffs, coves, and tiny communities (some just a few houses large) create an empty yet engaging landscape in Labrador.

About 5 kilometers (3 miles) after English Point, watch for a right-hand turn to **L'Anse-Amour.** The dusty 4-kilometer (2.5-mile) road leads out to Point Amour but first passes a historic burial mound and L'Anse-Amour, where a handful of homes lie along the bay and a sandy beach.

The **Maritime Archaic Burial Mound Historic Site** here is the oldest funeral monument in North America, dating back about 7,500 years. Excavated in the 1970s, the burial mound featured a wide pit where an adolescent had been wrapped and placed facedown, her/his head pointed west. The adolescent was buried with tools and weapons, and with a flat stone on the lower back. Rocks were piled in a mound over the grave. It's a significant site that provides a glimpse at how long this coast has been inhabited.

Keep following the cliff-side road around the hill, toward the water and **Point Amour Lighthouse** soon comes into view.

The tallest lighthouse in Atlantic Canada and the second tallest in Canada, Point Amour stands 33.2 meters (109 feet) tall. In summer, costumed guides provide tours of the lighthouse and keeper's quarters, which have been restored

Point Amour Lighthouse is the tallest in Atlantic Canada with walls that measure about 1.8 meters (6 feet) thick at the base.

to reflect the 1850s period. First lit in 1858, the lighthouse has walls that measure about 1.8 meters (6 feet) thick at the base.

And this coast is treacherous. In 1922, HMS *Raleigh* grounded on Point Amour while en route to Forteau Bay. It's said some officers aboard wanted to fly-fish in the area. Measuring 184 meters (604 feet) overall, the heavy cruiser sat stalled for four years before the British navy used explosives to demolish it.

Return along the road to Route 510, where rolling hills and sparse forest stretch to the inland horizon.

Continuing east, **Schooner Cove hiking trail** lies on the coastal side of the highway, just before L'Anse-au-Loup. The hike visits a site where the Maritime Archaic peoples first lived, Basque whalers rendered whale oil, and a whaling factory was built in the 1900s.

Stock up on supplies in L'Anse-au-Loup, and perhaps catch an exhibit at the **Labrador Straits Museum** in the town hall, and then drive over the Red Cliffs and through Diable Bay, Capstan Island, and West St. Modeste.

Pinware River

Where the **Pinware River** meets the Strait of Belle Isle, **Pinware River Provincial Park** features a smooth, sandy beach, abundant trout and salmon fishing, and short hiking trails. A campground and day-use area provide running water, pit toilets, and fire pits. The nearby **Pinware Hill** has yielded artifacts dating to about 9,000 years ago, making it one of the province's oldest habitation sites in North America.

From the park, Route 510 follows the Pinware River for about 20 kilometers (12.4 miles) through to **County Cat Pond.** Midway the treed scenery ends briefly at a bridge over the stunning **Pinware River gorge.** Often visitors will stop mid

The Pinware River gorge is not only scenic, but the river is excellent for salmon fishing.

bridge to photograph and admire, but for the safety of all, continue to the eastern side of the bridge where a sandy dirt road provides short-term parking.

The Pinware River, stocked with a healthy supply of salmon traveling upstream to spawn, is popular with anglers. As the road cuts east, glimpse views of large pond-lakes carved by glaciers and where hills dip down to the coast.

At County Cat Pond, where a few cottages sit within this mostly uninhabited landscape, the Pinware River tracks north. More ponds abut the road as the route cuts through a glacial landscape scattered with boulders.

Red Bay

The road meets **Red Bay** on the west side of the harbor, where two trails branch off to the shoreline. The 3-kilometer (1.9-mile) return **Tracey Hill Trail** is notable for its 689 steps to the top of its namesake hill. Picnic tables make mid-hike rests easier. An easier route, the **Boney Shore Trail** follows the coast to a **whale graveyard.** Bones mark the location where the carcasses of whales, killed by the Basque, washed ashore. A small interpretive site with a model right whale sits alongside the main road and marks the entrance to Red Bay.

On the east side of the bay, you'll see a road twisting up into the hills. It heads north for 340 kilometers (211 miles) to Cartwright and until recent years was unpaved.

At the town center, the **Right Whale Exhibit** explores the underwater world of endangered bowhead and right whales. The exhibit, at 50 Main Hwy., displays a **400-year-old whale skeleton,** scavenged from the sea floor of Red Bay.

On the east side of the harbor, find **Red Bay National Historic Site.** In the 1500s whalers from Basque Country in northern Spain spent summers on the Labrador shores, hunting bowhead and right whales. The Basques rendered the whale blubber into oil, barreled it, and shipped the oil back to Europe. Whale oil was valuable in Europe for use as fuel, and in soaps and pharmaceuticals.

Making summer-season journeys, the whalers would return to the Bay of Biscay for the winter. But harsh winters, when the ice moved in early, could strand the seafarers. Unprepared for the long, cold season, many of the whalers would not survive the Labrador winter.

Around **Red Bay Harbour,** archaeologists have uncovered more than 20 whaling stations. The visitor center shows a film about Red Bay discoveries, and displays excavated whalebones and a *chalupa,* or small wooden whaling boat built by the Basques. From the nails to clothes to graves, much has been uncovered in the Red Bay area. Model ships and interpretive panels retell the Basque story.

Look out to the lighthouse keeper's quarters at Red Bay Lighthouse and Saddle Island. A shuttle boat takes visitors out to the island where trails lead to the sites of tryworks (cauldrons used for rendering the fat from the whale blubber) and cooperages. To the northwest of the island, archaeologists have uncovered a cemetery containing the remains of 140 bodies in 60 graves.

Mid harbor you'll see a beached and rusting steel hull of a shipwreck.

Side Trip: Battle Harbour Historic District

About 90 kilometers (56 miles) north along the coast, take the ferry from **Marys Harbour** to visit a historic island-bound fishing settlement at Battle Harbour. The **Battle Harbour Historic District** is a re-created 1800s fishing station. During the height of the fishery, the community was called the "Capital of Labrador." A fire and decline of the fisheries crippled the community, but today costumed guides, hundreds of artifacts, and restored buildings bring the island outport back to its busiest days.

From Marys Harbour the highway pierces farther into the vast territory of Labrador, through to Port Hope Simpson and then Cartwright. The newest phase of the Trans-Labrador Highway connects Cartwright Junction to Happy Valley–Goose Bay: a total of about 550 kilometers (342 miles) over paved and unpaved surfaces from Red Bay.

25

Vikings

St. Anthony to L'Anse aux Meadows

General Description: Drive back in time a thousand years as this 30-kilometer (18.6-mile) scenic route travels out to shores where ancient seafarers once anchored at L'Anse aux Meadows National Historic Site. Empty coastal scenery, jam stands, and Viking interpreters create an eclectic but end-of-the-world feel at this northernmost end of the Northern Peninsula. Perhaps the Vikings also felt that they were reaching the end of the world as they landed on these shores more than a millennia ago. The glacier-raked scenery yields shallow ponds and frequent moose sightings. In fact Roddickton, just down the coast from St. Anthony, is known as the "moose capital."

Special Features: The Dark Tickle Company, Norstead: A Viking Port of Trade, L'Anse aux Meadows National Historic Site, Pistolet Bay Provincial Park, Burnt Cape Ecological Reserve.

Location: Northern Peninsula, Newfoundland.

Driving Route Numbers & Names: Route 430, Route 436, Route 437.

Travel Season: Summer rates as the best time to travel with the attractions at their peak: Interpretive sites are filled with guides demonstrating ancient chores, and local restaurants are serving desserts studded with berries like bakeapple and partridgeberry.

Camping: Pistolet Bay Provincial Park makes a lovely, quiet campground for visitors. There is a small RV campground outside L'Anse aux Meadows. Triple Falls RV Park is closest to the services in St. Anthony.

Services: St. Anthony, while not the prettiest town, offers plenty of services, including gas stations, medical care, and groceries. Hay Cove features historic bed-and-breakfasts close to the Viking-themed attractions, while St. Anthony offers a mix of motels and inns.

Nearby Points of Interest: Grenfell Historic Properties (interpretation center, museum, and trail).

Time Zone: Newfoundland time (GMT minus 3.5 hours).

The Drive

An amble through a glacier-carved landscape, the 30-kilometer (18.6-mile) trip to L'Anse aux Meadows takes on a dreamlike quality. It's a barren landscape, like in so many areas of Newfoundland, but without the sweeping views. A drive through these hillocks gives the feeling that you're finding a hidden destination, where ponds and stunted conifers are slipped between massive granite boulders.

Begin this route from Route 430, the Viking Trail, where **St. Anthony** lies at the precarious end of this road.

Located near the tip of the Northern Peninsula, the town lightens the severe winter weather with celebratory festivals. **The Grenfell Ride,** in March, recalls the journey of renowned physician Dr. Wilfred Grenfell from *Adrift on an Ice Pan*

Vikings

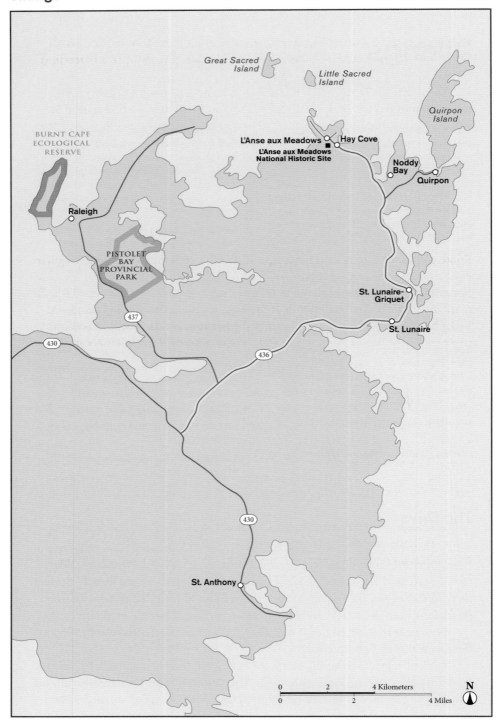

and turns it into the world's longest chain of snowmobiles. **The Iceberg Festival** in June offers boat tours, nature walks, and music, plus the giants of **Iceberg Alley.**

From this northern commercial center, you'll travel just 10 kilometers (6.2 miles) west over a forested, unscenic road to Route 436. If you don't start in St. Anthony, the turnoff for Route 436 is about 300 kilometers (186 miles) from the northern end of Gros Morne National Park—along a coastal road then through a horizon-filling view of bog, ponds, and barren.

Whichever way you arrive, be sure to watch carefully for moose that like to hang out eating the foliage near the highway.

St. Lunaire-Griquet

Route 436 winds through the landscape of ponds, coniferous scrub, and irregular hills, haphazard in their placement. About 10 kilometers (6.2 miles) past the junction with Route 430, the road meets the saltwater in St. Lunaire Bay. Small islands mark the inside harbor and mouth of the bay, including **Granchain Island**—its rocky headlands protecting the bay from the harshest winds. Flocks of seabirds circle above the fishing community and the bay, where fishing boats are docked at wharves.

A shop and café, **The Dark Tickle Company** is one of Newfoundland's best-known makers of homemade goods, and it is located in St. Lunaire. The shop produces jams, chocolates, teas, vinegars, and other items from local berries. Shiny orange **bakeapple berries** (cloudberries) and tart **partridgeberries** (lingonberries) are two Newfoundland-favorite varieties.

The business, which takes its name from a narrow channel of water called a tickle, also operates as an economuseum—where traditional crafters share their processes with visitors. Trails, a tearoom, and the berry patch make for a satisfying visit.

Although French fishermen plied these waters in the 1500s and the Vikings before that, the area was not mapped until 1784. It was then that **Liberge de Granchain,** a French sailor, charted the waters while stuck in the bay. On the island now named for him, bread ovens from the 16th-century visits of French fishermen are still visible. The Dark Tickle features an exhibit on Granchain and his work.

As the road turns north, the landscape evens out into larger hills. A sheer cliff marks White Cape Harbour and protects the entrance to the narrow waterway. A minute further along the drive, Dark Tickle Road is a turnoff to the island community of Griquet.

About 7 kilometers (4.3 miles) on, a right turn takes you on a circuitous route along the coast and through the residential community of **Quirpon Harbour.** Fishing boats, wharves, and vinyl-sided homes line the remote shoreline.

L'Anse aux Meadows

The protected national historic site is more than the archaeological site alone: the grounds encompass 80 square kilometers (31 square miles) of islands, bay, and bogs. Windswept bluffs, lush islands, and a changing ocean create a truly wild scene.

Between Hay Cove and L'Anse aux Meadows, turnoffs lead to **Norstead: A Viking Port of Trade** and **L'Anse aux Meadows National Historic Site.** But first follow Route 436 to its end.

In the community of **L'Anse aux Meadows,** the road splits around Medee Bay. Both routes are dead ends with weather-worn views. Seagulls drop sea urchins on the pavement to break open the tough shells. Off the coast Great Sacred, Little Sacred, Warrens, and Green Islands are clearly visible, with the larger Belle Isle farther offshore.

At **L'Anse aux Meadows National Historic Site,** a large visitor center over-looks the archaeological site, reconstructed leader's hall, and coastal walking trails. Helge Ingstad, an explorer and writer from Norway, discovered the site in 1960, in part by following the ancient sagas of Vinland. Local resident George Decker, who knew the humped ground as an old First Nations camp, led Ingstad to the site.

L'Anse aux Meadows is the earliest evidence of Europeans arriving in North America, and so predates the infamous journey of Christopher Columbus in 1492 and Prince Henry Sinclair's possible voyage in 1398. At the visitor center interpretive panels lead you through the tales of **Vinland**—of exiled murderers and Viking explorers. About 1,000 years ago Vikings from a colony in Greenland landed here and established an outpost. They explored farther south, seeking hardwood, but the base was burnt and abandoned a few seasons after. The full story remains a mystery.

L'Anse aux Meadows was protected as a historic site in 1969 and added to the World Heritage Site list in 1978.

Walk along a boardwalk to the reconstructed Viking base. A large sod hall is filled with weapons, sheepskins, and a flickering hearth. Bearded Viking interpreters sit around the fire, telling stories and answering visitors' questions. A group of crafters weave sailcloth, spin wool thread, and tie knotted belts. Around the hall, workers are perhaps building a replica boat or shaping nails in the forge. Slaves go out to the stream to fetch water and cook meals.

The grounds of L'Anse aux Meadows National Historic Site feature a recreated Viking leader's hall.

You can interact with all these characters, who explain their tasks or tell mythical stories, as well as dress for photos with an array of helmets, swords, and shields.

After exploring the living-history portion, head over to the actual ruins—now showing only as grassed-over bumps. Rectangular shapes outline where the buildings of the Viking encampment stood 1,000 years ago. The leader's hall, the largest building, is about the same size as a chieftain's hall in Iceland.

There is a second Viking history lesson in the area. **Norstead** recreates a Viking port of trade. The boathouse features a **full replica Viking cargo ship,** the *Snorri,* while the forge shows how nails were made. Enter the chieftain's hall to hear stories, or walk the grounds and watch a Viking battle. The site is similar to that at L'Anse aux Meadows, but with more hands-on activities.

Side Trip One: Raleigh

Just 4 kilometers (2.5 miles) in from the junction of Routes 430 and 436 (the road to L'Anse aux Meadows), another road branches off to a provincial park and

Fishing huts and coastal cliffs form the rugged scenery of the Northern Peninsula.

nature reserve. Route 437 follows Milan Arm to Pistolet Bay, Ha Ha Bay, and out to Ship Cove at its end.

Halfway to Raleigh, stop in at **Pistolet Bay Provincial Park.** The park is situated near a salmon river, and the campground offers 30 sites serviced with fire pits, washrooms, showers, laundry, and drinking water. The day-use area has access to a freshwater pond for swimming.

At **Raleigh,** the main road off Route 437 leads to **Burnt Cape Ecological Reserve.** A naked limestone landscape, the reserve is the rooting ground for rare plant species. The growing season is short here, with frosts occurring year-round, but the plants survive despite the peninsula's harsh climate. Guided hikes are available through Burnt Cape Cabins (709-452-3521; burntcape.com), or hike independently keeping on the reserve roads so as not to disturb the arctic plants.

A further 11 kilometers (6.8 miles) on Route 437, the road heads out to Ship Cove and Cape Onion. Look out over island and ocean views and consider that this rugged shore is where Vikings once anchored—but for unknown reasons decided again to leave.

Side Trip Two: St. Anthony

A town of perseverance, **St. Anthony** has attractions that center on a particularly hardy character: **Dr. Wilfred Grenfell**—a medical doctor who practiced here in the late 19th and early 20th centuries. In 1892 Grenfell arrived to evaluate life on the Labrador coast and then established a medical practice. In 1900, he became the first doctor in St. Anthony—an area that had been settled by migratory fishermen since the 1500s.

The extent to which Dr. Grenfell went to treat his remote patients can be best examined in his tale *Adrift on an Ice Pan.* In the epic, Dr. Grenfell and his dog team are stranded offshore on an unstable slush of ice. He survived by killing three dogs—named Moody, Watch, and Spy—and survived a day and a night on the ice pan before being rescued.

"Poor beast! I loved him like a friend—a beautiful dog—but we could not all hope to live. In fact, I had no hope any of us would, at that time, but it seemed better to die fighting," wrote Grenfell of the ordeal.

And of returning home he relayed: "Every soul in the village was on the beach as we neared the shore. Every soul was waiting to shake hands when I landed."

In town visitors can learn more at **Grenfell Historic Properties,** which include an interpretation center, museum, and walking trail.

26

Beothuks & Icebergs

Lewisporte to Boyd's Cove to Twillingate

General Description: Traverse causeways, islands, and historic Beothuk territory to travel to Twillingate, Newfoundland's most renowned iceberg-watching destination. A 120-kilometer (75-mile) scenic drive—with plenty of side roads to explore—ventures from the calm waters of Lewisporte, skirts the Bay of Exploits, and then island-hops out to Twillingate. Along the way, visit museums that explore historic fishing methods, recall outport life, and present the scant-known information about the extinct Beothuk peoples.

Special Features: Lewisporte Train Park, By the Bay Museum, Beothuk Interpretation Centre, Dildo Run Provincial Park, Prime Berth—Twillingate Fishery Museum, Twillingate Museum, Durrell Museum, Long Point Lighthouse, iceberg watching, whale watching, hiking, bird watching.

Location: Along the Bay of Exploits, on the northern coast midway between Grand Falls—Windsor and Gander.

Driving Route Numbers & Names: Route 340 (Road to the Isles), with many side trip options.

Travel Season: Travel in May or June for the best chances of seeing icebergs—although to catch the cold giants, it's essential to phone in advance or track the bergs at icebergfinder.com. Museums and attractions keep the longest hours from June through September.

Camping: Camp in Lewisporte for full services, or en route at Dildo Run Provincial Park, where there are flush toilets, showers, drinking-water taps, and fire pits. Notre Dame Provincial Park, located near the Trans-Canada Highway, has washrooms, showers, and laundry facilities.

Services: Gander and Grand Falls—Windsor are the easiest places to make a supply run before embarking on this scenic drive. Lewisporte offers groceries and gas, as does Twillingate at the road's end. Find medical assistance in Twillingate.

Nearby Points of Interest: Change Islands, Fogo Island, Pikes Arm Museum and Lookout, Moreton's Harbour Community Museum, Notre Dame Provincial Park, Silent Witness Memorial in Gander.

Time Zone: Newfoundland time (GMT minus 3.5 hours).

The Drive

This route is a 120-kilometer (75-mile) tangent north from the Trans-Canada Highway, the starting point for many drives in central Newfoundland. Following the coast along the **Bay of Exploits,** causeways link islands and lead out to the frigid northern coast where icebergs meander by.

Whether traveling east or west on the Trans-Canada Highway, take the Lewisporte-Twillingate exit at Notre Dame Junction. Nearby **Notre Dame Provincial Park** offers swimming plus campsites, flush toilets, showers, and laundry

Beothuks & Icebergs

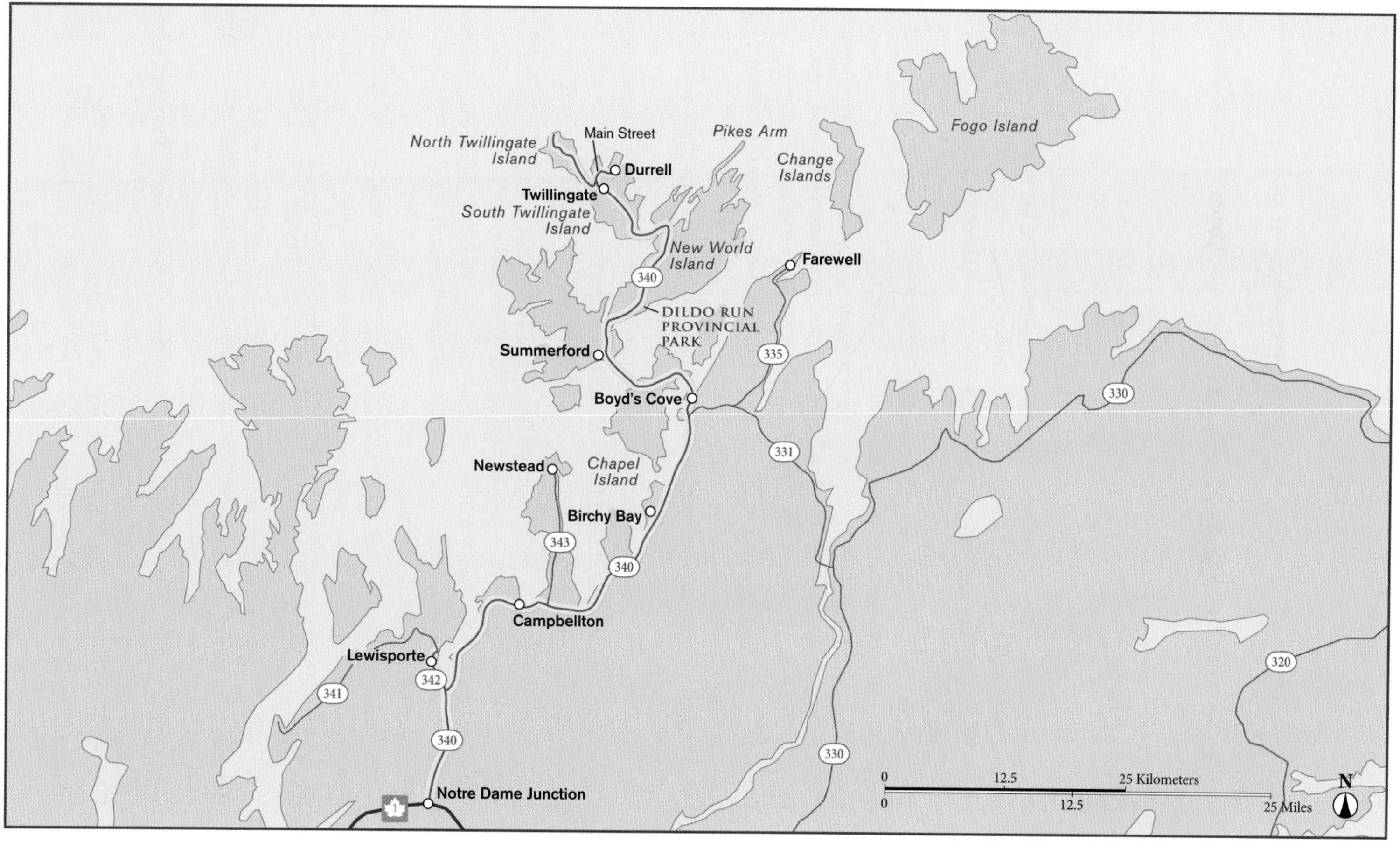

N

25 Miles

25 Kilometers

12.5

12.5

0

0

320

330

330

331

335

340

340

342

341

343

Fogo Island

Change Islands

Farewell

Pikes Arm

New World Island

DILDO RUN PROVINCIAL PARK

Main Street

North Twillingate Island

Durrell

Twillingate

South Twillingate Island

Summerford

Boyd's Cove

Chapel Island

Newstead

Birchy Bay

Campbellton

Lewisporte

Notre Dame Junction

facilities—roughly the same comforts as the provincial campground at **Dildo Run,** mid route.

From the highway exit, Route 340—also known as the **Road to the Isles**— heads north.

Lewisporte

An unscenic, 11-kilometer (6.8-mile) stretch cuts through forest to the head of Burnt Bay. For a break, stop in at the roadside **Lewisporte Train Park** on West Main Street, which features a passenger car, caboose, and interpretive railway displays. A large orange snowplow hints at the climate challenges the railway faced in Newfoundland.

The Newfoundland Railway connected Port aux Basques to St. John's, linking small settlements across the province. From the late 1890s to 1969, a passenger service ran across the province on the line, and then freight only through 1988. After Canadian National decommissioned the narrow-gauge rail lines, they became a provincial park—the 883-kilometer (549-mile) **T'railway.** Walkers, runners, ATV-ers, and cyclists use the trail in summer, and in winter the skiers and snowmobilers make use of this recreational corridor that crosses the island.

Main Street heads straight into downtown Lewisporte, while Route 340 continues to the right.

Head first into **Lewisporte,** via Main Street, where the **By the Bay Museum** shows local exhibitions, thoughtfully illuminating the history of the Bay of Exploits. Located in an old school, a craft gallery provides local handmade wares— from Newfoundland hand knits to jams. The town has a sheltered marina, and the wide waters of Burnt Bay are an attractive sight when filled with boats under sail.

Lewisporte was once a rich timber region, its hills thick with spruce, birch, and the now-rare white pine. The forest resources drew shipbuilders to establish operations here. Sheltered ocean access and the nearby railway at Notre Dame Junction all helped make Lewisporte a shipping center. During World War II, the port provided supplies to Canadian Forces Base Gander. Due to logging and fungal disease, however, the stands of white pine—a valuable building lumber—have been largely reduced.

Leaving Lewisporte, follow Main Street back to Route 340, which then cuts northeast for about 50 kilometers (31 miles) to Boyd's Cove. The road follows bays and passes through low, forested hills. En route in **Campbellton,** fishing wharfs and gentle waters make the area look more like a Nova Scotia coastal village than the usually rugged Newfoundland coastline.

Islands in Indian Arm—Sivier, Birchy, and Camel—are some of the dozens of large named islands that lie in the Bay of Exploits, and you'll see many more exposed at low tide that put the overall tally in the hundreds. The road to Comfort Cove (Route 343) leads out to a peninsula community. Side routes like this one to **Newstead** are scenic to explore but offer no definitive attractions beyond the views.

Coming to Loon Bay the road follows a narrow section of water and then continues along the eastern side of the bay. At the community of Birchy Bay, the main street provides another scenic detour and a snack stop.

At the junction just before **Boyd's Cove,** Route 340 continues on northwest to cross a causeway en route to Twillingate, while to the northeast, Routes 331 and then 335 head to Farewell Ferry on the tip of the Port Albert Peninsula. The ferry service connects to Change Islands and the much larger Fogo Island. The latter first appeared on French maps and was settled by English and Irish settlers.

Living in fishing outports along the island's tangled coast, Fogo Island residents refused to move inland during mid-century resettlement efforts. This retention of a more traditional way of life has made the island a favorite destination to experience Newfoundland culture.

Boyd's Cove

Finally, 50 kilometers (31 miles) from Lewisporte, Route 340 arrives at Boyd's Cove, located on the shore of an undescriptively named water channel known as The Reach.

Follow signs along South Side Road to the **Beothuk Interpretation Centre.** The interpretive center pieces together what is known about the now-extinct Beothuks, the original native inhabitants of Newfoundland. Through a combination of European conflicts, European diseases, and loss of territory, the Beothuk population was decimated; the last Beothuk—a woman in her late 20s named Shanawdithit—died in 1829 of tuberculosis.

At the interpretation center a short video shows interviews with Dr. Ralph Pastore, who excavated 4 of the 11 Beothuk dwellings here in the 1980s. See the powdered red ochre the Beothuk used for ceremonies, which also acts as a fly repellent, and view artifacts the Beothuk fashioned from European iron implements, such as nails flattened and sharpened into arrowheads.

The Beothuks avoided trade with the Europeans, and instead preferred to visit abandoned fishing communities in winter. When the fishermen returned to the seasonal outposts each spring, their encounters with the Beothuks escalated to violence because of the missing items and overlapping territories.

From the visitor center a trail and boardwalk lead down to the shoreline archaeological site and former Beothuk village. The sites have been filled in again after the excavations, now showing as mere numbered depressions in the grass.

Perhaps more special to see is Newfoundland artist Gerald Squires's bronze sculpture of a Beothuk woman. Proud and silent, the statue brings home the emotions that we can only imagine Shanawdithit felt in 1829: being the presumed last of your people.

Leaving Boyd's Cove, and still on Route 340, cross the first causeway—Reach Run Causeway—to Chapel Island. Next, the L. R. Curtis Causeway connects Chapel Island to Summerford and then continues to New World Island. The islands and causeways are like stepping stones in Dildo Run.

A side road ventures down to **Summerford,** on Strong's Island, which offers a few supplies. Farther north at **Virgin Arm,** another side trip on Route 345 heads out to **Moreton's Harbour,** where there is a community museum.

Views of North and South Trump Islands linger to the left, while the main route passes alongside **Dildo Run Provincial Park** on the right.

More than just its snicker-worthy name, the protected area has hiking trails and viewpoints that look out to Dildo Run. Among the twisted peninsulas, there are hundreds of teeny islands. Seemingly countless, the islands number about 365 according to provincial park literature. For facilities, the park offers a campground with flush toilets, showers, drinking water, laundry, and a sewage dump station.

Traveling north, Route 340 is surrounded with interesting scenery: Steeply mounded hills show rocky bedrock between thick coniferous forests, while small lakes and bays pierce the tree line.

Just after Newville, a side trip on Route 346 takes you east to **Pikes Arm Museum and Lookout**—a detour of 11 kilometers (6.8 miles) one-way.

Twillingate

Leaving New World Island, cross the Walter B. Elliott Causeway to arrive on South Twillingate Island. **Prime Berth–Twillingate Fishery Museum** sits immediately to the left when arriving on the island. At the collection of buildings on the shore, interpreters demonstrate the treasured techniques of fishing, including splitting and salting the cod. The museum introduces you to Twillingate's history—that of a fishery so rich that it prompted men to build wharves, boats, and stages and head out on the perilous sea. Stories, song, and photos piece together the mostly lost way of outport life.

In all directions, Route 340 affords gorgeous views of a convoluted coast. Coves and communities lie along the water in the dozens, a testament to the rich fishing grounds that once sustained the area. But as the route crosses South

A bronze statue in Boyds Cove is a silent reminder that the last Beothuk died in 1829.

Icebergs often float south to Twillingate, where the viewing deck at Long Point Lighthouse allows great views.

Twillingate Island and enters the community of **Twillingate,** the scenery starts to empty, and the windswept coastal barrens begin.

At a main junction, head left on Route 340 to North Twillingate Island or right on Main Street into Durrell. Both routes are not to be missed—the former delivers the most stunning views, and the latter offers an interesting museum.

Turn right to **Durrell,** following Main Street past Jenkins Cove. At Museum Road, look for the single-story red building that was built as an Arm Lads Brigade armory in 1910. Today the **Durrell Museum** displays a slice of Twillingate life, ranging from the old brigade uniforms to a stuffed polar bear that arrived in town on the ice floes in 2000. More exhibits revive the day-to-day of outport life—famed in movies and books such as *Random Passage* and *The Shipping News.* The museum itself overlooks Durrell Arm.

Follow Main Street back to rejoin Route 340, this time crossing the final causeway on the Road to the Isles to reach **North Twillingate Island.**

On this northern island, history is not forgotten either. There's a Women's Institute—a nonsectarian educational organization—building with a sense of another era. Nearby is the **Twillingate Museum,** itself housed in a 1915 cream-colored home with a wide porch overlooking the main street. Exhibits feature local stories, such as that of opera soprano Marie Toulinquet, who was born in Twillingate as Georgina Stirling. Other histories range from First Nations to mining and the Alphabet Fleet.

Made into near-legends in folk songs and paintings, the **Alphabet Fleet** were boats owned by the Reid Newfoundland Company. The boats ran mail, passengers, and supplies to remote Newfoundland outports—thereby connecting the communities to the inland world. The 13 boats were named for Scottish towns, from the SS *Argyle* to the SS *Meigle.*

Stop in Twillingate for lunch where wharf-side restaurants serve local seafood. Whale-watching and iceberg tours depart from the town. The **Fish Fun & Folk Festival** in Twillingate hosts a party with Newfoundland music and fireworks.

From the commercial center, Route 340 leaves the community and continues north past fishing stages and heritage homes of Crow Head to a viewpoint and lighthouse. The narrow twisting road, with its steep inclines and narrow profile, comes to an end at the rocky cliffs of Devils Cove Head. Viewing platforms and trails give a vantage over the water, and icebergs are sometimes visible in May and June—but don't come to town without checking on the icebergs first (icebergfinder.com).

The blocky Lego-like **Long Point Lighthouse** stands more than 100 meters (331 feet) above sea level and marks Newfoundland's **"Iceberg Alley."** The lighthouse, built in 1876, and interpretation center display exhibits, antiques, and crafts.

The small, gray **Gull Island** is shaped almost like an iceberg. And whatever the season, you can use the stationed binoculars to spot seabirds feeding around the island or perhaps whales on the horizon.

Side Trip: Change Islands & Fogo Island

From the prettily named community of **Farewell,** a ferry connects the tangled peninsulas of central Newfoundland to **Change Islands** and **Fogo Island.**

Fogo, the largest offshore island, was first settled by the Beothuks and then seasonally by European fishermen in the 1500s. Fishing has been the main industry ever since. The isolation of the culture and the refusal of locals to move during resettlement in the 1950s, 1960s, and 1970s have developed a distinct island spirit.

Theater productions, heritage fishing stages, age-old cemeteries, and a stunning coastline have all helped the weathered but vibrant culture of Fogo Island endure the changes of time.

27

Hidden Beaches & Abandoned Outports

Terra Nova National Park to Eastport to Salvage

General Description: This 38-kilometer (23.6-mile) scenic drive provides a short exploration from the Terra Nova National Park to a historic fishing community. Dramatic views of the national park, a water-bound causeway, beaches where access is restricted by the tides, and hikes to abandoned outports all allow visitors to experience a mostly uninhabited coast.

Special Features: Glovertown Museum—The Janes House, Terra Nova National Park, Eastport beaches, Beaches Arts & Heritage Centre, Salvage Fishermen's Museum, historic fish stages, hiking trails.

Location: On the northeastern shore of central Newfoundland, west of the Bonavista Peninsula.

Driving Route Numbers & Names: Route 310 (Road to the Beaches).

Travel Season: July and August offer the best weather to enjoy the beaches that give this route its name.

Camping: Two campgrounds in Terra Nova National Park—Malady Head and Newman Sound—offer full facilities including showers

and bathrooms. The wooded campgrounds, generally quiet and patrolled by security, have fire pits and picnic tables. Washrooms, however, are not as nice as the comfort stations at many private campgrounds.

Services: Glovertown near the park entrance has full services including firewood, gas, and supplies. The park is midway between hospitals in Clarenville to the south and Gander to the west. Fuel and basic supplies are available along the drive in Sandringham and Eastport.

Nearby Points of Interest: The Salvage Peninsula and Terra Nova National Park both lie above the Bonavista Peninsula, where heritage fishing villages are renowned for their scenic charm. In and near Bonavista find the Ryan Premises and Mockbeggar historic sites, Bonavista Museum, and Elliston's Root Cellars. On the southeastern side of the peninsula, visit the Trinity Museum, Lester Garland House, and Hiscock House.

Time Zone: Newfoundland time (GMT minus 3.5 hours).

The Drive

Tucked above the **Bonavista Peninsula** sits an often-overlooked area. Accessible only through a stretch of Terra Nova National Park, this 38-kilometer (23.6-mile) scenic route along the Eastport Peninsula is also known as the **Road to the Beaches.**

The sandy shores in Eastport alone are worth the trip. Liven the mix by adding explorations in the quaint fishing town of Salvage, with its red fishing stages and trail network to abandoned communities.

Hidden Beaches & Abandoned Outports

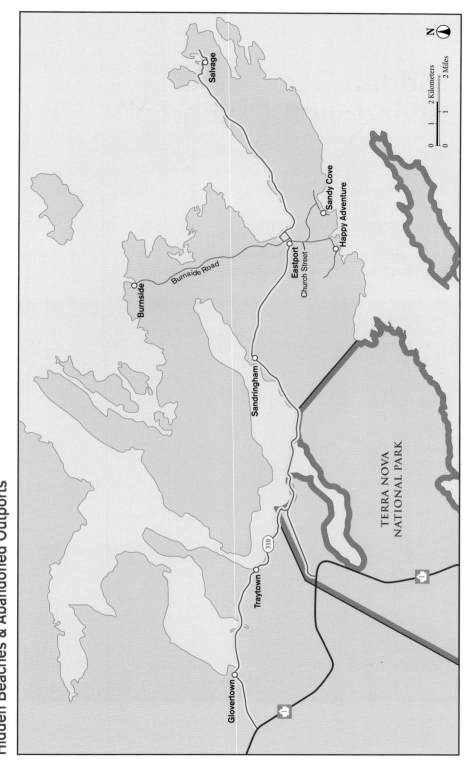

From the Trans-Canada Highway, take the turnoff for Glovertown and follow Route 310 through a string of commercial and residential buildings, stopping perhaps at the Glovertown Museum–**The Janes House** to learn about the resettlement of the Bonavista Bay outports to more central towns.

After Traytown, Route 310 begins to follow the coast of Terra Nova National Park and a bend of the far-reaching Northeast Arm. For a faster and alternate route, stay on the Trans-Canada Highway for an extra 9 kilometers (5.6 miles) to take the turnoff for Traytown and Malady Head.

Terra Nova National Park

Set aside in 1957, **Terra Nova National Park** was the province's first national park. A labyrinth of rocky peninsulas juts out into Bonavista Bay, creating

At sunset, catch the silhouettes of the glacier-rounded Appalachian hills and Terra Nova National Park.

sheltered boating areas and a diverse coastline. Hilly scenery of boreal forest forms an untouched backdrop to the water. Throughout the park hiking trails lead to abandoned outport communities and lookouts, while boat ramps and beaches provide access to the water. The park's main visitor center—where a touch tank, film, and exhibits introduce the park and its wildlife—and the larger Newman Sound campground, are located in the center of the park, further south along the Trans-Canada Highway.

But this scenic drive touches a different section of the national park by heading east on Route 310, passing **Malady Head campground.** The quiet, forested sites are family friendly and well maintained. All have picnic tables and fire pits, plus access to showers, washrooms, and a playground.

Just past the campground the route reaches a causeway. With water on both sides, the kilometer-long road is achingly pretty. Either stop on the east side of the causeway to look back at the glacier-rounded Appalachian hills, or plan to return close to sunset to see the silhouetted skyline of Terra Nova National Park.

Just before the road leaves the park boundaries, it passes a boat launch. The sheltered arm to the right is favored with canoeists.

Sandringham and Eastport

Route 310 follows the Northeast Arm through to **Sandringham.** Strung along the highway, the homes and few businesses of the town provide options to fuel and stock up. Follow the road through a forested section to reach **Eastport,** the center of the peninsula, and a junction of routes to Burnside, Sandy Cove, Happy Adventure, and Salvage.

The **Road to the Beaches**—named for Eastport's delightfully sandy shores— passes the **Beaches Arts & Heritage Centre** in Eastport, about 22 kilometers (13.7 miles) from Glovertown. Housed in the old community school, the heritage center hosts art exhibits, music shows, and theater performances, as well as the annual Winterset in Summer—a literary festival.

Stop in for hiking maps and information about **the Old Trails,** which follow the traditional paths between outport fishing communities on the peninsula. The hiking trails connect the beach community of **Sandy Cove** (just south of Eastport on Church Street) to the saltbox houses of **Salvage.** Along the approximately 12-kilometer (7.5-mile) hiking corridor of old footpaths and cart roads, the trails pass wildflower meadows and coastal viewpoints.

At the head of rectangular, sandy **Eastport Bay** (also called Salvage Bay), find the **Eastport beaches.** A rarity amid the rugged Newfoundland coastline, the beaches have made the area a favorite summer destination for locals. Along the shore find easily accessible Eastport Beach, tiny but quiet Seal Cove Beach, and

The High Tide Trail connects the Eastport beaches at high water.

the largest of the three—kilometer-long Northwest Beach. While all the beaches are accessible along the shoreline at low tide, the High Tide Trail connects them at high water. Eastport Beach, also called Southwest Beach, has a large parking area with change rooms, toilets, and picnic areas.

Settlers first arrived in Eastport in the mid-1860s, having left crowded Salvage at the end of the peninsula (so desirable because of its proximity to fishing grounds). Besides the beaches, the arable land on the Eastport Peninsula is another Newfoundland rarity. Topsoil is barely apparent in some areas of the province. The **Eastport Peninsula Agriculture Exhibition** celebrates this legacy on Canadian Thanksgiving weekend with events ranging from pie making to competitions for the weirdest looking vegetable.

In the 1960s Eastport Beach saw houses floated in from island communities—part of a resettlement plan to consolidate so the government could more easily provide health care and education.

From Eastport, take a drive south along Church Street and then follow Main Street to **Sandy Cove**—a fitting name for a community with such a wide stretch of sand. The beach looks out on Newman Sound and Swale Island in Terra Nova National Park. **Happy Adventure** is another small community on this side of the peninsula.

North from Eastport, Burdens Road becomes the road to Burnside (officially Route 310-32) and leads out past St. Chads on Damnable Bay—often pronounced "Damn the Bell." At the end of the road lies the community of Burnside, situated on Fair and False Bay. The drive, 8 kilometers (5 miles) one way, takes you to the departure point for the one-hour ferry to St. Brendan's on Cottel Island.

Salvage

The Road to the Beaches keeps close to the coast as it travels toward Salvage. Beyond the island-sheltered harbor, see the rocky bulge of Cow Head on the ever-nearing horizon. Islands—Sailors, Petty, and Hart—scatter the bay.

Long a fishing outport, the historic ochre-red fishing stages and saltbox houses make Salvage classically picturesque.

The saltbox houses and ochre-red fishing stages of **Salvage** hug Bishops Harbour. First settled in the 1600s, the community is often noted as one of the oldest continually settled places in the area. Migratory fishermen initially used the sheltered harbor as a base, and permanent settlement followed. From the mid-1800s through the 1930s, men and fishing schooners left for the summer Labrador fishery. They would return laden with salt cod for winter stocks and selling.

The local **Salvage Fishermen's Museum** on the main road lays out the history of the area and is located in the community's oldest building, a white two-story house dating to 1862. Also notable at the mouth of the harbor is the **Pickersgill Premises,** where two white saltbox houses and distinct red outbuildings sit isolated on the peninsula.

Throughout the community preserved fishing stages and boathouses cluster on the shore, alongside wharves and docked vessels. A seafood packaging company sits on the large community wharf, but the plant is now shuttered—showing the transition from working fishery to cutting off a community's lifeline. In 2001, the fish plant had burnt down, putting many workers out of a job before finally closing in 2013.

A project to restore the **Salvage Trails** provided employment after the 2001 fire. The trails are derived from old footpaths and rural roads between outports along this coast. Trails venture out to Net Point and other lookouts.

The trail network also connects to the Old Trails, which were being restored in 2018, and lead back to Sandy Cove via abandoned Broom Close Harbour and Little Barrow Harbour along Bonavista Bay.

All this can leave you a little lost in time, but never far from the main road.

Side Trip: Terra Nova National Park & the Bonavista Peninsula

Terra Nova National Park offers many days of exploration by boat tour, paddle, and hiking trail. Newman Sound and Clode Sound are the largest saltwater channels into the park.

To the south of the national park, **Bonavista Peninsula** has many well-known heritage attractions and great iceberg watching.

From the Trans-Canada Highway, Routes 230 and then 235 trace the shorelines of the hook-shaped Bonavista Peninsula. It's a sizeable land mass to explore, and at its tip the town of Bonavista features fishing heritage sites. The **Ryan Premises National Historic Site, Mockbeggar National Historic Site, Bonavista Museum,** and **Elliston's Root Cellars** all explore the area's long history as a commercial and seafaring center.

On the southeastern side of the peninsula, Trinity is perfectly picturesque with attractions scattered around the small, walkable community. The **Trinity Museum, Lester Garland House,** and **Hiscock House** each provide background to the photo-worthy setting.

Venturing south along the coast, visit the ***Random Passage* film set**—where sod-roof houses perched on the rocky shore re-created early-1800s outport life for the 2002 television miniseries.

28

Bell Island

Portugal Cove to Wabana, Bell Island

General Description: This 28-kilometer (17.4-mile) drive crosses the Bell Island Tickle to loop around Bell Island, Conception Bay's largest island. Once home to 12,000 people, the island grew prosperous by mining iron ore from its heavy rocks—originally used as boat ballast and to give weight to traditional killicks, or anchors. Tour a submarine mine or admire the painted murals depicting mining life. Visit the dock in Lance Cove that saw the only German land attack in North America during World War II. The treasures of the island include a memorial to lost sailors, a hike to artillery guns, and secret beaches below towering cliffs.

Special Features: Bell Island Ferry, Bell Island Gunsite, Lance Cove memorial, shipwrecks, Bell Island Community Museum, Underground Mine Tour, Bell Island Sports Hall of Fame, Grebes Nest, Bell Island Lighthouse.

Location: Conception Bay, the Avalon Peninsula.

Driving Route Numbers & Names: Bell Island Ferry, Beach Hill, Memorial Street, The Front, Lance Cove Road, Lance Cove Beach Road, Middleton Avenue, West Mines Road, Scotia Road, Hart Street/Cranes Lane, Petries Hill, Bennett Street, Main Street, Quigleys Line, Lighthouse Road, East End Road.

Travel Season: Although the ferry runs year-round, ice can hamper crossing from February through June. The Bell Island Community Museum, which gives underground mine tours, opens June to Sept. As it is the island's main attraction, a visit is best timed during these summer months.

Camping: There are no camping facilities on Bell Island, but the island is a good day-trip distance from Pippy Park in St. John's or Butter Pot Provincial Park near Holyrood. Both are fully equipped campgrounds for tents and RVs.

Services: Wabana, the largest town on Bell Island, features all the basics, including a hospital, grocery store, and a gas station. There are accommodations on the island—including The Grand Wabana Inn—and more options in Portugal Cove.

Nearby Points of Interest: Visit Bell Island as part of a coastal drive from St. John's, exploring Conception Bay's rich historical and natural sites: Pouch Cove Museum, Butter Pot Provincial Park, Hawthorne Cottage National Historic Site, Cupids Cove Plantation Provincial Historic Site, Cupids Legacy Centre, Conception Bay Museum, and Harbour Grace Airstrip.

Time Zone: Newfoundland time zone (GMT minus 3.5 hours).

The Drive

World War II history, submarine mines, and a controversial ball-lightning strike provide a magnetic complement on **Bell Island.** With only one main road that trims the island, you'll spend little time driving on this 28-kilometer (17.4-mile) island loop and lots touring an iron-ore mine and spotting the wartime shipwrecks.

Bell Island

Old mine collars still poke above ground, a testament to Bell Island's history of mining iron ore.

Unfortunately, on summer weekends you'll also spend time in ferry lines. The ferry operates on a no-reservations policy, so if at all possible arrive during off-peak times. Avoid weekday rush hours and midmorning to early evening on weekends. Ferries run daily, with more than a dozen trips; however, in winter conditions the tickle—a narrow channel of water—can pack with ice, making the crossing impassable.

Bell Island Tickle

Portugal Cove Road, Route 40, leads from St. John's and passes the airport en route to **Portugal Cove** on the shore of Conception Bay. You may see the ferry "lineup," along the right shoulder of the road before the ferry. Avoid blocking driveways and keep in mind that the line moves quickly for the short 20-minute crossing.

Board either the MV *Flanders* or the MV *Legionnaire* in Portugal Cove. Transportation regulations require passengers to head to the upper decks—an appreciated opportunity to admire the views during the crossing. There are washrooms and a small canteen on board.

In 1940 a tragic accident saw two ferries—the *W. Garland* and *Little Golden Dawn*—collide just off the Bell Island shore. The *W. Garland,* carrying 24 passengers plus crew, sank in four minutes. The mostly empty *Little Golden Dawn* stayed afloat longer. Twenty-two died, and a memorial to the disaster stands near the beach at the island ferry dock.

Bell Island's vertical cliffs, rising up to about 45 meters (148 feet) in places, give a stony-faced welcome to the island.

As the ferry docks at Beach Hill, look to the left to see the **Bell Island Gunsite.** A hiking trail leads up to the promontory where you can see guns that fired on German U-boats during World War II.

A testament to the small size of the island, which measures only 3.5 kilometers (2.2 miles) wide and less than 10 kilometers (6.2 miles) long, is catching sight of the **Wabana water tower.** The town is the final stop for this drive.

Drive up the steep hill from the ferry and take a left at the intersection with Memorial Street, then continue on a route known as The Front. The road quickly clips along at about 90 meters (295 feet) in elevation. Despite the road being set slightly inland, the high vantage allows clear views of Conception Bay. Heading southwest along the road, look out to Little Bell and Kellys Islands. Bell Island was once called Great Belle Isle, but the name was shortened over time.

Irish and English settlers, drawn to the arable soil here, first came to Bell Island in the 1740s. Follow the road through these long-settled farm fields, and about 6.5 kilometers (4 miles) from the ferry terminal, turn left onto O'Neals Hill and then Lance Cove Beach roads to head down to the waterfront.

Follow the rural roads as they twist down to a bayside monument. An anchor memorializes the torpedoing of four ships transporting island iron ore during World War II. On September 5, 1942, a German U-boat attacked and sank the SS *Sargarnaga* and SS *Lord Strathcona.* Less than two months later on November 2, 1942, a second U-boat attack was launched against the SS *Rose Castle* and freighter PLM. *27.* In the second attack one of the torpedoes missed its target, hitting Scotia Pier. The explosion was the only land attack on North America during the war. At low tide the ship wreckage is said to be still visible along the shore.

Lance Cove is also the site of a very different (and far more controversial) blast. In 1978, a 10-megaton explosion shocked residents. Reported to be ball lightning—a rarely observed phenomena that has a longer duration and more globular appearance than streak lightning—it left blast holes in the ground, exploded television sets, and melted the insulation on power lines. Happening mid Cold War, the blast is also said to have drawn investigations from Canadian, US, and Russian military personnel.

From Lance Cove, the drive follows the main island road as it rounds a sharp right bend at Freshwater and becomes Middleton Avenue. Although not visible from the road, Bell Rock sits off the island cliffs here at the western edge of the island.

There are places named **Freshwater Cove** on both sides of the island, owing to sailors stopping on Bell Island to replenish their stocks of potable water. From this Freshwater, the straight road cuts through a forested path along the north edge of the island toward Wabana.

Wabana

Rich in red hematite, or iron ore, Bell Island saw its first mine open in the 1890s. The island's heavy rock was used historically as ship ballast and as the weight for killicks, or anchors made from wood and rock. First surface mine operations, and later submarine mines, extracted more than 3 billion tons of iron ore from Bell Island.

As the route arrives on the outskirts of **Wabana**—which is derived from an Abenaki First Nations word that means "place of first light"—the town's houses splay out amid a spacious scribble of roads. The mazelike streets are untypical of the bay-clustered houses you'll see in most Newfoundland communities. Old mineshafts, like the collar of No. 4 Mine, occasionally break the surface from below the depths, and piles of waste ore give the feeling of a quarry pit. It's an intriguing mess.

Heading northeast into town, follow signs for the No. 2 Mine to **Bell Island Community Museum.** One of six mines on the island, the No. 2 mine is open for tours, taking visitors into the submarine shaft. See the iron ore carts where the miners loaded ore, hear about horses that lived in belowground stables and pulled the carts, and feel the chill of the shafts that miners first navigated by candle-light. The temperature in the mines is about 8 degrees Centigrade (47 degrees Fahrenheit).

Piles of rust-colored waste ore surround the museum. The small one-story building houses an array of donated local artifacts as well as a large collection of Bell Island mining photos by famed portrait photographer Yousuf Karsh.

Fueled by a strong industry, the Bell Island population quickly grew in the first half of the 20th century. By 1961 more than 12,000 lived on the island. The No. 2 mine closed in 1949, and Bell Island's last mine closed in 1966, owing to the increasing costs to excavate the iron ore.

On **Petrie's Hill,** find the local curling club where exhibits of the **Bell Island Sports Hall of Fame** retell the island's sport triumphs. It's open summer only.

Wabana also has services such as a hospital, grocery store, and gas station. On a drive through town, murals provide vivid reminders of mining life.

In the distant horizon, to the northeast of Wabana, you'll see a dark peninsula capped with the community of Biscayan Cove beyond Pouch Cove.

For an adventurous and scenic detour (over Bell Island's roads that often sport multiple names), turn off West Mines Road to link with Scotia No. 1 Road. (Nearby the close-in-name Scotia Road is an old route that cuts south clear across the island, once a direct route to transport ore from the Wabana mines to the loading dock at Scotia Pier.)

Follow Scotia No. 1 Road past Foleys Road and McCarthy Street, and then bear left on Hart Street/Cranes Lane as it becomes a dirt road that parallels the

Rocky trails lead from a rock stack to a blasted tunnel—the Grebes Nest—on Bell Island.

shoreline. For some vehicles it may be best to pull off, park, and then walk the short distance down to the cliffs by foot.

From the cliff tops, you'll see the rock stack that divides the beaches. A trail leads under questionably stable cliffs down to sea caves, a beach, and a tunnel blasted through the rock. Both sides of the sea stack provide coast to explore.

To the north, waves have carved dramatic sea caves in the island's cliffs.

To the south, the trail approaches a head-high tunnel opening in the cliff. Blasted through the rock with dynamite and reinforced with wooden poles, it's known as **Grebes Nest**. While the safest option is to admire the tunnel opening from the shoreline, many make the trip through the tunnel to spend a day at the beach on the other side.

Another excursion from Wabana is to follow Quigleys Line northeast to visit the lighthouse. Lighthouse Road leads to the tip of the island and the small **Bell Island Lighthouse**—which benefits from its natural elevation. Watch for sea birds, such as the sleek black guillemots.

But if ferry waits are long, it may be best to take your place in line as it snakes down the hill on the road shoulder. Although tedious, the pre-crossing wait does create a great opportunity to visit the hillside **World War II gun battery** if you missed it when arriving on Bell Island.

Side Trip: St. John's

Portugal Cove Road leads from the Bell Island ferry right toward the Newfoundland capital of **St. John's,** with its many natural, historical, and cultural attactions.

Begin a visit to the city at **Signal Hill National Historic Site,** where the elevated vantage has sweeping views of the downtown and the Atlantic Ocean. The Cabot Tower is the site's distinct landmark, but there are trails, gun batteries, and other historic buildings to explore. Nearby the **Johnson GEO Centre** takes visitors underground to see the geology that gives this province its nickname of "The Rock". **The Rooms** combines a museum, archives, and art gallery and its exhibits unveil tales and hardships of Newfoundland life.

For local culture, visit the small fishing community of **Quidi Vidi,** which also has a brewery, as well as the live music bars on **George Street.** Here, it's not hard to find a "screech-in"—the tongue-in-cheek ceremony for non-Newfoundlanders that includes taking a shot of liquor, reciting some verse, and kissing a cod.

29

Irish Loop

Bay Bulls to Ferryland to Cape Race to Salmonier

General Description: A 315-kilometer (196-mile) scenic drive follows the southeastern coast of the Avalon Peninsula, a route popularly known as the Irish Loop. From rocky but forested coves in Bay Bulls and Witless Bay, the route heads south to barren lands near Cape Race. Archaeological digs, fossil shores, and a hike to a community destroyed by a tidal wave feature along the route. Whale and puffin tours venture from the land to see the region's rich offshore wildlife, while moose and caribou herds inhabit the wilderness areas.

Special Features: Puffin and whale watching, East Coast Trail, La Manche Provincial Park, La Manche town site, Colony of Avalon, Ferryland Museum, Ferryland Lighthouse Picnics, Avalon Wilderness Reserve, Chance Cove Provincial Park, Mistaken Point Eco Reserve, Cape Race Lighthouse, Holyrood Pond Interpretation Centre, St. Vincent's Fishermen's Museum, Salmonier Provincial Wildlife Park.

Location: Southern Avalon Peninsula, Newfoundland.

Driving Route Numbers & Names: Irish Loop, Route 10, Route 90.

Travel Season: While the weather is usually fine and pleasant from June through September, avoid most bugs with a visit in August or early September.

Camping: La Manche Provincial Park provides the best camping facilities on the circuit. Comfort stations (with showers, washrooms, and laundry), drinking water, a playground, and fire pits provide solid services. The pretty valley park is also noted for bird-watching opportunities. Chance Cove Provincial Park offers only basic camping with pit toilets, but the stunning shoreline location adds its own unique appeal.

Services: Fueling up in Bay Bulls and Trepassey will keep the gas tank full for this route. For major supplies or medical care, return to the St. John's area for the best options.

Nearby Points of Interest: Cape Spear National Historic Site, Cape St. Mary's Ecological Reserve, Castle Hill National Historic Site, O'Reilly House Museum.

Time Zone: Newfoundland time (GMT minus 3.5 hours).

The Drive

Embark on a 315-kilometer (196-mile) coastal drive from the forested rocky coves south of St. John's to the barren tip of the Avalon Peninsula. Wildlife sightings are the treat of the journey, from the whales and puffins near Witless Bay to the moose and caribou at Salmonier Nature Park. A community swept away by a tidal wave, an archaeological dig, and one of the Atlantic's brightest lighthouses (which also first received the *Titanic* distress call) all create mysteries along the way.

If traveling to Bay Bulls from Conception Bay or points farther west, cut across a glacier-raked landscape from exit 37 on the Trans-Canada Highway and along Route 13.

Irish Loop

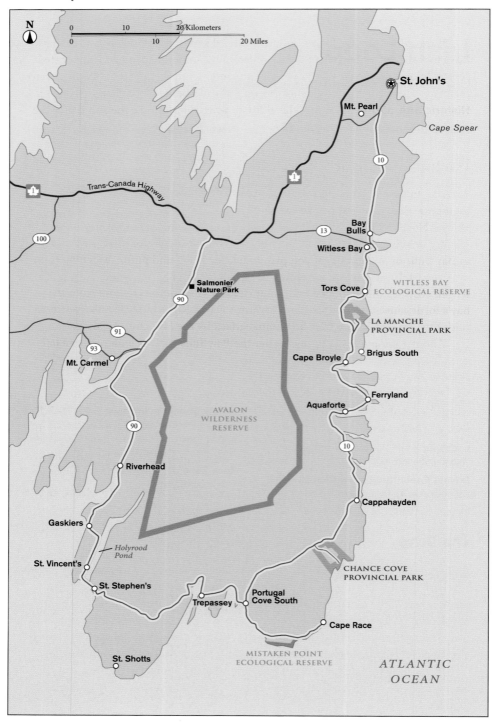

If traveling from St. John's, follow Route 10 south as it parallels part of the **East Coast Trail,** a more than 300-kilometer (186-mile) mapped and signposted coastal hiking route that this drive will encounter a number of times. Perhaps start the drive with a side trip to the lighthouse and museum at **Cape Spear National Historic Site,** at the end of Blackhead Road, where you can see the sun rise at the easternmost point of North America.

Whales, Puffins & Wild Coasts

Arriving in **Bay Bulls** on Route 10, stop in at the visitor information center (alongside the grocery store) where you'll find hiking maps and plenty of brochures. North Side and South Side Roads lead around the harbor in Bay Bulls. Fishing vessels and wildlife-watching boats make it a busy spot. Allow a half day in Bay Bulls or Witless Bay if you plan to take a whale- and puffin-watching tour.

The **St. Peter and St. Paul Roman Catholic Church** in town is notable for its gateposts: cannons topped with saint statues. The cannons remain from the bay's fortifications, put in place by Governor David Kirke in 1638. Subsequent raids saw the Dutch land here and a final attack by the French in 1796.

About 2 kilometers (1.2 miles) after the Bay Bulls visitor center, make a left onto Deans Road. The road is a scenic route to Witless Bay, becoming Harbour Road at Bear Cove Head and crossing Lower Pond.

As you arrive in **Witless Bay,** look out to Gull Island, the northernmost island in the **Witless Bay Ecological Reserve** chain. The reserve is home to the largest Atlantic puffin colony in North America, with more than 260,000 nesting pairs of the provincial bird. More than 600,000 breeding pairs of Leach's storm petrels as well as black-legged kittiwakes, common murres, razorbills, and northern fulmars also nest at the reserve.

As you travel along the coast you'll see the reserve's Gull, Green, Great, and Pee Pee Islands, as well as other rocky knolls. On each of the four islands in the reserve, puffins make their nests by burrowing into the grassy turf before laying a single egg. Leach's storm petrels also dig into the hillsides.

As the forest meets the ocean, the coniferous trees seem almost cemented to the shore in order to withstand the powerful storms.

From Harbour Road in Witless Bay, the route reconnects with Route 10. Turn left to journey 8 kilometers (5 miles) south to **Tors Cove,** passing through Mobile Bay en route.

A lookout and interpretive sign with a history of the community lie alongside the main route for a quick stop and photo, but I prefer to venture down to explore this sheltered and picturesque spot. Follow the winding Cove Road to the shoreline, where a dirt road leads out past a fish plant to a crumbling wharf. Here, you'll

The Witless Bay Ecological Reserve is home to the largest Atlantic puffin colony in North America.

have clear views of the bay's islands: Fox Island and Ship Island closest to the shore, and Great Island and Pee Pee Island, which are part of the seabird reserve.

Leaving Tors Cove you'll note the large water pipe running from Tors Cove Pond to the community.

Just past Tors Cove, a side road ventures off Route 10 along a residential coastline to Burnt Cove, St. Michaels, and East Bauline (pronounced like "Pauline" with a B). It's a one-way route, but one that affords more coastal views for those on a relaxed time schedule. East Bauline is one of many trailheads for the East Coast Trail, and this particular section follows the coast to the old La Manche village site.

If you're not walking the trail, retrace the road to Route 10.

La Manche

From Tors Cove, Route 10 bends inland for good reason: It skirts the swath of valley and coast encompassed by **La Manche Provincial Park.** Hiking, bird watching, swimming, and canoeing on the La Manche River are all popular park activities. An 82-site campground offers laundry, washrooms, and showers, making the park a comfortable overnight destination.

Just south of the park boundaries, La Manche Road leads to a trailhead for an easy-to-moderate hike along another part of the East Coast Trail to the **old La Manche town site,** suspension bridge, and an inviting swimming hole. The forested trail passes ponds and rocky outcrops before reaching the former village.

On both sides of the water, see concrete foundations that tell the tale of the community washed away by a powerful winter storm and tidal wave on January 25, 1966. No one was killed, and the community opted to resettle elsewhere following the destructive ocean swell. Allow about 1.5 hours for the out-and-back journey.

Back on Route 10, the road keeps inland through mostly forested scenery.

About halfway between Tors Cove and Ferryland, Brigus Road on the left makes a scenic detour to Brigus South for photos of a typical Newfoundland fishing village.

A minute further on the main route, you'll pass the unassuming, dirt-surfaced Horse Chops Road. It leads to a special place, cutting into the heart of the peninsula to the **Avalon Wilderness Reserve.** The 1,070-square-kilometer (413-square-mile) tract of wilderness encompasses caribou migration lands and moose territory over rolling barrens, ponds, and forest. The caribou herd is the most southerly one in Canada.

Passing through Cape Broyle (get gas and moose burgers here) and Calvert, the treed scenery ends abruptly in Ferryland.

Ferryland to Barren Lands

Arriving in **Ferryland,** watch for the town building and visitor center on the right. But a stop is unnecessary unless seeking maps or accommodation information. Route 10 traces the coast, and the town's substantial attractions are easy to find.

Near the large stone **Holy Trinity Roman Catholic Church** (for which fishermen shipped in the stone from an island that is 2 kilometers [1.2 miles] off-shore), find the **Ferryland Museum.** The museum itself, in the old courthouse building, houses exhibits ranging from a jail cell to details on shoreline shipwrecks.

Just past the museum, a road branches left to Ferryland Head.

Sir George Calvert of England, who became the first Lord Baltimore, sponsored the founding of a colony here in 1621 and it would become one of the first English settlements on the continent.

The **Colony of Avalon** presents what the settlers (and later, Baltimore himself) left behind. Gold rings, cannonballs, silver thimbles, pipes, glass windows, and gravestones have been unearthed by the dig, and some are on display at the interpretive center. Watch diggers in the site uncovering items and conservationists putting the pieces together like a jigsaw.

The area was first visited by the Beothuk and then migratory fishermen. Permanent settlement came when Sir George Calvert purchased title and established a colony on the lollipop-shaped land called the Downs. After a little more than one Newfoundland winter at the colony, Calvert headed for warmer climes in Maryland in 1629, leaving the colony under a representative.

In 1638 Sir David Kirke arrived at Avalon. Having captured Nova Scotia and Quebec and been awarded Newfoundland when a treaty returned those regions to the French, Kirke deposed Calvert's representative and took residence at Ferryland as governor of Newfoundland.

Legal tensions between Kirke and Calvert ensued, but it is perhaps Sara Kirke who deserves the greatest attention: The widow ran a successful fish mercantile for decades after her husband died in prison.

Also on Ferryland Head sits the **Ferryland Head Lighthouse,** which is renowned for its **Lighthouse Picnics**—a gourmet, homemade-quality picnic served on the rocky bluffs around the red metal lighthouse. Fresh molasses bread, homemade lemonade, and gingerbread with custard are just a selection from the tempting menu. It's a 25-minute walk out to the 1870 lighthouse.

The Ferryland community celebrates with the **Southern Shore Shamrock Festival** in late July, when Irish and Newfoundland musicians entertain the crowds.

Returning to Route 10, the road dips around the lovely **Aquaforte Harbour.** Watch for the power-generating wind turbines that sit on the far hill. Treed slopes lead down to a bay that has an almost turquoise hue on a fine day.

Past Aquaforte and Fermeuse—names which show that this coast was long visited by migratory French fishermen—a side road leads out to **Port Kirwan.** Even a short detour on this road will take you to the odd complement of a huge boulder next to the **St. Charles Borromeo Church.** Farther down this road find picnic tables and a fishing wharf.

Back on Route 10, another detour leads into **Renews**—a small town with narrow streets to explore. Tales of shipwrecks and a daring rescue by Captain William Jackman—who rescued 27 people by swimming out to a sinking schooner an incredible 27 times—show the resilient spirit of folk along the coast. The *Mayflower* stopped here in 1620 to resupply en route to its historic landing in Massachusetts.

As the barrenness of the land increases on the journey past Cappahayden, the route soon bears southwest to follow the inland trajectory of the Southern Shore Highway.

Chance Cove to Cape Race

Flat lands, scattered boulders, waterlogged bogs, and hardy grasses reach from the road to the horizon along the 32-kilometer (20-mile) stretch from Cappahayden to Portugal Cove South. When there is forest, the trees are stunted and sparse. Off-the-grid hunting camps prompt musings about a disconnected life. Watch the barrens for wildlife.

For a break in the emptiness, 13 kilometers (8 miles) from Cappahayden turn down to **Chance Cove Provincial Park.** Bump along the 6-kilometer (3.7-mile) dirt road to a parking lot where short trails lead to fabulous views. The day-use park has no attendant on-site and limited services, which include pit toilets and picnic tables. Although not a tended campground, camping is permitted in the parking area for RVs or by the picnic tables for tents.

The former village of Chance Cove once stood here, but was mysteriously abandoned by all its residents. Ghost tales recall the 1863 shipwreck of the steamer *Anglo Saxon* off Chance Cove. Of the 444 on board, only about half were saved and many of the dead were buried here. For the years following, it is said that screams were heard off the coast until the entire community left one night. No one knows where they went. Years later, after fishermen used the community as a summer camp, they torched the houses.

At the very least it's a good campfire horror story—but maybe not for those who plan to camp here.

Back on Route 10, a rare break in the barren landscape is the **Cape Race LORAN-C transmitter.** The original 411-meter (1,348-foot) tower has collapsed, but it was the tallest structure in Canada prior to the construction of the CN Tower in Toronto. The use of long-range transmission has diminished with the popularity and easy use of GPS technology.

Finally the drive arrives in **Portugal Cove South,** where you'll first encounter the **Edge of Avalon Interpretive Centre.** The center provides details on the nearby attractions at Cape Race and Mistaken Point. From the center, you can continue west to Trepassey or southeast to Cape Race.

Toward Cape Race, there's a 20-kilometer (12.4-mile) half-paved, half-dirt road skirting the inland side of the **Mistaken Point Ecological Reserve.** The reserve is a world heritage site because it features fossils of the world's oldest creatures, which lived in the ocean 580 to 541 million years ago. The reserve is accessible by guided tour only, which must be booked ahead (information available at the Edge of Avalon Interpretive Centre).

At the end of the point find **Cape Race Lighthouse.** A national historical site, the lighthouse is known for its powerful light that has saved many a ship

Mistaken Point Provincial Ecological Reserve and the Cape Race Lighthouse are worth the drive to the end of the road.

from being wrecked on the foggy point. Views are wide and flat, looking out at the Atlantic Ocean's expanse—if you're lucky, you may catch a sight of whales.

Near the lighthouse, and also along the Cape Race road, get the long and the short of Morse code at the **Myrick Wireless Interpretation Centre.** The Marconi wireless station, originally built in 1904, received the first distress call from the RMS *Titanic* in 1912.

Return on the same road back to Portugal Cove to continue the journey through southern Avalon.

The Portugal Cove South area celebrates its roots with the annual **Cape Race–PCS Heritage Days** in August. Beach bonfires, guided tours, and traditional tasks like butter churning and rug hooking cast a wide net for the festival.

In Portugal Cove pass the dunelike piles of rocks, washed ashore by powerful storms, and round the bend to Biscay Bay, where a flatter beach is a more sheltered haven. The road then cuts across Cape Mutton toward Trepassey.

Spectacular barren bluffs, the Atlantic Ocean, and even a glimpse of Cape Pine Lighthouse treat as you arrive at Trepassey Harbour. For those driving the route over two days, **Trepassey** makes a good halfway point. Accommodations in town are limited, so inquire ahead for rooms during high season, July and August.

Amelia Earhart flew from here as the first female passenger to cross the Atlantic Ocean on the *Friendship* in 1928. Her better-known solo flight across the Atlantic Ocean departed from Harbour Grace on Conception Bay in 1932.

The town's name is said to come from the French trépassé, meaning passed away—and one take on the name's history is that it refers to those lost in shipwrecks off the foggy coast.

Holyrood Pond

As the road skirts Trepassey Harbour and passes through Daniels Point, the distances seem to lengthen with the emptiness of the scenery. The landscape is blown clean of trees, and the scrape of the glaciers has left ponds and boulders deposited like litter.

Midway between Trepassey and St. Stephen's, St. Shott's Road presents two coastal detours. One fork continues out to a small fishing community, while a slow-going gravel road ventures out to **Cape Pine Lighthouse**—another dangerous point that has witnessed many shipwrecks in foggy conditions. The side trip to St. Shott's adds a slow 25 kilometers (15.5 miles) round trip from Route 10.

About 30 kilometers (18.6 miles) past Trepassey, the road dips into the pleasant discovery of Peter's River—a treed valley that livens up the clean-swept landscape.

Holyrood Pond Interpretation Centre, a sharp, red building, marks the inland Holyrood Pond. Popular with anglers, the pond is a 21-kilometer (13-mile) landlocked fjord that provides habitat for more than 30 species of saltwater and freshwater fish. A wide, weather worn beach separates the pond from the ocean, and the storm barriers are worth a stop to peer over.

On the west side of the pond, St. Vincent's tempts with tales of watching the whales from the shore. Stop in at the St. Vincent's **Fisheries Museum,** located on the main road and behind Sacred Heart Catholic Church, to get tips on when and where.

For the next 8 kilometers (5 miles) of the route, now mapped as Route 90, the road climbs above Holyrood Pond and affords gentle views of the often-calm inland waters. As the route bends northeast through Gaskiers, you may catch views of St. Mary's Bay, edged on the far side with Cape St. Mary's and a many-thousand-strong gannet colony at Bird Rock.

Trees, twisting roads, and more small towns strike a contrast to the earlier barrens of the Avalon Peninsula.

Salmonier Provincial Nature Park is great for families with a boardwalk and easy wildlife viewing.

Amid excellent moose territory, the road reaches the wonderful **Salmonier Provincial Nature Park**. The free attraction is great for families with its boardwalk, easy wildlife viewing, friendly staff, and good facilities. Watch for shy moose, hiding caribou, playful mink, and alert owls in the park. Arrive at morning feeding times to watch the animals devour their breakfasts.

From Salmonier, it's then just a short 11-kilometer (6.8-mile) journey to reconnect with the Trans-Canada Highway—completing the Irish Loop around the southern Avalon Peninsula.

Side Trip: Cape St. Mary's

Although less of a scenic drive than the Irish Loop, a journey to **Cape St. Mary's** may be the headline highlight of a visit to the Avalon Peninsula. **Cape St. Mary's Ecological Reserve,** off Cape St. Mary's Road (located at the southern end of Routes 92 and 100), features a huge gannet colony that nests on Bird Rock and the surrounding cliffs.

Gannets nest by the thousand on Bird Rock at Cape St. Marys.

A 1.4-kilometer (0.9-mile) hike leads down to a viewing cliff within meters of the birds, which included 24,000 Northern gannet and 20,000 black-legged kittiwake in 2018. Amid the gannets, with their 2-meter (6.6-foot) wingspan, try to spot common and thick-billed murres, cormorants, and seagulls.

This route pairs well with a return ferry journey to Nova Scotia and the Maritimes. The Argentia, NL–North Sydney, NS ferry makes the 16-hour crossing just twice a week from mid-June to mid-September. Reservations (particularly for bunks and cabins) and confirming sailing times are highly recommended well in advance.

If arriving in Placentia a day or two early, a series of historical museums and sites can fill the time.

Castle Hill National Historic Site presents reenactments of the French and English conflicts over Newfoundland's rich fishing grounds. When the British blockaded the harbor here, the French—given the little arable land in the area—were forced to abandon the fort. The 1713 Treaty of Utrecht made the fortress officially British territory, and the French moved south to build Fortress Louisbourg on Cape Breton Island.

Learn about more recent local history at **O'Reilly House Museum,** including tales of the inshore fishery and the 1960s resettlement, when many who lived on island outports relocated to more central communities—sometimes by floating their house to the new location!

Appendix A: More Information

Drive 1

Campobello Island ferry
East Coast Ferries
P.O. Box 301, Lords Cove
Deer Island, NB E5V 1W2
(506) 747-2159 or (877) 747-2159
eastcoastferries.nb.ca

Campobello Public Library & Museum
3 Welshpool St.
Welshpool, NB E5E 1G3
(506) 752-7082
visitcampobello.com/librarymuseum

Deer Island–Letete ferry
(506) 662-3724
coastaltransport.ca

Head Harbour Lightstation
210 Lighthouse Rd.
Wilson's Beach, NB E5E 1M2
(506) 752-2454
campobello.com/lighthouse

Herring Cove Provincial Park
136 Herring Cove Rd.
Campobello Island, NB E5E 1B8
(506) 752-7010
parcsnbparks.ca/HerringCove

Roosevelt Campobello International Park
459 Hwy. 774
Campobello Island, NB E5E 1A4
(506) 752-2922 or (877) 851-6663
fdr.net

Drive 2

Ministers Island Historic Site
199 Carriage Rd.
Ministers Island, NB E5B 0A4
(506) 529-5081
ministersisland.net

St. Andrews Welcome Centre
24 Reed Ave.
St. Andrews, NB E5B 1A1
(506) 529-3556
standrewsbythesea.ca

Wild Salmon Nature Centre
24 Chamcook Lake No. 1 Rd.
Chamcook, NB E5B 2Z4
(506) 529-1384
wildsalmonnaturecentre.ca

Drive 3

Fundy Parkway
229 Main St. (mailing address)
St. Martins, NB E5R 1B7
(506) 833-2019 or (866) 386-3987
fundytrailparkway.com

Quaco Museum
236 Main St.
St. Martins, NB E5R 1B8
(506) 833-4740 (seasonal)
quaco.ca

St. Martins Visitor Information Centre
424 Main St.
St. Martins, NB E5R 1B9
(506) 833-2006 (seasonal) or
(506) 833-2010 (village office)
stmartinscanada.com

Drive 4

Albert County Museum
3940 Rte. 114
Hopewell Cape, NB E4H 3J8
(506) 734-2003
albertcountymuseum.com

Bank of New Brunswick Museum
5985 Rte. 114
Riverside-Albert, NB E4H 4B8
(506) 882-2015

Cape Enrage
650 Cape Enrage Rd.
Waterside, NB E4H 4Z4
(506) 887-2273 or (833) 796-2273
capeenrage.ca

Fundy National Park
P.O. Box 1001
Alma, NB E4H 1B4
(506) 887-6000
pc.gc.ca/en/pn-np/nb/fundy/index.aspx

Hillsborough Visitor Information Centre
2861 Main St.
Hillsborough, NB E4H 2X7
(506) 734-2240

Hopewell Rocks
131 Discovery Rd.
Hopewell Cape, NB E4H 4Z5
(877) 734-3429
thehopewellrocks.ca

New Brunswick Railway Museum
2847 Main St.
Hillsborough, NB E4H 2X7
(506) 734-3195
nbrm.ca

Riverside-Albert Village Office
(visitor info)
5823 King St.
Riverside-Albert, NB
(506) 882-3023

Steeves House Museum
40 Mill St.
Hillsborough, NB E4H 2Z8
(506) 734-3102
steeveshousemuseum.ca

Drive 5

Beaverbrook Art Gallery
703 Queen St.
Fredericton, NB E3B 1C4
(506) 458-2028 (reception)
beaverbrookartgallery.org

Canadian Military Engineers Museum
Mitchell Building (J-10), CFB/ASG
Gagetown
Oromocto, NB E2V 4J5
(506) 422-2000 ext. 1897
cmemuseum.ca

Fredericton Region Museum
571 Queen St.
Fredericton, NB E3B 1C3
(506) 455-6041
frederictonregionmuseum.com

Fredericton Tourism
397 Queen St.
Fredericton, NB E3B 1B5
(506) 460-2129
tourismfredericton.ca

Government House
51 Woodstock Rd.
Fredericton, NB E3B 9L8
(506) 453-2505
gnb.ca/lg/ogh/index-e.asp

Kings Landing
5804 Rte. 102
Prince William, NB E6K 0A5
(506) 363-4999
kingslanding.nb.ca

Legislative Assembly of New Brunswick
706 Queen St.
Fredericton, NB E3B 5H1
(506) 453-2527
gnb.ca/legis

Mactaquac Provincial Park
1265 Rte. 105
Mactaquac, NB E6L 1B5
(506) 363-4747
parcsnbparks.ca

New Brunswick Military History Museum
Building A-5, CFB/ASG Gagetown
Oromocto, NB E2V 4J5
(506) 422-1304
nbmilitaryhistorymuseum.ca

New Brunswick Sports Hall of Fame
503 Queen St.
Fredericton, NB E3B 5H1
(506) 453-3747
nbsportshalloffame.com

Oromocto Visitor Information Centre
311 Restigouche Rd.
Oromocto, NB E2V 2H5
(506) 446-5010 (seasonal)
oromocto.ca

Queens County Court House Museum
16 Court House Rd.
Gagetown, NB E5M 1A4
(506) 488-2483
queenscountyheritage.com

Saint John River cable ferries
(888) 747-7006

School Days Museums
Justice Building Annex, east entrance
Queen Street
Fredericton, NB
(506) 459-3738
museum.nbta.ca

Tilley House and Gagetown Visitor Information Centre
69 Front St.
Gagetown, NB E5M 1A4
(506) 488-2966 (seasonal)
queenscountyheritage.com

Drive 6

Atlantic Salmon Museum
263 Main St.
Doaktown, NB E9C 1A9
(506) 365-7787
atlanticsalmonmuseum.com

Beaubears Island Shipbuilding National Historic Site
35 St. Patrick's Dr., Nelson
Miramichi, NB E1N 4P6
(506) 622-8526
beaubearsisland.com

Beaverbrook House
518 King George Hwy.
Miramichi, NB E1V 1N1
(506) 622-5572
beaverbrookhouse.com

Central New Brunswick Woodmen's Museum
6342 Hwy. 8
Boiestown, NB E6A 1Z5
(506) 369-7214
woodmensmuseum.com

Doak Historic Site
386 Main St.
Doaktown, NB E9C 1E4
(506) 365-2026

Metepenagiag Heritage Park
2156 MicMac Rd.
Red Bank, NB E9E 2P2
(506) 836-6118
metpark.ca

Miramichi Visitor Information Centre
21 Cove Rd.
Miramichi, NB E1V 0A6
(506) 778-8444
discovermiramichi.com

Drive 7

Caraquet Visitor Information Centre
39 West St-Pierre Blvd.
Caraquet, NB E1W 1B7
(506) 726-2676
caraquet.ca

Éco-musée de l'Huître (Oyster Museum)
675 West St-Pierre Blvd.
Caraquet, NB E1W 1A2
(506) 727-3226
rmne.ca/eco-musee-huitre

Ecological Park of the Acadian Peninsula
65 Du Ruisseau St.
Lamèque, NB E8T 1M2
(506) 344-3223

Founding Cultures Museum
184 Acadie St.
Grande-Anse, NB E8N 1A6
(506) 732-3003
museedescultures.ca

Musée Acadien de Caraquet (Acadian Museum)
15 East St-Pierre Blvd.
Caraquet, NB E1W 1B6
(506) 726-2682
museecaraquet.ca

New Brunswick Aquarium and Marine Center
100 Aquarium St.
Shippagan, NB E8S 1H9
(506) 336-3013
aquariumnb.ca

Shippagan Visitor Information Centre
200 Hôtel-de-ville Ave.
Shippagan, NB E8S 1M1
(506) 336-3993
shippagan.ca

Village Historique Acadien
5 Rue du Pont
Bertrand, NB E1W 0E1
(506) 726-2600
vhanb.ca

Drive 8

Bouctouche Visitor Information Centre
14 Acadie St.
Bouctouche, NB E4S 2T2
(506) 743-8811
villedebouctouche.ca

Bonar Law Historic Site and Richibucto River Museum
31 Bonar Law Ave.
Rexton, NB E4W 1V6
(506) 523-7615
bonarlawcommon.com

Irving Eco-Centre
1932 Rte. 475
Bouctouche, NB E4S 4W9
(506) 743-2600 or (888) 640-3300
jdirving.com

Kent Museum
150 Couvent Lane
Bouctouche, NB E4S 3C1
(506) 743-5005
facebook.com/museedekent

Kouchibouguac National Park
186 Rte. 117
Kouchibouguac, NB E4X 2P1
(506) 876-2443 or (888) 773-8888
pc.gc.ca/kouchibouguac

Le Pays de la Sagouine
57 Acadie St.
Bouctouche, NB E4S 2T7
(506) 743-1400 or (800) 561-9188
sagouine.com

Musée des Pionniers de Grande-Digue
468 B Rte. 530
Grande-Digue NB E4R 5K3
(506) 532-6823
grande-digue.com

Olivier Soapery
831 Rte. 505
Sainte-Anne-de-Kent, NB E4S 1J9
(506) 743-8938
oliviersoaps.com

Parlee Beach Provincial Park
45 Parlee Beach Rd.
Pointe-du-Chêne, NB E4P 8V5
(506) 533-3363
parcsnbparks.ca/ParleeBeach

Pascal-Poirier Historic House
399 Main St.
Shediac, NB E4P 2B7
(506) 532-7022

Shediac Visitor Information Centre
229 Main St.
Shediac, NB E4P 2A5
(506) 532-7788
shediac.ca

Drive 9

Age of Sail Heritage Centre
8334 Rte. 209
Port Greville, NS B0M 1T0
(902) 348-2030 (seasonal)
ageofsailmuseum.ca

Bass River Heritage Museum
5666 Hwy. 2
Bass River, NS B0M 1B0
(902) 647-2648
bassrivermuseum.ca

Cape Chignecto Provincial Park
1108 West Advocate Rd.
Advocate Harbour, NS B0M 1A0
(902) 392-2085 or (888) 544-3434
parks.novascotia.ca

Cape d'Or Scenic Area
Cape d'Or Road
Advocate Harbour, NS B0M 1A0
(902) 670-8314

Cobequid Interpretive Centre
3246 Hwy. 2
Economy, NS B0M 1J0
(902) 647-2600

Five Islands Provincial Park
618 Bentley Rd.
Five Islands, NS B0M 1K0
(902) 254-2980 or (888) 544-3434
(camping reservations)
parks.novascotia.ca

Fundy Geological Museum
162 Two Islands Rd.
Parrsboro, NS B0M 1S0
(902) 254-3814
fundygeological.novascotia.ca

Glooscap Country Bazaar
3323 Hwy. 2
Economy, NS B0M 1J0
(902) 647-2920

Joggins Fossil Cliffs
100 Main St.
Joggins, NS B0L 1A0
(902) 251-2727 or (888) 932-9766
jogginsfossilcliffs.net

Ottawa House
1155 Whitehall Rd.
Parrsboro, NS B0M 1S0
(902) 254-2376 (summer only)
ottawahousemuseum.ca

Ship's Company Theatre
18 Lower Main St.
Parrsboro, NS B0M 1S0
(902) 254-3000 (box office) or
(800) 565-7469
shipscompanytheatre.com

That Dutchman's Farm
132 Brown Rd.
Upper Economy, NS B0M 1J0
(902) 647-2751
thatdutchmansfarm.com

Thomas' Cove Coastal Reserve
Economy Point Road
Economy, NS
colchester.ca/thomas-cove-coastal-
reserve

Truro Tidal Bore Viewing Visitor Centre
103 Tidal Bore Rd.
Lower Truro, NS B6L 1T9
(902) 897-6255

Truro Welcome Centre
493 Prince St.
Truro, NS B2N 3H7
(902) 893-2922
truro.ca

Drive 10

Fort Edward National Historic Site
67 Fort Edward St.
Windsor, NS B0N 2T0
(902) 798-2639 (seasonal) or
(902) 532-2321
pc.gc.ca/fortedward

Grand Pré National Historic Site
2205 Grand-Pré Rd.
Grand-Pré, NS B0P 1M0
(902) 542-3631 or (866) 542-3631
pc.gc.ca/grandpre

Haliburton House
424 Clifton Ave.
Windsor, NS B0N 2T0
(902) 798-2915
haliburtonhouse.novascotia.ca

Howard Dill Enterprises
400 College Rd.
Windsor, NS B0N 2T0
(902) 798-2728
howarddill.com

Randall House Museum
259 Main St.
Wolfville, NS B4P 1C6
(902) 542-9775 (seasonal)
wolfvillehs.ednet.ns.ca

Robie Tufts Nature Centre
117 Front St.
Wolfville, NS
wolfville.ca/robie-tufts-nature-centre
.html

Shand House Museum
389 Avon St.
Windsor, NS B0N 2T0
(902) 798-2915 (Haliburton House)
shandhouse.novascotia.ca

West Hants Historical Society Museum
281 King St.
Windsor, NS B0N 2T0
(902) 798-4706
westhantshistoricalsociety.ca

Windsor–West Hants Visitor Information Centre
321 Gerrish St.
Wolfville, NS B0N 2T0
(902) 798-2690 (seasonal)
town.windsor.ns.ca

Wolfville Visitor Information Centre
11 Willow Ave.
Wolfville, NS B4P 2G5
(902) 542-7000
wolfville.ca

Drive 11

Admiral Digby Museum
95 Montague Row
Digby, NS B0V 1A0
(902) 245-6322
admiraldigbymuseum.ca

Annapolis Royal Historic Gardens
441 St. George St.
Annapolis Royal, NS B0S 1A0
(902) 532-7018
historicgardens.com

Annapolis Royal Visitor Information Centre and Annapolis Tidal Generating Station
236 Prince Albert Rd.
Annapolis Royal, NS B0S 1E0
(902) 532-5454
annapolisroyal.com

Digby Visitor Information Centre
110 Montague Row
Digby NS B0V 1A0
(902) 245-2201 (seasonal)
digbyarea.com

Fort Anne National Historic Site
323 St. George Street
Annapolis Royal, NS B0S 1A0
(902) 532-2397
pc.gc.ca/fortanne

O'Dell House Museum
136 St. George St.
Annapolis Royal, NS
(902) 532-7754
annapolisheritagesociety.com

Port-Royal National Historic Site of Canada
53 Historic Lane
Port Royal, NS B0S 1K0
(902) 532-2898
pc.gc.ca/portroyal

Sinclair Inn Museum
230 St. George St.
Annapolis Royal, NS B0S 1A0
(902) 532-0996 (seasonal) or
(902) 532-7754
annapolisheritagesociety.com

Upper Clements Parks
2931 Hwy. 1
Annapolis Royal, NS B0S 1A0
(902) 532-7557 or (888) 248-4567
upperclementsparks.com

Drive 12

Fort Point Museum
100 Fort Point Rd.
LaHave, NS B0R 1C0
(902) 688-1632
fortpointmuseum.com

Halifax & Southwestern Railway Museum
11188 Hwy. 3
Lunenburg, NS B0J 2C0
(902) 634-3184
hswmuseum.ednet.ns.ca

LaHave Islands Marine Museum
100 LaHave Islands Rd.
LaHave, NS B0R 1C0
(902) 688-2973
lahaveislandsmarinemuseum.ca

Ovens Natural Park
326 Ovens Rd.
Feltzen South, NS B0J 2W0
(902) 766-4621
ovenspark.com

Rissers Beach Provincial Park
5366 Hwy. 331
Petite Riviere, NS
(902) 688-2034 or (888) 544-3434
(camping reservations)
parks.novascotia.ca

Drive 13

Amos Pewter
589 Main St.
Mahone Bay, NS B0J 2E0
(902) 624-9547
amospewter.com

Bluenose II
68 Bluenose Dr.
Lunenburg, NS B0J 2C0
(855) 640-3177
bluenose.novascotia.ca

Chester Playhouse
22 Pleasant St.
Chester, NS B0J 1J0
(902) 275-3933
chesterplayhouse.ca

Fisheries Museum of the Atlantic
68 Bluenose Dr.
Lunenburg, NS B0J 2C0
(902) 634-4794
fisheriesmuseum.novascotia.ca

Graves Island Provincial Park
230 Graves Island Rd.
East Chester, NS
(902) 275-4425 or (888) 544-3434
(camping reservations)
parks.novascotia.ca

Hooked Rug Museum of North America
9849 St Margarets Bay Rd.
Hubbards, NS B0J 1T0
(902) 858-3060
hookedrugmuseumnovascotia.org

Knaut-Rhuland House Museum
125 Pelham St.
Lunenburg, NS B0J 2C0
(902) 634-3498
lunenburgheritagesociety.ca/krhouse
.htm

Lunenburg Academy of Music Performance
97-101 Kaulback St.
Lunenburg, NS B0J 2C0
(902) 634-8667
lampns.ca

Lunenburg Visitor Information Centre
11 Blockhouse Hill Rd.
Lunenburg, NS B0J 2C0
(902) 634-8100 or (888) 615-8305
lunenburgns.com

Mahone Bay Museum
578 Main St.
Mahone Bay, NS B0J 2E0
(902) 624-6263
mahonebaymuseum.com

Mahone Bay Visitors Information Centre
165 Edgewater St.
Mahone Bay, NS B0J 2E0
(902) 624-6151
mahonebay.com

Oak Island
Oak Island Drive
Western Shore, NS
friendsofoakisland.com
oakislandtours.ca

Peggy's Cove Visitor Information Centre
96 Peggy's Point Rd.
Peggy's Cove, NS B3Z 3S2
(902) 823-2253
peggyscoveregion.com

St. John's Anglican Church
64 Townsend St.
Lunenburg, NS B0J 2C0
(902) 634-4994
stjohnslunenburg.org

SS *Atlantic* Memorial
178 Sandy Cove Rd.
Terence Bay, NS B3T 1Y5
(902) 852-1557
ssatlantic.com

Drive 14

Acadian House Museum
79 Hill Rd.
Head of Chezzetcook, NS B0J 1N0
(902) 827-5992
acadiedechezzetcook.ca

Cole Harbour Heritage Farm Museum
471 Poplar Dr.
Cole Harbour, NS B2W 4L2
(902) 434-0222
coleharbourfarmmuseum.ca

Evergreen House, Dartmouth Heritage Museum
26 Newcastle St.
Dartmouth, NS B2Y 3M5
(902) 464-2300
dartmouthheritagemuseum.ns.ca

Fisherman's Cove
4 Government Wharf Rd.
Eastern Passage, NS B3G 1M7
(902) 465-6093
fishermanscove.ns.ca

Lawrencetown Beach Provincial Park
4348 Lawrencetown Rd.
Lawrencetown, NS
parks.novascotia.ca

Martinique Beach Provincial Park
2389 Petpeswick Rd.
East Petpeswick, NS
parks.novascotia.ca

McNabs and Lawlor Islands Provincial Park
Halifax Harbour
parks.novascotia.ca
mcnabsisland.ca

Musquodoboit Harbour Railway Museum
7895 Hwy. 7
Musquodoboit Harbour, NS B0J 2L0
(902) 889-2689
mhrailwaymuseum.com

Porters Lake Provincial Park
1160 West Porters Lake Rd.
Porters Lake, NS
(888) 544-3434 (camping reservations)
parks.novascotia.ca

Quaker House, Dartmouth Heritage Museum
57 Ochterloney St.
Dartmouth, NS
(902) 464-2253
dartmouthheritagemuseum.ns.ca

Rainbow Haven Beach Provincial Park
2248 Cow Bay Rd.
Rainbow Haven
parks.novascotia.ca

Shearwater Aviation Museum
34 Bonaventure St.
Shearwater, NS B0J 3A0
(902) 720-1083
shearwateraviationmuseum.ns.ca

Shearwater Flyer, Salt Marsh, and Altantic View trails
halifax.ca/recreation

Drive 15

Antigonish Heritage Museum
20 East Main St.
Antigonish, NS B2G 2E9
(902) 863-6160
antigonishheritage.org

Arisaig Lighthouse
137 Arisaig Point Rd.
Arisaig, NS B2G 2L1
(902) 863-1101

Arisaig Provincial Park
5704 Hwy. 245
Arisaig, NS
parks.novascotia.ca

Ballantynes Cove Tuna Interpretive Centre
57 Ballantyne's Cove Wharf Rd.
Ballantyne's Cove, NS B2G 2L2
(902) 863-8162

Cape George Heritage School Museum
5758 Hwy. 337
Cape George, NS
capegeorgetrails.ca

Cape George Point Lighthouse
152 Lighthouse Rd.
Cape George Point, NS
parl.ns.ca/lighthouse

Drive 16

Cabots Landing Provincial Park
1904 Bay St. Lawrence Rd.
Sugarloaf, NS
parks.novascotia.ca

Cape Breton Highlands National Park
37639 Cabot Trail
Ingonish Beach, NS B0C 1L0
(902) 224-2306
pc.gc.ca/capebreton

Cape Smokey Provincial Park
40301 Cabot Trail
Cape Smokey, NS
parks.novascotia.ca

Giant MacAskill Museum
504 Route 312, P.O. Box 41
Englishtown, NS B0C 1H0
(902) 929-2875 (seasonal)

**Les Trois Pignons: Museum of
Hooked Rug and Home Life**
15584 Cabot Trail
Chéticamp, NS B0E 1H0
(902) 224-2642
lestroispignons.com

**North Highlands Community
Museum**
29243 Cabot Trail
Cape North, NS B0C 1G0
(902) 383-2579
northhighlandsmuseum.ca

Whale Interpretive Centre
104 Harbour Road
Pleasant Bay, NS B0E 2P0
(902) 224-1411 (seasonal)

Drive 17

Argyle Shore Provincial Park
Route 19
(902) 859-8790
tourismpei.com/provincial-park/argyle-
shore

**Borden-Carleton Visitor Information
Centre**
100 Abegweit Dr., Gateway Village
Borden-Carleton, PE C0B 1X0
(902) 437-8570 or (800) 463-4734

Cape Jourimain Nature Centre
5039 Rte. 16
Bayfield, NB E4M 3Z8
(506) 538-2220 or (866) 538-2220
capejourimain.ca

**Skmaqn–Fort Amherst–Port-la-Joye
National Historic Site**
191 Hache Gallant Drive, off Route 19
Rocky Point, PE C0A 1H2
pc.gc.ca/skmaqn

Victoria Seaport Lighthouse Museum
Water Street
Victoria, PE
victoriabythesea.ca/SeaportMuseum
.html

Drive 18

Acadian Museum
23 Main Dr., Highway 2
Miscouche, PE C0B 1T0
(902) 432-2880
museeacadien.org/an

Bideford Parsonage Museum
784 Bideford Rd., Route 166
Bideford, PE C0B 1J0
(902) 831-3133

The Bottle Houses
6891 Rte. 11
Cap-Egmont, PE C0B 2E0
(902) 854-2987
bottlehouses.com

College of Piping
619 Water St. East
Summerside, PE C1N 4H8
(902) 436-5377 or (877) 224-7473
collegeofpiping.com

Eptek Art & Culture Centre
130 Heather Moyse Dr.
Summerside, PE C1N 5Y8
(902) 888-8373
peimuseum.ca

Green Park Provincial Park
364 Green Park Rd., Route 12
Port Hill, PE
tourismpei.com/provincial-park/green
-park

Green Park Shipbuilding Museum & Yeo House
360 Green Park Rd., Route 12
Port Hill, PE
(902) 831-7947
peimuseum.ca

Indian Art & Crafts of North America
4 Eagle Feather Trail
Lennox Island First Nation, PE
(902) 831-2653
indianartpei.com

International Fox Museum
33 Summer St.
Summerside, PE
(902) 432-1296
culturesummerside.com

Lennox Island Mi'kmaq Cultural Centre
8 Eagle Feather Trail
Lennox Island, PE C0B 1P0
(902) 831-3109
lennoxisland.com

Linkletter Provincial Park
Linkletter Beach Road, Route 11
Linkletter, PE
(902) 888-8366
tourismpei.com/provincial-park/
linkletter

PEI Shellfish Museum
144 Bideford Rd.
Ellerslie, PE
shellfishpei.ca

Summerside Visitor Information Centre
124 Heather Moyse Dr.
Summerside, PE C1N 5Y8
(902) 888-8364 or (877) 734-2382
exploresummerside.com

Union Corner Provincial Park and Schoolhouse Museum
Route 11
Union Corner, PE
(902) 859-8790
tourismpei.com/provincial-park/union-corner

Wyatt Historic House Museum
85 Spring St.
Summerside, PE
(902) 432-1296
culturesummerside.com

Drive 19

Cedar Dunes Provincial Park
265 Cedar Dunes Park Rd., Route 14
West Point, PE C0B 1V0
(902) 859-8785 or (877) 445-4938
tourismpei.com/provincial-park/cedar
-dunes

North Cape Interpretive Centre
21817 Route 12
North Cape, PE C0B 2B0
(902) 882-2991
northcape.ca

Stompin' Tom Centre
14024 Route 14
Skinners Pond, PE C0B 2B0
(902) 882-3214
stompintomcentre.com

West Point Lighthouse Museum
364 Cedar Dunes Park Rd. Lot 8
West Point, PE C0B 1V0
(902) 859-3605 or (800) 764-6854
westpointlighthouse.com

Drive 20

Cavendish Visitor Information Centre
7591 Cawnpore Lane
Cavendish, PE C0A 1M0
(902) 963-7830
cavendishbeachpei.com

Dalvay-by-the-Sea National Historic Site
16 Cottage Crescent
PEI National Park
Grand Tracadie, PE C0A 1P0
(902) 672-2048
dalvaybythesea.com

The Dunes Studio Gallery and Café
3622 Brackley Point Rd., Route 15
Brackley Beach, PE C1E 2P2
(902) 672-2586 or
(902) 672-1883 (restaurant)
dunesgallery.com

Farmers' Bank Museum and Doucet House
2188 Church Rd.
Hunter River, PE C0A 1N0
(902) 963-3168
farmersbank.ca

Green Gables Heritage Place
8619 Cavendish Rd.
Cavendish, PE C0A 1M0
(902) 963-7874
pc.gc.ca/greengables

Lucy Maud Montgomery Birthplace
6461, junction of Routes 6 and 20
New London, PE
(902) 886-2099
lmmontgomerybirthplace.ca

Prince Edward Island National Park
North-central coast of PEI
(902) 672-6350
pc.gc.ca/pei

Stanley Bridge Marine Aquarium
32 Campbellton Rd., Route 6
Stanley Bridge, PE C0A 1E0
(902) 886-3355

Drive 21

Cape Bear Lighthouse
42 Black Brook Rd., Route 18
Cape Bear, PE C0A 1V0
(902) 962-2917
capebearlighthouse.com

Kings Castle Provincial Park
1887 Gladstone Rd., Route 348
Gladstone, PE C0A 1V0
(902) 962-7422
tourismpei.com/provincial-park/kings-castle

Northumberland Provincial Park
12547 Shore Rd., Route 4
Wood Islands, PE C0A 1B0
(902) 962-7418 or (877) 445-4938
tourismpei.com/provincial-park/northumberland

Panmure Island Lighthouse
62 Lighthouse Rd., Route 347
Panmure Island, PE C0A 1R0
(902) 969-9380

Panmure Island Provincial Park
350 Panmure Island Rd., Route 347
Panmure Island, PE C0A 1R0
(902) 838-0668 or (877) 445-4938
tourismpei.com/provincial-park/
panmure-island

Rossignol Estate Winery
11147 Shore Rd., Route 4
Little Sands, PE C0A 1W0
(902) 962-4193
rossignolwinery.com

Wood Islands Ferry
Terminal: 23 Service Rd.
Wood Islands, PE C0A 1B0
(902) 962-2016 or (877) 762-7245
peiferry.com

Wood Islands Lighthouse
173 Lighthouse Rd.
Wood Islands, PE C0A 1B0
(902) 962-3110

Wood Islands Welcome Centre
13056 Shore Rd., Route 4
Wood Islands, PE C0A 1B0
(902) 962-3761
woodislands.ca

Drive 22

Basin Head Provincial Park and Basin Head Fisheries Museum
336 Basin Head Rd.
Kingsboro, PE C0A 2B0
(902) 357-7233 (museum)
tourismpei.com/provincial-park/basin-head (park)
peimuseum.ca (museum)

East Point Lighthouse
404 Lighthouse Rd.
East Point, PE C0A 1K0
(902) 357-2106 (gift shop)
eastpointlighthouse.com

Elmira Railway Museum
457 Elmira Rd., Route 16A
Elmira, PE C0A 1K0
(902) 357-7234 (seasonal)
peimuseum.ca

Magdalen Islands ferry
435 Chemin Avila Arseneau
Cap-aux-Meules, QC G4T 1J3
(418) 986-3278 or (888) 986-3278
ctma.ca/en

Red Point Provincial Park
249 Red Point Park Rd., Route 16
Red Point, PE C0A 1K0
(902) 357-3075 or (877) 445-4938
tourismpei.com/provincial-park/red-point

Souris Beach Gateway Park
8 Main St.
Souris, PE
sourispei.com

Souris East Lighthouse
134 Breakwater St.
Souris, PE
(902) 940-5148 or
(902) 687-2251 (gift shop)
sourislighthouse.com

Souris Visitor Information Centre
95 Main St.
Souris, PE C0A 2B0
(902) 687-7030 (seasonal)

Drive 23

Bonne Bay Passenger Ferry
Woody Point, NL
(709) 458-2016 or (888) 458-2016
bontours.ca

Gros Morne National Park
P.O. Box 130
Rocky Harbour, NL A0K 4N0
(709) 458-2417
pc.gc.ca/grosmorne

Jacob A. Crocker House
221 Main St.
Trout River, NL
(709) 451-5376 (town office)
townoftroutriver.com

Drive 24

Gateway to Labrador
Route 510
L'Anse Au Clair, NL A0K 3K0
(709) 931-2013
labradorcoastaldrive.com

Labrador Marine
(709) 535-0810 or (866) 535-2567
labradormarine.com

Pinware River Provincial Park
Route 510
Pinware, NL
(709) 927-5516 or (877) 214-2267
tcii.gov.nl.ca/parks

Point Amour Lighthouse
L'Anse Amour Road
L'Anse Amour, NL
(709) 927-5825 (seasonal)
pointamourlighthouse.ca
seethesites.ca

Red Bay National Historic Site
P.O. Box 103
Red Bay, NL A0K 4K0
(709) 920-2142
pc.gc.ca/redbay

Right Whale Exhibit Museum
50 Main Hwy.
Red Bay, NL
(709) 920-2197 (town)

Drive 25

Dark Tickle Economuseum
75 Main St., P.O. Box 160
St. Lunaire-Griquet, NL A0K 2X0
(709) 623-2354
darktickle.com

L'Anse aux Meadows National Historic Site
P.O. Box 70
St-Lunaire-Griquet, NL A0K 2X0
(709) 623-2608 (May to Oct);
(709) 458-2417 (Oct to May)
pc.gc.ca/meadows

Norstead: A Viking Port of Trade
Route 436
L'Anse aux Meadows, NL
(709) 623-2828 or (877) 620-2828
norstead.com

Drive 26

Beothuk Interpretation Centre
66 South Side Rd.
Boyd's Cove, NL A0G 1G0
(709) 656-3114
seethesites.ca

By the Bay Museum
235 Main St.
Lewisporte, NL A0G 3A0
(709) 535-1911

Dildo Run Provincial Park
Route 340
Virgin Arm, NL
(877) 214-2267
tcii.gov.nl.ca/parks

Durrell Museum
17 Museum Rd.
Durrell, NL A0G 1Y0
(709) 884-2780 (seasonal) or
durrellmuseumandcrafts@gmail.com
visittwillingate.com/durrellmuseum

Lewisporte Train Park
477 Main Street
P.O. Box 219
Lewisporte, NL A0G 3A0
(709) 535-2737

Notre Dame Junction Visitor Information Centre
P.O. Box 782
Lewisporte, NL A0G 3A0
(709) 535-8547 (seasonal)

Prime Berth—Twillingate Fishery Museum
Twillingate Island
(709) 884-5925 (June to Sept) or
(709) 884-2485
primeberth.com

Twillingate Museum
Route 340 P.O. Box 369
Twillingate, NL A0G 4M0
(709) 884-2825
tmacs.ca

Drive 27

Beaches Arts & Heritage Centre
8-10 Church St.
P.O. Box 136
Eastport, NL A0G 1Z0
(709) 677-2360
beachesheritagecentre.ca

Glovertown Museum
11 Memorial St.
Glovertown, NL A0G 2L0
(709) 533-6004
glovertown.net/tourism

Terra Nova National Park
Off the Trans-Canada Highway
Glovertown, NL A0G 2L0
(709) 533-2942 or (709) 533-2801
pc.gc.ca/terranova

Drive 28

Bell Island Ferry
(709) 729-3835
tw.gov.nl.ca/ferryservices

Bell Island Mine Museum and No. 2 Mine Tours
13 Compressor Hill
Wabana, Bell Island, NL
(709) 488-2880 or (888) 338-2880
bellislandminetour.com

Bell Island Sports Hall of Fame
Curling Club, Petrie's Hill
Wabana, Bell Island, NL A0A 4H0
(709) 488-2326 (summer only)

Drive 29

Avalon Wilderness Reserve
flr.gov.nl.ca/natural_areas/wer/r_aw

Chance Cove Provincial Park
Route 10
Chance Cove, NL
(877) 214-2267
tcii.gov.nl.ca/parks

Colony of Avalon
1 The Pool Ferryland, NL A0A 2H0
(709) 432-3200 or (877) 326-5669
colonyofavalon.ca

East Coast Trail
P.O. Box 8034
St. John's, NL A1B 3M7
(709) 738-4453
eastcoasttrail.ca

Edge of Avalon Interpretive Centre
Route 10
Portugal Cove South, NL A0A 4B0
(709) 438-1100
edgeofavalon.ca

Ferryland Lighthouse Picnics
Ferryland Head
Ferryland, NL A0A 2H0
(709) 363-7456
lighthousepicnics.ca

Irish Loop Tourism Visitor Information Centre
609 Southern Shore Hwy., Foodland Plaza
Bay Bulls, NL A0A 1C0
(709) 334-2609
theirishloop.com

La Manche Provincial Park
Route 10
La Manche, NL
(709) 685-1823 (seasonal)
tcii.gov.nl.ca/parks

Mistaken Point Eco Reserve
Cape Race Road, NL
(709) 438-1011
flr.gov.nl.ca/natural_areas/wer/r_mpe

Salmonier Provincial Wildlife Park
P.O. Box 190
Holyrood, NL A0A 2R0
(709) 229-7888
flr.gov.nl.ca/wildlife/snp

St. Vincent's Fishermen's Museum
180 Main Rd.
St. Vincent's, NL
(709) 525-3063 or (709) 525-2544

Additional Reading

Barrett, Wayne, and Harry Thurston. *Atlantic Canada Nature Guide.* Toronto: Key Porter, 1998.

Creighton, Helen. *Bluenose Ghosts.* Halifax, NS: Nimbus Publishing, 2009.

Day, Frank Parker. *Rockbound.* Toronto: University of Toronto, 2005.

Grenfell, Wilfred Thomason. *Adrift on an Ice Pan.* St. John's, NL: Creative, 1992.

Hubbard, Mina, Roberta Buchanan, Anne Hart, and B. A. Greene. *The Woman Who Mapped Labrador: The Life and Expedition Diary of Mina Hubbard.* Montreal: McGill-Queen's University Press, 2005.

Montgomery, L. M. *Anne of Green Gables.* Oxford, UK: Oxford University Press, 2007.

Proulx, Annie. *The Shipping News.* New York: Scribner, 2003.

Running Wolf, Michael B., and Patricia Clark Smith. *On the Trail of Elder Brother: Glous'gap Stories of the Micmac Indians.* New York: Persea Books, 2003.

Young, Ron. *Dictionary of Newfoundland and Labrador: A Unique Collection of Language and Lore.* St. John's, NL: Downhome, 2006.

Appendix B:
Agencies & Organizations

New Brunswick

New Brunswick Provincial Parks
parcsnbparks.ca

Tourism New Brunswick
P.O. Box 6000
Fredericton, NB E3B 5H1
(800) 561-0123
tourismnewbrunswick.ca

Nova Scotia

Nova Scotia Provincial Parks
(888) 544-3434 (camping reservations)
or (866) 230-1586 (general enquiries)
parks.novascotia.ca

Nova Scotia Tourism
8 Water St., P.O. Box 667
Windsor, NS B0N 2T0
(902) 742-0511 or (800) 565-0000
novascotia.com

Prince Edward Island

Prince Edward Island Provincial Parks
tourismpei.com/pei-provincial-parks

Tourism Prince Edward Island
(902) 437-8570 or (800) 463-4734
tourismpei.com

Newfoundland & Labrador

East Coast Trail
P.O. Box 8034
St. John's, NL A1B 3M7
(709) 738-4453
eastcoasttrail.ca

Newfoundland and Labrador Heritage
heritage.nf.ca

Newfoundland and Labrador Provincial Parks (camping)
(877) 214-2267
nlcamping.ca

Newfoundland and Labrador Tourism
P.O. Box 8700
St. John's, NL A1B 4J6
(709) 729-2830 or (800) 563-6353
newfoundlandlabrador.com

Index